FORGOTTEN FRONTIER

Don

To one of the finest men
I know. You have done much
For Rock Springs and we are
going to miss you.

Dudley

3/16/90

A. Dudley Gardner is a historian and archaeologist. He is director of historical studies at Western Wyoming College and a member of the Wyoming Governor's Consulting Committee on Historic Preservation. **Verla R. Flores** is an instructor of business at Western Wyoming College.

FORGOTTEN FRONTIER

A HISTORY OF
WYOMING COAL MINING

A. Dudley Gardner
and
Verla R. Flores

WESTERN WYOMING COLLEGE

WESTVIEW PRESS
BOULDER, SAN FRANCISCO, & LONDON

Front cover photograph: McDonald's Coal Mine, Big Horn County, Wyoming, circa 1900 (*photo by J. E. Stimson, courtesy of the Wyoming State Archives, Museums and Historical Department, Stimson Collection*). Back cover photograph: Miners outside the Reliance Mine in Sweetwater County, Wyoming, circa 1900 (*courtesy of the Sweetwater County Museum*).

Unless otherwise credited, photographs in the text are the property of Western Wyoming College. All photographs are used by permission. Text graphics and captions are by Steven D. Creasman; text illustrations are by Sharon Dolan.

Published in 1989 in the United States of America by Westview Press, Inc., 5500 Central Avenue, Boulder, Colorado 80301, and in the United Kingdom by Westview Press, Inc., 13 Brunswick Centre, London WC1N 1AF, England

Library of Congress Cataloging-in-Publication Data
Gardner, A. Dudley.
  Forgotten frontier : a history of Wyoming coal mining/A. Dudley
Gardner, Verla R. Flores.
    p. cm.
  ISBN 0-8133-1008-3—ISBN 0-8133-1007-5 (pbk.)
  1. Coal mines and mining—Wyoming—History. I. Flores, Verla R.
II. Title.
TN805.W8G37 1989
978.7'03—dc20   89-38402
                                                                 CIP

Printed and bound in the United States of America

⊗ The paper used in this publication meets the requirements of the American National
    Standard for Permanence of Paper for Printed Library Materials Z39.48-1984.

10   9   8   7   6   5   4   3   2   1

Contents

—

Acknowledgments

"Time flies like an arrow," say the Chinese. The same can be said of history; it passes swiftly and to the mark but is seen clearly only after the arrow has struck its target. The history of Wyoming coal mining is like an arrow still on its way to the target—still in motion and not easily perceived. Yet part of the path can be charted. The history of Wyoming coal mining has proven to be an uneven flight—a history of economic ups and downs, tragedies and triumphs, and uncertainties. So in the midst of the arrow's flight, we attempt to chart its course.

The course of Wyoming history began with daring people. It was through the efforts of men mining coal that many Wyoming towns had their beginning. It was through the sacrifices of women and men that towns continued. Some towns, however, were abandoned once the mines closed. Yet the memory of the once-thriving camps survives. "Gone but not Forgotten" is a common inscription on tombstones in deserted coal camps. Through this book we attempt to pay tribute to the men and women of Wyoming's coal camps who are gone but not forgotten. Their lives helped to make and shape Wyoming; we owe them much.

To trace this history of Wyoming, we spent hours in the homes of miners and their families. They told us about their lives and shared food with strangers. Each of these people is listed in the bibliography and deserves our thanks. To Alice Antilla in Kemmerer, Homer Alley in Sheridan, the William Harrises in Frontier, and Amy Pivik in Rock Springs, we extend our gratitude for opening their homes and providing food and shelter. They extended this courtesy because they, like other miners and miners' families, want others to know of the courage and grit it took to make Wyoming home.

In writing this work, the expertise of David Johnson was called upon to generate the information about early railroads in Wyoming, Jay Gould, and statewide expansion of the railroads. His efforts were quiet but of great importance to this work.

Dr. Duane Smith, Dr. William Snell, Dr. Eugene Berwanger, Dr. David Kathka, Dr. Lawrence Cardoso, and Dr. Richard Flores served as readers for this effort. Jim Beveridge, Joe Bozovich, Dr. John Collins, Henry Chadey, Kathy Karpan, Ray Lovato, Charles Love, Arthur Rosatti, and Anita Smalstig provided invaluable advice. Val Brinkerhoff did the photographic work for this effort. The effort of librarians and archivists throughout the region aided in this research effort. A special thanks is extended to the University of Wyoming, Laramie; State Archives and Museums, Cheyenne; Wyoming Secretary of State, Cheyenne; the U.S. Geological Survey Library, Denver; the Nebraska State Archives, Lincoln; and the Union Pacific Museum, Omaha. The archivists and librarians at these institutions helped us greatly. Thanks go to Kevin Thompson, Ted Hoefer, Linda Wadleigh, Russel Tanner, Margie Shanks, Chris Plant, Cheryl Harrison, Yan Zhaoxing, Steve Shea, and John Anselmi for their research efforts and hours in the field surveying historic coal towns and providing insight. Also, student readers provided additional fresh perspective on the text, especially Johanna Stainbrook and Mike and Debbie Allen. To the farsighted and diligent efforts of Gary Beach and Steve Whissen of the Wyoming Department of Environmental Quality, more than thanks is needed. They understand the importance coal mining played in the development of Wyoming and provided the thought that began this effort.

In addition to the readers and the Wyoming Department of Environmental Quality, our deepest debt is owed to our families—to Jodie, Will, and Emma Gardner, who went without weekend outings for the length of this effort and provided a reservoir of kindness and warmth when the candle burned dimly, and to Dick Flores who not only read the manuscript but also provided much needed support. Then there are the special people who typed and retyped this effort. Debbie Braithwaite and Carole Howard-Carter not only typed but provided the props needed to finish this project. Mrs. Braithwaite continually revised and retyped without complaint or criticism of the time demands placed on her. We want to acknowledge Tonya Auble's contributions in providing desk-top composition for this effort. To these people and the faculty, staff, and librarians at Western Wyoming College, our heartfelt thanks.

This work reflects part of the history of Wyoming coal mining. Much more needs to be written. To those that have produced written histories, historical overviews, and manuscripts we cited here, we extend thanks. To the archaeologists and historians who are studying Wyoming's past and attempting to preserve its lasting legacy, we applaud your efforts. The flight of time is not complete, but the history that has passed shows coal miners will be a part of the future. To those that are attempting to preserve the mining history of Wyoming and the West, we are grateful. And to men such as Steven Creasman and Gary Beach, who have the courage to dream and the willingness to persevere in attempting to save America's past, thank you. With the help of such unselfish individuals this work has been strengthened, but the responsibilities of accuracy fall to the authors alone.

ix

This effort was not for profit. The work on which this publication was based was financed through the Wyoming Department of Environmental Quality, Land Quality Division, Abandoned Mine Lands Program, by the U.S. Department of the Interior, Office of Surface Mining Reclamation and Enforcement, as authorized by the Surface Mining Control and Reclamation Act of 1977. The contents of this publication do not necessarily reflect the views and policies of the Wyoming Department of Environmental Quality, Land Quality Division, or the U.S. Department of the Interior, Office of Surface Mining Reclamation and Enforcement, nor does mention of trade names or commercial products constitute their endorsement or recommendation for use by the United States Government.

Royalties from the sale of this book will go to the Western Wyoming College Museum of Natural History to fund displays relating to Wyoming coal mining history.

A. Dudley Gardner
Verla R. Flores

Miners outside the Reliance Mine in Sweetwater County, Wyoming, circa 1900. (Courtesy of the Sweetwater County Museum)

Introduction

When we think of settling the West, we often imagine trappers, gold miners, or ranchers seeking new lands and new opportunities. The settlement of the West, however, was not accomplished by these people alone; the region was also settled by men and women engaged in a less glamorous occupation: coal mining. Like the trappers and traders who preceded them, the coal miners sought new lands and new opportunities. Although the coal miner and his family often traveled to their destination by railroad and wagon, they moved to areas just as unsettled as the earlier pioneers had encountered. In the desert landscape of what is now Wyoming, they built towns like Almy, Carbon, Winton, Dines, Cambria, Monarch, Sublet, and Dana. When the mines closed, the miners moved on, but usually to mine a new coal field and build a new town. To the coal miners fell the burden of settling the land skipped over by the gold miners, farmers, and ranchers. These men and women settled areas previously unoccupied and were true pioneers.

These pioneers came from all over the world. Initially they came from England, Wales, China, and various parts of the United States. As the mining industry grew and the need for workers increased, immigrants from Sweden, Italy, Greece, Austria, Hungary, Japan, Korea, Poland, Russia, Slovenia, Scotland, and Finland came to Wyoming seeking employment in the coal fields. Japanese immigrants arriving in San Francisco by boat were transported by train to treeless Wyoming coal towns like Superior. The transition from the green Island of the Rising Sun to the high desert of southwestern Wyoming took some getting used to. One mail-order bride from Japan cried for days upon her arrival in Superior. Nor was she alone in her feelings. Countless groups of people were shocked to find that their new homeland lacked water and trees. Accustomed to Mediterranean climates or the forests of northern Europe, women who had followed their husbands to dusty or snowbound villages felt isolated from all that was familiar. Initially, the only positive aspect of their new location was the availability of work. Italians moved next door to Poles. Greeks moved near "Finns." Soon an area that had recently been a sagebrush flat or hillside was transformed into a community. These pioneers, living and working side by side with immigrants who might not even speak the same language, changed the landscape.

Coal was the magnet that drew people to the previously uninhabited areas of what would become Wyoming. Beginning in 1868 when the first steam engine began to climb the Continental Divide of the Wyoming Rockies, coal was regarded as one of the most valuable assets of the area. Towns developed wherever coal and the means of transportation coincided. Throughout the nineteenth and into the twentieth century, towns were built almost overnight in previously isolated areas. The area still remains relatively unpopulated because once the mines closed the towns were abandoned and buildings removed for use elsewhere. The vast landscapes that are still evident today in Wyoming prompted one twentieth century writer to call the area "the Empty Quarter." Though coal drew the miners to the area, they never quite conquered the land. Therefore, when the energy crisis hit America in the 1970s, a new wave of settlers rushed into Wyoming. Trailers replaced the dugouts and the stone houses built by earlier pioneers, but the attraction of the least populated state in the United States was coal and other fossil fuels. Drawn by the possibility of finding good paying jobs and a better life, people came, but once again they left when the employment opportunities changed. In turn, the landscape absorbed the remnants of these modern pioneers. The vast, unlimited skyline that greeted the first coal miners and their families to Wyoming continues to greet new dreamers seeking their fortune.

This study centers on the state of Wyoming, but the story is regional and national in scope. It deals with the tenacity of pioneers attracted to an area to seek a new life. These pioneers came from all over Europe, Asia, and America to work the coal mines. People from Austria lived next to Greeks. Japanese and Chinese drawn from Asia found themselves with common goals in trying to adapt to living in an inhospitable environment. Black Americans found jobs in the West when opportunities were limited in the East. The common focus was extracting coal. The history presented here points out how the men and women succeeded in turning an empty land into a productive region. The by-product was the settlement and growth of Wyoming.

1

Wyoming Coal Mining: The Early Years

Wyoming is a wide open land made up of basins, prairies, and mountains. From border to border these different land forms create a varied appearance, but it is the wide open spaces that give the state continuity.

Climate, topography, and geology have combined to make the state unique. The environment and remoteness of the region have kept the state's population small. Wyoming remains the least populous state of the United States; yet it is the ninth largest in area. Mountains, basins, and plains separate the people of Wyoming from one another, and vast, untouched areas tend to isolate them from the rest of the United States. As John Rolfe Burroughs said of southwest Wyoming, it is an area "where the Old West stayed young."[1] This statement, in many ways, applies to the entire state.

The mountains of Wyoming are part of the Rocky Mountains, but instead of being formed in long, continuous ranges running from north to south, they are interrupted by prairies or basins or mountains running from east to west. The uplifting forces that created the mountains made Wyoming the second highest state in the Union. This idea is often difficult to grasp. For example, Laramie, on the flat eastern plains, is situated at an elevation of 7100 feet.

The flanks of the Uinta Mountains, which run from east to west, serve as the southern boundary of southwestern Wyoming. The Western Wyoming Range, which runs from north to south, forms the western border. In addition to the Western Wyoming Range in northwestern Wyoming, there are also the Teton, Wind River, Gros Ventre, and Absaroka mountains and the uplifted plateau that forms Yellowstone National Park. Not only do these ranges give Wyoming some of its most spectacular scenery, but they also serve as the headwaters of a surprising number of America's largest rivers. Although the Yellowstone, Green, and Snake rivers drain into separate oceans, they share the mountains of northwest Wyoming as their point of origin. The grandeur of Wyoming's landscape was described as early as the 1800s. One traveler crossing the mountains of western Wyoming in 1851 wrote, "On the divide we look eastward and see the Green river valley in all of its grandeur, with its snowy range, the source of the river trending northward as far as the eye can reach...."[2]

In the northcentral section of the state, the Big Horn Mountains separate the Great Plains from the Big Horn Basin. East of the Big Horns, in the middle of the grasslands, the Black Hills rise as hilly islands in the midst of a sea of prairie grass. The southeastern quarter of Wyoming contains the Laramie, Medicine Bow, and the Sierra Madre ranges, but these three ranges never truly touch the Big Horn or Wind River mountains. Instead, separate, smaller uplifts, like the Shirley, Seminoe, and Green mountains, bend westward in a broken arch that runs from the Sierra Madres to the Wind River Mountains. Between these uplifts and mountains are open expanses of prairies and basins.

The prairies exhibit gently rolling hills punctuated by buttes and uplifts. Pine trees can be found in the uplifts, but it is the sea of unending grasses and sagebrush that catches attention. The monotony of endless stretches of prairie grass was noted by emigrants traveling westward in the 1840s and 1850s, and motorists on the modern interstate often comment on the treeless stretches. These grasses, however, have endured through blizzards and droughts alike, and they once supported large herds of bison that made places like the Powder River Basin in northeastern Wyoming one of the most valued hunting grounds of the Plains Indians.

The climate of Wyoming is similar to that of steppes found throughout the world. Steppes are treeless expanses with seemingly unlimited vistas. The open expanses lend themselves to harsh weather in the form of long winters, high winds, and arid summers. Except for the eastern plains and the basins around Cody and Riverton, the growing season in Wyoming is too short to grow field corn. At Laramie the average growing season lasts only 113 days.[3] Jackson Hole, in the northwest, has virtually no growing season. Across the state the amount of available moisture also varies. In the mountains the precipitation can range from 20 to 40 inches per year, but at Green River in southwest Wyoming the average annual precipitation is a scant 8.9 inches. Interestingly, in Wyoming short growing seasons generally correspond with the areas that receive the most moisture. The opposite is true of areas with longer growing seasons. So where there might be enough growing days to raise crops, there is little moisture. Then there is the wind. The winds of Wyoming are legendary. Some say the wind never stops, but Wyoming residents know better. As old-timers claim, "there are days when the wind doesn't blow but a little bit." Although moisture may fall in the form of rain or snow, the winds evaporate the moisture, which makes farming almost impossible without irrigation. Only on the eastern plains is dryland farming possible.

The intermountain basins of the state contain the beauty of vast, silent expanses broken only by buttes and sandstone outcroppings. The sands of these basins are covered with sagebrush, spiny hopsage, Indian ricegrass, pricklypear cactus, and a host of other wild flowers and plants that have adapted to living in a high elevation desert. In some places, nothing but phlox and rocks are evident; here the landscape is stark. The dominant plant, however, is sagebrush. Although sagebrush extends into the prairies and mountains, it is in the basins that this species is most evident. One traveler who crossed the state in 1863 decried sagebrush as "the dreariest mockery of vegetation that ever grew." He went on to call it "an exotic from the Valley of Desolation, a ghost of departed brush heaps, [a] ghostly skeleton of a plant, of an ashy pale color and as dry as the sand it stands in."[4] Sagebrush and prairie grasses provide the covering over the geological formations that contain most of Wyoming's coal. Coal basins underlie practically the entire state; it is on the prairies, however, that it is most economical to mine coal.

It was obvious even to the fur trappers and early explorers, who understood little about the geology of the area, that coal was abundant. The mineral was found in outcrops along cliff faces and eroding out of ridge sides and drainages. Eventually, when the overlying strata were stripped away, coal seams ranging from four to forty feet thick were exposed. Wyoming was (and is) rich in coal. On the windswept plains and in the high intermountain basins, a black bonanza awaited the pioneer entrepreneurs.

Early Discoveries

Possibly the first people to use coal in Wyoming were Native Americans. There is no conclusive archaeological evidence that Indians actually extracted coal from outcrops within the borders of the state, but in nearby North Dakota, archaeologists have found traces of lignite coal in a fire hearth dating to 4000 years ago. Also, at excavations conducted at the Sakakawea Village site in Mercer County, North Dakota, three pounds of coal were recovered from a sweat lodge dating to the early nineteenth century.[5] Even though these sites lie outside the boundaries of Wyoming, it is more than likely that the Indians of this area knew about and understood the nature of coal.

Trappers seeking beaver furs in the Rocky Mountains during the early 1800s were the first Americans to write about the presence of coal in Wyoming. Prior to 1803, the area that would become Wyoming had been claimed by both Spain and France. The Louisiana Purchase of 1803 brought the lands east of the Continental Divide under the jurisdiction of the United States, and it was not long before fur trappers began trapping for beaver in the streams of the region.

In 1831 a young French-born American, B. L. E. Bonneville, took leave of the U.S. Army. With a party of "one hundred ten men ... most of whom were hunters and trappers," he set out to explore the Rockies. Captain Bonneville left Fort Osage, Missouri, in May of 1832 and did not return to Missouri until August 1835. Bonneville spent a good portion of his western travels in present-day Wyoming. Washington Irving, the author of *Rip Van Winkle* and *The Legend of Sleepy Hollow*, published Bonneville's journal material in the book *Adventures of Captain Bonneville*. In his flamboyant writing about Bonneville's journeys, Irving related that the Crow Indians held a place called Burning Mountain on the Powder River in "superstitious awe." He wrote, "Here the earth is hot and cracked; in many places emitting smoke and sulphurous vapors, as if covering concealed fires."[6] Burning coal seams still abound in the West.

Osborne Russell, who trapped in the Rockies, kept a journal describing his life in the fur trade between 1834 and 1843. In July 1835 he reported finding "rich beds of iron and bituminous coal" near the site of present-day Cody. In 1837 Russell, in describing the area adjacent to the Popo Agie River near Lander, noted that "beds of iron and coal are frequently found in this part of the country."[7] Other trappers, such as Jim Bridger, were also aware of the presence of coal. Bridger informed Captain Howard Stansbury, a member of the United States Army Corps of Topographical Engineers, that he had used coal at his trading post for years.[8] Bridger's trading post, established in 1843, was located on the banks of the Black's Fork River in southwestern Wyoming near good outcrops of bituminous coal.

During the 1840s, settlers began moving westward in ever increasing numbers. Following trails used by the Indians and the trappers, the settlers found a way to travel over these mountains. Oregon, and later California, would be their destination, but most of these westward travelers took advantage of the natural break in the Rocky Mountains found at South Pass, Wyoming. At first emigrants to Oregon and California sought new lands to farm; but with the discovery of gold in California in 1848, their reason for migrating westward changed. The increasing numbers of people, more interested in seeking California gold than in farming, saw Wyoming as a high, dry desert to cross and not as a place to settle. They did, however, keep diaries of their journeys, and one of the things they noted was the existence of coal.

The overland emigrants, the frontier army, and the wagon road surveyors carried on an almost accidental process of discovering coal. Joel

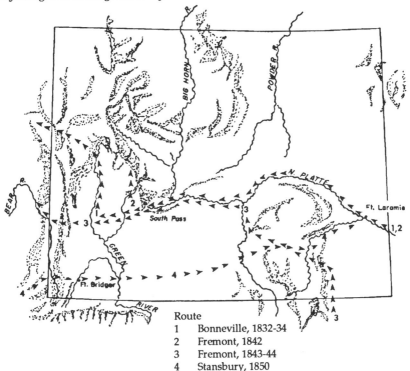

Route
1   Bonneville, 1832-34
2   Fremont, 1842
3   Fremont, 1843-44
4   Stansbury, 1850

Routes of early explorers that noted and mapped the occurrence of coal in the region that was to become Wyoming.

Palmer, who crossed the eastern plains of Wyoming in July 1845 by following the Oregon Trail, noted a coal deposit on Deer Creek (at the site of Glenrock).[9] In describing the area where he camped, this Oregon-bound traveler wrote, "stone coal was found near the road. This would make a suitable place for a fort," he went on to add, "as the soil and timber is better than is generally found along the upper Platte."[10] The coal seam noted by Palmer would be mentioned by other westward travelers. Albert Carrington, traveling with the Pioneer Band of Mormons during the 1847 emigration to the Salt Lake Valley, also pointed out this deposit to other members of his party. The Latter Day Saints would later use coal from this area to fuel their lucrative blacksmith shop at Mormon Ferry, approximately 28 miles to the west. The presence of coal along Deer Creek became well-known to travelers, and the coal "was commercially mined during the late nineteenth century."[11] Joseph Goldsborough Bruff, who was part of the

1849 Gold Rush to California, reported finding coal two days before reaching Independence Rock on the Sweetwater River.[12] In an enthusiastic report, Osborne Cross, a major in the United States Army, reported to his superiors in 1849 that, "the country from Deer Creek to the Sweetwater abounds in coal in great quantities I have no doubt."[13] These travelers along the Oregon Trail provided information about the extent of Wyoming coal deposits.

John Charles Fremont wrote one of the earliest reports of coal deposits along what would be called the Overland Trail crossing southern Wyoming. Fremont carried out an expedition to provide preliminary mapping of the major trails over the Rocky Mountains for the Army Corps of Topographical Engineers.[14] In his report of the *Expedition to Oregon and North California in the years 1843-1844*, Fremont mentioned coal found along the North Platte River between the sites of Saratoga and Fort Steele, Wyoming. Fremont wrote that several coal beds were located in "precipitous bluffs" along the river. He went on to say, "In some of the beds the coal did not appear to be perfectly mineralized, and in some of the seams, it was compact and remarkably lusterous."[15]

In 1849 and 1850 Howard Stansbury conducted a survey of the Great Salt Lake and portions of southern Wyoming for the Bureau of Topographical Engineers. When he returned east from Salt Lake in 1850, Stansbury traveled over what would become the Overland Trail. In his journal he reported finding coal from Evanston eastward to Rock River (virtually the entire length of Wyoming). He mentioned coal deposits along Bitter Creek and near the Green River. In fact, Stansbury labeled the entire area the "Coal Basin." Near Rock Springs he noted "a bed of bituminous coal cropping out of the north bluff of the valley with every indication of its being quite abundant."[16] He went on to mention coal outcroppings in the vicinity of Point of Rocks. After reaching the North Platte River, Stansbury again encountered coal. Coal was noted along Rattlesnake Creek between the North Platte River and Elk Mountain.[17] James Hall, who wrote the Geological Appendix to Stansbury's report, stated, "The importance of this mineral in that distant region cannot be too highly estimated, and the geographical position and extent of the beds should be one of the first points ascertained in the location of any route of communication between the East and West."[18] This geologist understood early the significance coal would play in establishing a transcontinental transportation route.

South of Evanston, along the future route of the transcontinental railroad, coal was mined in 1859 to provide fuel for Fort Bridger's blacksmith shop. This coal seam was first reported by William Clayton in his 1848 *Latter Day Saints Emigrants Guide*, which described the Mormon Trail from Fort Bridger to Salt Lake City.[19] Early development of this seam occurred about ten miles southeast of present-day Evanston where a U.S. Military Coal Reservation was established and a mine opened in 1859.[20] The coal beds were never extensively worked, and when Fort Bridger was abandoned in 1890, the coal reservation was returned to the public domain. This mine and others near the Emigrant Trail provided information about potential coal reserves along the future transcontinental railroad line. Stansbury's initial observations while traveling eastward were borne out by small mines along his route of exploration.

The Overland Trail name was taken from the Overland Stage Line Company. Along this route, stage stations were placed seven to seventeen miles apart.[21] Many of these stations used locally available coal to heat the stations or fuel the blacksmith shops. In 1865 James Evans, who was responsible for surveying the proposed Union Pacific rail line, described in detail coal mines found adjacent to several of the stage stations along the Overland Trail. At the Black Butte Stage Station, thirty miles from the summit of Bitter Creek and south of Point of Rocks, he reported, "several seams have been opened, one 5 feet, and one 3 and a half feet of clean coal. ... This is the hardest and best quality of coal found on the line."[22] Evans' 1865 report also described the mining of coal at Sulphur Springs Stage Station in what would become Carbon County. In his description he noted,

This opening has been worked systematically, and is carried in a distance of 40 feet, with but little appreciation in the quality of the coal, it being like that found to the eastward, brittle and imperfectly mineralized. The station of the Overland Stage Company, at Sulphur Springs, is the headquarters of one of the divisions of their line; their blacksmith and repair shops are here. The object in making the coal opening was to save the hauling of coal from Bitter Creek.[23]

Evans also noted that coal was evident from the North Platte eastward to Rock Creek.

In 1862 Fort Halleck was established at the north end of Elk Mountain to provide travelers protection from Indian attacks along the Overland Stage Line. Evans noted in 1864 that coal was being mined near Fort Halleck for blacksmithing purposes.[24] Apparently coal was also used for heating the buildings at the fort. Dr. J. W. Finfrock, assistant surgeon for the post in 1864, mentioned acquiring a load of coal. In his personal diary he reported obtaining a load of coal brought in from a road north of camp.[25] Unfortunately, the account does not include the distance from Fort Halleck to the coal mine.

Although the mines associated with the Overland Trail and military posts were small, they provided evidence that coal was available in the

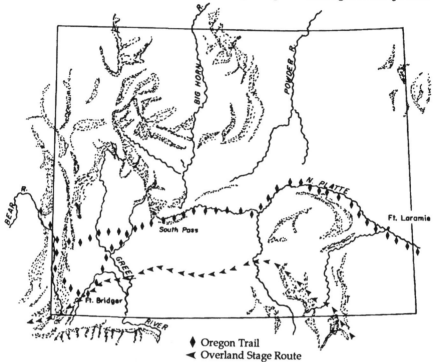

Routes of the Oregon Trail and Overland Stage Line through Wyoming. The rich coal deposits along the Overland led to the selection of this route for the transcontinental railroad.

area. Through the mining efforts of the stage station operators, the fact that coal was available in significant amounts became common knowledge. When the Union Pacific Railroad route to the West Coast was chosen, the availability of coal played an important role in the decision to use southern Wyoming as the corridor west.

During the 1860s, attention was focused on the southern half of future Wyoming. There were, however, government surveys in other areas of the state. Kemble Warren, William Raynolds, and James Sawyers explored northwestern Wyoming and surrounding areas. In the mid-1850s Kemble Warren traveled throughout Nebraska, the Dakotas, and eastern Montana and noted extensive deposits of coal in and around the Black Hills and in the Powder River Country.[26] In 1859 and 1860 Captain William F. Raynolds led explorations of the Lower Yellowstone to find a new route to link Fort Laramie in eastern Wyoming with Fort Benton on the Upper Missouri in Montana. Raynolds' party included a young geologist who was destined to become the director of the Geological Survey of the Territories, Ferdinand V. Hayden. Hayden reported the presence of extensive lignite beds, up to eight feet thick, between the Platte River and Pumpkin Buttes.[27] In the summer of 1865, James A. Sawyers received a commission from the Department of the Interior to survey a wagon road from the mouth of the Niobrara River north to the rapidly growing Montana gold fields. "By early August, the road builders were traveling through the Powder River Country, where they came across several sizeable deposits south of where Gillette stands today." Sawyers felt this coal, "the best I have ever seen in the west; from the amount seen cropping out, I should think it almost inexhaustible."[28] Government surveys of the mid-1800s revealed the extent of Wyoming's coal deposits.

While reports provided by emigrants, trappers, explorers, and the Army Corps of Topographical Engineers documented the presence of coal, simple knowledge of the presence of coal was not enough to bring the Wyoming coal industry into existence. The resources were present, but the means of getting the coal to market was lacking. At the time, large local markets were nonexistent. Henry Englemann, a geologist who accompanied Lieutenant Francis T. Bryan in his efforts to locate and improve a road connecting Fort Riley and Bridger's Pass in 1856 and 1857, provided insightful comments about the possibility of extracting this coal. Working in basically the same areas where Fremont and Stansbury had found deposits along the Upper North Platte, the Laramie Plains, and on Sage Creek, Englemann commented that with proper treatment the coal could be used in the manufacture of iron from ore deposits in the area. The geologist went on to note that such an industry would require a population center, although an influx of population was something the geologist doubted would ever happen. Englemann went on to conclude that the value of the coal beds "would be enormous if they were in a cultivable [sic] country; but as it is, they are probably of no use, unless a railroad should be constructed through the country, and require them for fuel."[29]

Parallel Ribbons of Steel

The development of the Wyoming coal industry is intertwined with the building and expansion of the Union Pacific Railroad. The Union Pacific Railroad created the market for Wyoming coal, both as a source of fuel for its own fleet of steam locomotives and as a means of transporting coal to western and midwestern cities. To understand the beginnings of the Wyoming coal industry, it is necessary to examine the rise of the Union Pacific Railroad.

The idea of a transcontinental railroad began almost with the birth of American railroading in the East. The earliest proposal was in the form of an anonymous article in 1832 in the *Emigrant,* a weekly paper published in Ann Arbor, Michigan.[30] The writer's idea was to extend a railroad from New York City, past the Great Lakes, through the Platte River Valley, and on to the Oregon Coast. This concept of a transcontinental railroad tying the country together captured public interest. That this idea could capture such public interest was due to the prevailing spirit of the age. This was the period of Manifest Destiny, that romantic notion that the United States was destined to spread from the Atlantic to the Pacific and encompass North America. Railroads were seen as instruments of Manifest Destiny. By 1860 the experience and the technology to build a transcontinental railroad were present. All that was needed was the will to do so, and money.

By 1850 the people of the United States had settled across the Mississippi River and were firmly planted on the Pacific Coast, but between California and the rest of the country lay the "Great American Desert," a region thought by most to be "a desert hopeless and irreclaimable."[31] In the 1850s this notion began to change. Gold had been discovered in California in 1848, and the mining boom soon extended to include Nevada, Oregon, Idaho, Colorado, and Montana. Not only was gold found in abundance, but silver, copper, and coal were also available. More than $100,000,000 worth of coal had been removed from western coal fields outside the state of Wyoming prior to the coming of the railroad.[32] Farmers were also beginning to move into Kansas and eastern Nebraska. The Mormons were settling and farming areas around the Great Salt Lake and producing grain surpluses, which they hoped to trade. The West Coast was beginning to produce riches of its own, and it was in great need of people to both mine and farm the area. The Coast also needed merchandise and equipment from the East to facilitate the economic exploitation of minerals and land.

It became clear to certain visionaries that great profit could be reaped by a transcontinental railroad. These men ran heavy public relations campaigns before Congress, the press, and the people through the 1840s and 1850s. In March of 1853, Congress authorized Secretary of War Jefferson Davis to carry out surveys of five routes across the country. These surveys were inconclusive for two reasons. First, they had to be completed in ten months. This was not sufficient time to gather detailed information, such as determining grades or curves. The second reason was more crucial. The region in which the terminus of the railroad was located would be in a position to dominate the economy of the West Coast. Davis, who would later become president of the Confederacy, wanted to be certain that the southern route, from Texas to Southern California, would be the choice. Northerners in Congress would not let the South gain such an advantage;

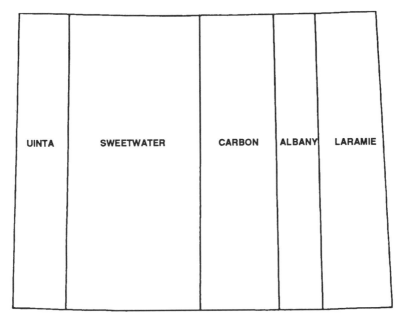

| UINTA | SWEETWATER | CARBON | ALBANY | LARAMIE |

Wyoming Counties in 1869

and because of these sectional disagreements, the whole matter of a transcontinental railroad remained in limbo until the Civil War.

The Civil War removed many of the obstacles to building a transcontinental railroad. With the southern route no longer under consideration, the best route west roughly paralleled the Overland Trail and Stage Route. From Omaha, Nebraska, the route extended west along the Platte River through Nebraska. At the junction of the North Platte and the South Platte, the route followed the South Platte almost to the Colorado border. From there the route moved due west to present-day Cheyenne. From Cheyenne the route climbed the 7000 foot Evans Pass over the Laramie Mountains and onto the Laramie Plains. From there the line crossed the northern flanks of the Medicine Bow Mountains into the Platte River Valley. Taking advantage of a natural break in the mountains near the site of present-day Rawlins, the line proceeded westward and crossed the Continental Divide over a small rise in the Red Desert. The route continued through the Wyoming Basin, across the Overthrust Belt, and into the Great Salt Lake Basin where it would meet the Central Pacific, which was laying track eastward from Sacramento, California.

This route had many advantages over other proposed routes. The railhead at Omaha was the closest to the major rail junction at Chicago. Once a bridge was built across the Missouri River, freight and passengers bound for Chicago or Omaha could travel existing Chicago and North-western trackage. The route along the Platte River through Nebraska was advantageous due to the abundance of water needed by the locomotives to produce steam and the presence of wood, which was still used as fuel for locomotives in the early 1860s as well as being used for railroad ties and trestles. Also, the route took advantage of very easy grades over the Rocky Mountains. The standard locomotives used by the Union Pacific at that time could not manage a grade of more than 116 feet to the mile.[33] The Wyoming Basin, which divides the Southern and Middle Rocky Mountains, provided the easiest and cheapest means of crossing the Continental Divide. The Union Pacific had to dig only four tunnels, three of which were through the Wasatch Mountains in Utah; whereas the Central Pacific, which was laying track eastward over the Sierra Nevadas, had to dig fifteen tunnels.[34] The Wyoming Basin also offered the inducement to the railroads of large deposits of coal. Most American railroads in the late 1860s were switching from wood to coal to fuel their steam locomotives. Coal is a more efficient source of heat, burning hotter and longer than wood. This made coal more economical to use, especially in the West where good wood is scarce.

   Another factor influencing the location of the route was the desire of the Mormon settlers around the Great Salt Lake to be connected to the railroad. Mormon interest in the transcontinental railroad was evidenced as early as the 1851-1852 session of the Utah Territorial Legislature.[35] Brigham Young himself supported the railroad. A railroad would make the journey of Mormon emigrant parties easier as well as less expensive. The railroad would also be a boon to local merchants and farmers who would be able to trade their wares with the surrounding area. Mormon leaders were in contact with Union Pacific officials as early as 1864 fixing the route that the railroad would take into the Salt Lake Basin.[36] Finally, when the Union Pacific and the Central Pacific met at Promontory, in May 1869, the shortest and most direct route between the East and the most populous regions of the West Coast was established. The main purpose of the first transcontinental railroad was to connect the major settlements of California and the mining towns of Nevada with the rest of the country and to facilitate trade between these two regions. The transcontinental route was the easiest, cheapest, and most direct route available to accomplish this task. The coal of Wyoming provided an additional incentive for the railroad to cross through the southern half of the future state.

   By the early 1860s, the need for a transcontinental railroad and the likelihood that long-term profits could be made became apparent to many people in the North. With government aid, a transcontinental railroad was feasible. Congress defined the form of government aid in the Pacific

Railroad Act of 1862 and modified it in the Pacific Railroad Act of 1864. The most important part of the bill stated that the Union Pacific would be granted ten sections of land (6400 acres) for every mile of track laid.[37] This land was to be distributed in alternating sections, the government keeping all even-numbered sections and the railroad being alloted odd-numbered sections. The act of 1864 liberalized the 1862 act after it became apparent that investors were still not willing to become deeply involved. The 1864 act doubled the land grant to twenty sections per mile. This change would become especially important in Wyoming where the Union Pacific also obtained the mineral rights to the sections received in the land grant. It gave the Union Pacific control over vast amounts of coal and a monopoly over the transportation of coal from its own mines as well as mines on land leased or bought from the government.

Early Settlement

Prior to the coming of the railroad, Wyoming had neither towns nor large settlements. Except for the military establishments of Fort Bridger, Fort Laramie, and a few other military outposts, there were no true settlements within the borders of the future state. Trappers, traders, and a small number of stage coach station operators lived in the area, but they were few in number. There were no population centers from which to obtain workers for an onsite work force to build the railroad or to open coal mines. For the first time in American history, a railroad would be built through an area before it was settled. The railroad preceded the settlement of the Wyoming Rocky Mountain frontier, and as it moved westward, it created new frontiers.

To extract the needed coal, mine shafts had to be opened, tipples constructed to load the coal on waiting trains, and steam plants constructed to hoist the coal out of the mines. Men were needed to mine, load, and haul the black fuel to the surface and to load trains and repair equipment. To serve the needs of the miners and those working outside the mines, shopkeepers, butchers, bakers, saloonkeepers, and a host of others were required. Towns appeared overnight in areas where not even trees had stood before. Post offices and telegraph offices were established early on. Towns usually had mercantile shops, bakeries, butcher shops, boarding houses, and the ever-present saloon. The company store, which became a fixture in the late nineteenth century, was not yet in place in the 1860s, but a company mine office was to be found in most mining towns. Other services, such as those of a doctor and laundress, could be obtained. All of these came into existence to serve the coal miners. These towns were isolated islands, dependent upon the transcontinental railroad for almost all of the necessities of life.

Building materials for the new towns had to be hauled in from elsewhere. The railroad provided the means of bringing some milled lumber into the mining towns, but usually this wood was used in mine structures or in the businesses of the town. The rapidity with which towns sprang up meant that suitable housing was not available for everyone. The average worker might obtain wood from the mountains or stream valleys, but he could rarely afford to purchase lumber. Then in many areas, distances to trees prevented the miners from readily obtaining wood suitable for building houses.

To meet their immediate needs, men excavated dugouts into creek banks. Rectangular in shape, these structures had six foot ceilings; interior dimensions varied according to personal preferences. Poles supported the roof, and a board siding made up the front. A door and window were usually located in the front. The roof might have been partially wood, but it was covered with dirt. Dugouts often served as a miner's first home until he could build a structure from native sandstone or find enough wood to build a house.

A great number of people experienced life in a dugout when they first moved onto the Great Plains or the Rocky Mountains. The principal advantage of a dugout was that it was warm in the winter and cool in the

Dugouts were typical housing during the early phase of coal town development. This type of structure gave way to more substantial housing as the towns grew. This artist's rendition of the dugouts along Bitter Creek in Rock Springs was taken from an undated photograph. The structures in the background are the barracks of Camp Pilot Butte, established in 1885.

summer. Dugouts did, however, have numerous faults. After a heavy rain or during heavy runoff from snow melt, many occupants were forced to leave their homes. This was especially a problem in the Rock Springs area where dugouts along Bitter Creek were subjected to periodic flooding. Since the roofs of these dirt structures were by no means waterproof, they would drip for days when they became saturated. One pioneer woman living on the Plains in a dirt home remembered "frying pancakes with someone holding an umbrella over her and the stove. In case of sickness, someone had to hold an umbrella over the patient in bed."[38] Even worse was the potential of the roof collapsing under the weight of the water. In Wyoming, where rain was generally not a major problem, large accumulations of snow were a mixed blessing. The snow served as insulation, but if not monitored, the weight of the snow could cause the roof to collapse.

Dugouts had few openings, so ventilation was poor. One Nebraska woman stated that, "the window or door should be left open as much as possible to provide ventilation."[39] This provided some air flow through the structure, but it also permitted intruders, such as snakes, insects, and other animals, to enter. In some areas insects and snakes were a constant torment. "The muslin draped under the ceilings to keep the constantly falling dirt off the table and beds also caught falling insects."[40] In addition to letting in insects, the openings allowed clouds of dust to cover tables, chairs, bedding, and the occupants. From dust-filled homes to dust-filled mines, airborne dirt was part of the miner's life.

The Early Mines and Coal Towns

The first coal town in Wyoming Territory was Carbon, built in 1868. By September of 1868, initial mining efforts had begun near Rock Springs.[41] Shortly thereafter work commenced at Almy, north of present-day Evanston, and in February 1869 a crew of miners was sent into the area to open the Wyoming mine. Between 1868 and 1870, mines were opened east of Rock Springs at Black Butte, Hallville, Point of Rocks, and Van Dyk. A short distance west of Rock Springs, the Blair mine was set into operation.[42] Each of these mines near Rock Springs experienced varying degrees of success, but the most significant ventures were the mines at Almy, Rock Springs, and Carbon.

The mines at Carbon were initially operated by parties outside the Union Pacific Railroad Company. The reason for founding the town, however, was to take advantage of the coal obtained as part of the land grant made by the United States Government to the Union Pacific Railroad. In 1868, "Thomas Wardell, William Hinton, Michael Quealy, and others entered into an agreement with railroad authorities which permitted them to open and develop mines on land granted to the railroad by the United States Government."[43] This mining company, known as the Wyoming Coal and Mining Company, also opened mines at Rock Springs and Almy. Thomas Wardell became the principal party responsible for running the company, and he, along with his partners, was influenced by Union Pacific's corporate policies. It was at Carbon that the Wyoming Coal and Mining Company had its beginnings.

The mines at Carbon were located along the northern flanks of the Medicine Bow Mountains. Coal mines were generally numbered or lettered sequentially according to which mine was opened first. Carbon mines followed this convention, and No. 1 was opened in 1868. It had to be closed, however, in 1881 due to recurring water accumulations. Carbon No. 2, which also opened in 1868, remained in operation until 1900. In all, seven mines were opened between 1868 and 1892, but Carbon No. 2 proved to be the most reliable. Between 1868 and 1902, when the mines closed, 4,680,346 tons of coal had been extracted at Carbon.[44] The Wyoming Coal and Mining Company's choice of Carbon as its first mining venture proved profitable.

Miners were brought in from Missouri and the British Isles to extract the coal at Carbon. Men from Norway, Sweden, Denmark, Germany, China, and Finland were also employed, but at least initially a preference was given to American and British miners.[45] The preference for British miners was common among mid-nineteenth-century coal mine operators. Between 1850 and 1880, the majority of immigrants seeking employment in American coal mines were of British descent. "American coal operators and state mining officials considered the Welsh and English to be the most capable miners because many had learned the trade in their native lands."[46] The coal mine operators regarded these English-speaking miners as craftsmen and often recruited them to work in their mines. After 1880, immigrants from elsewhere in Europe and Asia gradually began to dominate the ranks of foreign-born miners in Wyoming.[47] Initially, however, it was primarily immigrant miners from the British Isles and American mines that extracted coal from the Wyoming Coal and Mining Company mines.

The first death at Carbon was not the result of a mine accident; it was the result of an Indian raid. Searching for mules that had strayed from a corral, a stable boss was shot with arrows and fatally wounded a mile and a half from town. The townspeople, fearing an Indian attack, took refuge in the mine shaft; but the town itself was never raided. At times it was reported that lone travelers were killed and stock was stolen, but these isolated incidents did not result in a direct confrontation between the townspeople and the Native Americans.[48]

Carbon was the first coal town in Wyoming Territory with its initial construction starting in 1868. This panoramic view of Carbon in about 1875 shows the town at its zenith after having been taken over by the Union Pacific Coal Company. (Courtesy of the Union Pacific Railroad Museum Collection, Omaha, Nebraska)

Carbon never became strictly a company town. There was enough private enterprise and private property within the city to prevent this. A general store, a meat market, saloons, a shoe shop, a barber shop, a blacksmith shop, and a livery barn were operated in town. The first religious building was a Methodist church, built in 1873. Joseph Cruise built the first hotel and sold it to Mr. and Mrs. Adam Arnold before it was completed. Called the Wyoming House, it was famous throughout the area. It was managed by the Arnolds from March 1873 until 1902 when the town was abandoned. The housing, however, frequently consisted of dugouts and shanties. "Most of the [dugouts] were built into the side of a hill, and through necessity, had no windows except in front of the house. . . . After a storm, it was quite a frequent occurrence to have a cow fall in through the roof to disturb the tranquility of a household." By 1870 Carbon had 244 residents.[49] Its entire growth could be attributed to the coal industry.

Carbon's living conditions were primitive at best. Water was not available in town, so it had to be hauled from the Medicine Bow River in tank cars and dumped into cisterns lined with boards. These cisterns provided water for home use by the miners and their families. Although the water was free, there was still the problem of hauling it from the cistern to the shanty or dugout. For a price of 25 cents a barrel, you could have water hauled from the cistern to your barrel.[50] The price of hauling the water was somewhat steep; but on a windy winter morning, the cost probably did not seem too high. The lack of water also minimized the amount of vegetation that could be grown in town. One lady commented that "Horseshoe Canyon was the only green spot three miles from town where Sunday School picnics and other outdoor life was spent. There was a spring in the Canyon where fresh water could be used."[51] Water was at a premium.

Cattlemen and cowboys from the surrounding area were attracted to Carbon to take advantage of town services. In one account, *History of Union Pacific Coal Mines*, more reminiscent of a western novel than an historical account, the author wrote of the saloon, "With his foot on the bar rail, one hand conveniently near his holstered gun, cowboy would face miner across the dim room, thick with smoke and the smell of hard liquor. The combination of cowboy, miner, and hard liquor often resulted in a shooting." In the Union Pacific's official history, the author pointed out that "The stories told of Carbon's saloons would match the wildest of barrack-room ballads of any country."[52] The history goes on to detail shootings and lynchings in Carbon.

The mines and the community at Rock Springs were similar to Carbon in numerous ways. When Thomas Wardell arrived with his Missouri miners in 1868, he set about opening the No. 1 mine at Rock Springs. This mine would become one of the largest coal mines in the West. Rock Springs coal was considered the highest quality coal found along the Union Pacific mainline.

By early 1869, Rock Springs was becoming one of the more important coal mining camps on the Union Pacific mainline. The *Wyoming Tribune* for December 11, 1869, asserted, "Wardell's coal mine is a great success. Twenty or thirty miners are constantly employed and an excellent quality of coal is produced in large quantities. Many car loads are shipped east and west each day."[53] Miners from England, Scotland, Wales, and Ireland joined the Missouri miners, and production from the mines at Rock Springs continued to climb. The Rock Springs mines, located in the Bitter Creek Valley, rapidly expanded after 1869.

By 1870 there were a number of coal mines operating along the Bitter Creek Valley. These included the mines at Rock Springs and Black Butte; the Van Dyk mine; the Blair mine; the Point of Rocks mine; and the mine at Hall (Hallville), located about thirty miles east of Rock Springs. A December 1869 article published in the *Wyoming Tribune* reported of the Hallville mines, "one hundred car loads per week are being shipped to Omaha and the east." The article also noted that the town of Hallville had

The No. 1 mine in Rock Springs was opened by the Wyoming Coal and Mining Company in 1868. Shown here in 1880, the mine was taken over by the Union Pacific in 1874 and eventually abandoned in 1910. (Courtesy of the American Heritage Center, Photo Archives, University of Wyoming)

a combination restaurant and hotel called the Junior Ford House, which was going "full blast" and copied the "illustrious prototype in Cheyenne." In a somewhat exaggerated statement the paper went on to say, "People are finding houses here, and a town will be shortly built."[54] The houses proved to be small stone structures, dugouts, or tents. The Junior Ford House never reached the size of its counterpart in Cheyenne. It was not too long afterwards that the entire venture was abandoned. Thicker seams of coal were available elsewhere. By 1889 not even the state coal mine inspector's reports made mention of the Hallville mine and accompanying buildings.

Other mines along Bitter Creek, such as Black Butte, Point of Rocks, Blair, and Van Dyk, had more checkered careers. They were operated for short periods at various times from 1869 into the early twentieth century. None of these mines, however, would experience the success of the Rock Springs ventures of Thomas Wardell and the Wyoming Coal and Mining Company.

Silas Reed, the surveyor general of the Wyoming Territory which was created in 1868, gave a detailed description in 1871 of the mines along the Bitter Creek Valley. In describing the mines at Rock Springs, he reported that during the year 1870, the Wyoming Coal and Mining Company "mined 21,109 tons of coal, and the total number of tons produced from November 1868 to December 31, 1870, was 38,308. Of this total amount the Union Pacific Railroad consumed 35,359, and 2,949 tons were shipped to private parties."[55] In addition to the railroad mines, Reed mentioned that "capitalists" from San Francisco were operating mines at Van Dyk and Hallville. Reed, who was paid to advertise the advantages of settling in Wyoming, extolled the virtues of Rock Springs coal and claimed it to be "literally inexhaustible." In describing its qualities, the report went on to claim, "It is superior to all other coal in this region for domestic and mechanical purposes. . . . For blacksmiths' use, it has superseded charcoal, both in Wyoming and Colorado, and is the only coal used in this Territory by blacksmiths."[56]

During the 1870s, both coal production and the population of Rock Springs increased. The *Cheyenne Daily Leader* for October 5, 1875, claimed:

> The Newcastle of Wyoming is now bringing forth from the bowels of the earth, the coal which is to make us comfortable during the next winter and to keep the Union Pacific railroad running, in spite of any snow blockade that may occur. . . . The Rock Springs mines, as it is well known, furnish the best coal yet discovered in Wyoming, east of Evanston; the deposits in this section are inexhaustible, being far more extensive than those of Pennsylvania, Illinois, and Iowa combined.[57]

In order to accommodate the Rock Springs coal miners, a variety of services were available, including hotels, a meat market, a Chinese laundry, and a dry goods store.[58] Living quarters for the miners in the 1870s were simple dugouts. The miners carved these into the banks of the Bitter Creek drainage. A correspondent to E. C. Hussey's *Home Building from New York to San Francisco*, published in 1876, reported that "Rock Springs had about one hundred of these dug-out dwellings and that other mining settlements in the region had similar homes."[59]

In 1874 the Wyoming Board of Immigration published a pamphlet entitled *The Territory of Wyoming, Its History, Soil, Climate, Resources, Etc.* This publication described the types of structures and the mines at Rock Springs. It also mentioned the presence of a newly opened, independent mine, the Excelsior, located south of the railroad line between Union Pacific No. 1 mine and the Blairtown mine. In describing the coal mining town of Rock Springs, the Board of Immigration claimed, "The town

Chinese were first brought to Wyoming as laborers on section crews for the newly constructed railroad. Some eventually went into private business in the new coal towns, as illustrated in this undated photograph of a Chinese proprietor and his store in Rock Springs. (Courtesy of the American Heritage Center, Photo Archives, University of Wyoming)

Northeast Rock Springs, near No. 1 mine. Mining offices and businesses were built close to the newly established mine and railroad. The photograph, taken between 1875 and 1885, shows the construction of newer more substantial buildings as the mines prospered. (Courtesy of the Sweetwater County Museum)

contains several good stores, a church, school house, and numerous residences. Nearly all the buildings are of stone, and are built in a neat, substantial manner."[60] This statement, of course, contradicts the 1876 statement that Rock Springs had "about one hundred dug-out" dwellings, but it was the job of the Board of Immigration to attract new settlers to the region; they wanted to expound on the positive aspects of the town. Mentioning dugouts in the flood plain of Bitter Creek could have been counterproductive.

By 1876 Rock Springs could boast of one newspaper. The *Rock Springs Exposer*, according to its editor, had a circulation that "exceeds any other hand printed newspaper in Wyoming Territory." The paper carried a number of advertisements extolling the virtue of local merchants. Some of the advertisements appear to have been written by the merchants themselves.[61]

A reflection of how fast Rock Springs grew in the early years is seen in the amount of coal the newly opened mines produced. An article in the November 10, 1876, issue of the *Rock Springs Exposer* stated that the Union Pacific Coal Company proposed to build new offices. This new facility was "necessitated by the increase of their business" at Rock Springs. In 1868 the coal mines along the Union Pacific Railroad produced 6925 tons. By 1875 this amount had climbed to 208,222 tons, and in 1880 the output reached 527,811 tons.[62]

The Almy mines were the last major mines opened by the Wyoming Coal and Mining Company in the eventful years of 1868 and 1869. Accounts vary slightly concerning the initial discovery and development of coal mines at Almy. The Union Pacific Coal Company credits Thomas Wardell with discovering the coal beds in the winter of 1868. As mentioned earlier, Wardell held the coal contract with the Union Pacific at Carbon. He went west from Rock Springs that winter searching for new deposits before all trackage had been laid. Satisfied with the coal prospects, he sent a crew of miners to the site in February 1869 to open the Wyoming mine.[63] Elizabeth Stone, who wrote the earliest history of Uinta County where Almy was located, presented a different version. Stone contended that two men named Mears and Shaffer located claims in the summer of 1868 three miles north of the Evanston townsite (at Almy). They were employed by Major Laurence of the Union Pacific Engineering Corps. The Bear River Coal Company was formed in August, and the first coal was extracted from the No. 2 mine in September 1868.[64]

In early 1869, the Bear River Coal Company consolidated with the Rocky Mountain Coal Company. Henry Simmons served as president, and James T. Almy, for whom the camp was named, was his clerk. In January 1870 this company was reincorporated under the name of the

An undated photograph of one of the mines at Almy. Almy was off the Union Pacific mainline, which required the use of freight wagons to haul coal to the railroad. A spur line was eventually constructed. (Courtesy of the Wyoming State Archives, Museums and Historical Department, Cheyenne)

Rocky Mountain Coal and Iron Company. This company was controlled by the Central Pacific Railroad Company, which operated railroads on the West Coast. Central Pacific's desire to have a steady supply of coal available for their West Coast line was the primary goal in establishing the Rocky Mountain Coal and Iron Company. At Almy, the Central Pacific and Union Pacific both had a direct interest in obtaining Wyoming coal. Here the competition for the same resource led to a land dispute. Stone credited Wardell with opening a mine on grounds purchased from Shaffer sometime in 1868, meaning that the Union Pacific was not the first interest on the Almy scene. A dispute arose over land ownership, and Wardell was forced to locate a new mine, known as the No. 1 or the Wyoming, a short distance to the south. Established by the Wyoming Coal and Mining Company, this mine supplied coal for the Union Pacific Railroad.[65]

Regardless of which interest first developed Almy coal, the massive outcrops stretched for a distance of six miles. On sections located on Union Pacific lands, the coal was supplied to that railroad. On alternate government sections, the coal was supplied to the Central Pacific Railroad by the Rocky Mountain Coal Company or its successor, the Rocky Mountain Coal and Iron Company.[66] When Ferdinand Hayden visited the Almy mines in 1871 he claimed, "I regard them as more valuable and the coal of a better quality than any I have ever seen west of the Mississippi."[67] Hayden's observations were made before it was discovered that gases had a tendency to accumulate in the Almy mines. Although the coal was of relatively high quality, the Union Pacific mines were closed in 1900, and the Rocky Mountain Coal and Iron Company mines discontinued operation in 1914.[68]

Almy mines were slightly different from the mines at Carbon and from those near Rock Springs. Instead of being located on the mainline, the Almy mines were scattered along a seven mile stretch north of the transcontinental railroad at Evanston. Almy itself was about six miles north of town. In order to ship the coal from Almy to the mainline, a rail spur was required. Almy was also near the flanks of the Uinta Mountains and the Bear River Divide. Since these mountains were near at hand and because it lay along the Bear River Valley, Almy residents had little difficulty obtaining water and wood. One example of the richness of the Bear River Valley is the continued use of this valley by the Indians after the miners arrived. The meadow west of Almy was a favorite camping ground for the Indians who frequented the area. As a result, horse trading and even horse races were held between the miners and the Indians.

During the initial mining period at Almy, the miners built their own homes from quaking aspen cut in the nearby hills. The logs were chinked with mud to keep the wind and snow from whistling through the walls.

The cabins were then white-washed inside and out to give them a finished appearance. These cabins were so drafty and hard to heat that in the middle of winter "Mothers often had to keep their children in bed all day long to keep them warm."[69]

Even though wood was available in the nearby mountains, expansion of the mines at Almy created a housing shortage in the late 1860s and early 1870s. Dugouts were excavated into the hills around Almy. After a short time, however, the mining company began to actively take an interest in constructing houses at Almy. In the 1870s, uniformly built homes began to make their appearance.[70] Thus, company housing made its entrance into the Wyoming coal fields.

Because Almy was located along a fertile valley, the miners could also find employment at ranches; some even filed for homesteads. Homesteads provided supplementary income. To the wives of these miners fell the chores left undone by the men working in the mines. "While their husbands made the daily trek to the mines to work twelve or fourteen hour shifts, the women milked the cows, branded the cattle, mowed the hay fields, and harvested the vegetable gardens."[71] These early homesteads did not offer better housing, but the ability to produce one's own food helped improve the life style of the miners and their families. Some miners eventually abandoned mining in favor of ranching, but others continued to do both, attempting to make a living along the Bear River Valley.

Like those of Carbon and Rock Springs, the early miners at Almy came from Wales, Scotland, England, and Ireland. Miners from the eastern United States were also employed early in the Almy mines, but the preference for using miners from the British Isles continued. In 1870 it was reported that 38 miners lived near the Rocky Mountain Coal Mine while 140 were reported at the Wyoming Coal Mine. In addition to the miners from the British Isles and the eastern states, 32 Chinese were living in Uinta County as were 3 blacks and 25 Indians.[72] Although it is held that Chinese workers did not enter the mines until 1874, by 1870 Asian immigrants were working in a variety of professions and as maintenance workers along the Union Pacific Railroad. Chinese workers were also serving in various capacities in the Rock Springs and Carbon areas. After 1874, the number of Chinese immigrants working in the coal mines increased.

Changes in the Infant Industry

The year 1874 brought with it great changes in the coal industry. Coal mining, though not entirely restricted to the Union Pacific land grant corridor, was centered in areas where coal could easily be transported.

Mines used by ranchers and military posts were scattered throughout the territory, but the larger industrial mines were located near the transcontinental railroad. Initially the mining was done by the Wyoming Coal and Mining Company, which was contracted to sell the coal to the railroad. Due to federal government criticism of this mining operation, the railroad's contract with the Wyoming Coal and Mining Company was terminated in 1874, and the Union Pacific established its own coal mining venture. As T. A. Larson, the noted Wyoming historian, observed, "No doubt the Union Pacific profited handsomely from its coal, using it as fuel, selling it at high prices, and charging outrageous freight rates." The value of the coal mines to the Union Pacific cannot be overestimated. In fact, Union Pacific President Charles Francis Adams, Jr., testified in 1887 that the coal mines were "the salvation of the Union Pacific; those mines saved it. Otherwise, the Union Pacific would not have been worth picking up."[73] When the Union Pacific formed its coal company in 1874, this began Union Pacific's domination of coal mining in Wyoming and the Intermountain Region. The Union Pacific Railroad could control coal mining in the region because they controlled transportation. Since Union Pacific owned the only means of transporting the coal out of the region, it found it easy to maintain this virtual monopoly.

The importance of Wyoming coal to the Union Pacific Railroad was apparent to no less a financial genius than Jay Gould. In the early 1870s, Gould had invested heavily in Union Pacific stock and was elected to the board of directors and the executive committee in 1874. By that year it was clear to more people than just Gould that the relationship between the Union Pacific Railroad and the Wyoming Coal and Mining Company, which operated the Rock Springs, Carbon, and Almy mines, was not satisfactory to the railroad. When Thomas Wardell received the leases to the coal lands within the Union Pacific's land grant in 1869, he negotiated a 15-year contract to sell coal to the railroad on a sliding scale ranging from $6 to $3 over the life of the contract. In addition, Wardell would receive a 25 percent rebate on all coal shipped by the Union Pacific to other customers.[74] Under this contract, the railroad found itself paying high prices for its own coal to a company it neither controlled nor had any real influence over. What was more, the profits from the Wyoming Coal and Mining Company went not to the Union Pacific, but to the mining company's shareholders. For five years following the railroad's completion in 1869, this unsatisfactory arrangement was allowed to continue. It took Jay Gould one day to resolve it. The day after he was elected to the board of directors, he simply abrogated the contract, seized the mines, and incorporated them into the Union Pacific. Wardell sued to recover the leases, but after six years in the courts, the case was dismissed.[75]

Thomas Wardell, while not possessing the mettle of a Jay Gould, was a significant figure in the early growth of Wyoming's coal industry. As one of the principal founders of the Wyoming Coal and Mining Company, Wardell managed the first major coal mining company in the future state. Wardell remained at the helm of the mining company from 1869 to 1874. He had gained his experience in mining in Missouri. Using this experience, he helped open mines at Carbon, Almy, and Rock Springs. These mines would become the mainstay of the Union Pacific Railroad in the 1870s and 1880s. After Jay Gould seized control of the coal mines, Wardell eventually found his way back to Missouri. Undaunted by his failure to regain the Union Pacific contract in Wyoming, Wardell continued in the mining industry in Missouri. His latter years are obscure, but in the late 1880s he was reportedly killed in Bevier, Missouri. Wardell died from a gunshot fired during a labor dispute in the mines at Bevier.[76]

The mining organization acquired by Gould in 1874 was beset by problems. Production was low, costs were high, and labor problems abounded. While labor unrest and inefficiency plagued the coal mines, the parent company had problems of its own. The Union Pacific had incurred huge debts during its construction. This debt made operating capital scarce. As a result, maintenance and upkeep were difficult and expansion of the system even more so. In order to reduce the debt, the Union Pacific had to generate more traffic along its own line and cut costs. The coal department could meet both these criteria, but only in such a manner as would put management and labor on a collision course. Gould's goals upon taking control of the Almy, Rock Springs, and Carbon mines were to increase output and lower costs. When Gould took over the mines, coal was being produced at around $2 per ton. Gould wanted this reduced to $1.30 a ton. To enable this reduction, Gould began to hire Chinese miners. The first Chinese miners, who went to work in Almy in the fall of 1874, were paid $32.50 a month compared to $52 a month paid white miners.[77] The Almy miners, alarmed by the increasing numbers of Chinese working in the mines, went on strike in November of 1874, but nothing changed except that more Chinese were hired. The trend continued through 1875 as more Chinese appeared in Almy as well as in Rock Springs where miners striking to protest wage reductions were replaced.

This policy of hiring Chinese did have the effect for which it was intended. At Almy, the replacing of white miners with Chinese saved the company some 25 cents a ton, or around $40,000 per year.[78] Production increased, and the coal department of the Union Pacific became a profitable and growing concern. Credit for the turn around belongs to Jay Gould; however, the process he began in 1874 and 1875 would result in tragedy some ten years later.

In 1874 the Board of Immigration for the Territory of Wyoming commented on the immediate changes resulting from the take over of the coal
mines by Union Pacific. In describing the direct effects of the policy
changes at the Uinta County mines, the Board of Immigration stated,

> This industry has received a severe blow at the hands of the railroad
> company, whose policy at present, is to drive all coal out of market, except
> that taken from the company's mines. The tariff on coal has been raised, and
> the price of coal reduced by the company in such a manner, that the other
> companies cannot compete with them; as a natural result some of the best
> mines in the Territory are to-day closed and lying idle, and hundreds of men
> thrown out of employment. It is to be regretted that the company have seen
> fit to pursue such a policy, but it is hoped that this plan will soon be
> abandoned, and that the company will resume the generous and satisfactory
> course formerly pursued.[79]

The Board of Immigration's purpose for existing was to attract settlers.
Choosing to report incidents such as this was not common practice. The
change from privately operated mines to company operated mines created
a disruption. Privately operated mines, such as those at Van Dyk and
Blairtown, would feel the effects immediately.

The Union Pacific mining practices were similar to those of other
nineteenth-century coal mine operators. These practices were especially
apparent in areas of pricing and labor relations. Labor relations problems
first occurred in 1871 when Thomas Wardell fired the men striking against
the Wyoming Coal and Mining Company. Wardell replaced the strikers
with Scandinavians at $2 per day, a wage considerably lower than that
previously paid. To lessen tension, federal troops were sent from Fort
Steele to maintain order at Rock Springs and Carbon. "When Union Pacific
took over the mines, it continued Wardell's practices."[80]

Railroad executives in the 1870s were uniformly opposed to unionism.
Therefore, when Union Pacific took over the mines, its policy was to fire
anyone who went out on strike against the company. In the summer of
1875, Union Pacific officials cut the pay for mining coal from 5 cents a
bushel to 4 cents for every bushel leaving the mine. Since Union Pacific also
controlled the prices of food, clothing, and mining supplies in the coal
towns, the miners felt that the cost of these items should be dropped to
allow the miners to afford their needed supplies. When Union Pacific
refused to drop the price of goods, the miners at Carbon and Rock Springs
went out on strike. Their demands centered on the restoration of the 5-
cent-per-bushel rate. The Union Pacific Railroad responded quickly.
Strikers were promptly discharged and replaced by Chinese miners. "The

strikers then offered to go back to work at 4 cents, but they could get nothing more than an offer of free transportation to Omaha." The Union Pacific, expecting trouble, requested federal troops to protect its mines. Four companies of U.S. Army regulars were dispatched: two were sent to Carbon and two to Rock Springs. The main function of the troops was to protect company property. With the strikers gone, troops did not have to stay long, and an important change began to take place in the Union Pacific coal mines. Finding the Chinese "easier to deal with," the Union Pacific increased their numbers until they outnumbered all other nationalities in the Wyoming mines.[81]

In 1874 the coal industry stood on the verge of expansion. From the small mines run by stage station operators to the railroad mines initiated in 1868, the infant industry had already undergone sweeping changes; but in 1874 changes were put in place that would lead to large-scale expansion of Wyoming coal mining. Union Pacific was putting into motion changes that would take Wyoming mining from its frontier infancy into becoming part of a nationwide industrial network. Mining technologies developed in Europe would serve as the basis for this expansion. But as the need for more coal increased, so did the need for more men to mine the coal. In the sparsely populated Territory of Wyoming, finding enough men to work underground meant hiring immigrants from Asia and Europe. Men who had never mined coal before would be recruited to work underground. They had to learn mining techniques from experienced miners. The coal mining industry in the Territory of Wyoming was entering a new era.

Notes

[1] John Rolfe Burroughs, *Where the Old West Stayed Young* (New York: Bonanza Books, 1962).

[2] P. V. Crawford, "Journal of a Trip Across the Plains in 1851," *Quarterly of the Oregon Historical Society* 25 (June 1924): 148-150.

[3] U.S. Department of the Interior, *Draft Green River-Hams Fork Regional Coal Environmental Impact Statement* (Denver: Bureau of Land Management, 1978), I-19.

[4] A. Howard Cutting, *A Journal of an Overland Trip, 1863*, (Ms. on file, Henry H. Huntington Library and Art Gallery, San Marino, California), June 2, 1863, entry.

[5] William S. Bryans, A History of Transcontinental Railroads and Coal Mining on the Northern Plains to 1920 (Ph.D. dissertation, University of Wyoming, 1987), 32-33; Arleyn Simon and Kelly Keim, *The Marsh Hawk Site 32BI317, Billings County, North Dakota*, vol. 1 (Grand Forks, North Dakota: Department of Anthropology and Archaeology, 1983), 323-325.

⁶ Washington Irving, *Adventures of Captain Bonneville*. Reprinted. (Portland, Oregon: Binfords and Mort, 1950), 10, 160.

⁷ Osborne Russell, *Journal of a Trapper*, ed. Aubrey L. Haines. (Lincoln: University of Nebraska Press, 1965), 25, 58.

⁸ Howard Stansbury, *Exploration and Survey of the Valley of the Great Salt Lake of Utah Including a Reconnaissance of a New Route Through the Rocky Mountains* (Washington, D.C.: Robert Armstrong Public Printer, 1853), 234.

⁹ Bryans, Railroads and Coal Mining, 38.

¹⁰ Joel Palmer, *Journals of Travels over the Rocky Mountains* (Cincinnati: J. A. and U. P. James, 1847), 30.

¹¹ Bryans, Railroads and Coal Mining, 39; Dale L. Morgan, "The Mormon Ferry on the North Platte, The Journal of William A. Emprey," *Annals of Wyoming* 21 (July-October 1949): 135.

¹² Joseph Goldsborough Bruff, *Gold Rush: The Journals, Drawings, and other Papers of Joseph Goldsborough Bruff*, ed. Georgia Willis Read and Ruth Gaines (New York: Columbia University Press, 1944), 52.

¹³ Bryans, Railroads and Coal Mining, 39, 59.

¹⁴ Carl A. Ubbelohde, Maxine Benson, and Duane A. Smith, *A Colorado History* (Boulder, Colorado: Pruett Publishing Company, 1976), 44.

¹⁵ Donald Jackson and Mary L. Spence, *Travels from 1838 to 1844, The Expeditions of John Charles Fremont*, vol. 1 (Urbana: Illinois University Press, 1970), 461.

¹⁶ Stansbury, *Exploration and Survey of the Valley of the Great Salt Lake of Utah*, 234.

¹⁷ Ibid., 246.

¹⁸ Ibid., 406.

¹⁹ William Clayton, *The Latter Day Saints Emigrant Guide* (St. Louis: Chambers and Knapp, 1848), 24.

²⁰ A. R. Veatch, *Geography and Geology of a Portion of Southwestern Wyoming*, U.S. Geological Survey Professional Paper No. 56 (Washington, D.C.: Government Printing Office, 1907), 117.

²¹ W. Turrentine Jackson, *Wells Fargo in Colorado Territory* (Denver: Colorado Historical Society Monograph Series, 1982), 24.

²² James A. Evans, *Report of Jas. A. Evans of Exploration from Camp Walbach to Green River, 1865* (Omaha, Nebraska: Union Pacific Historical Museum, File K-13-1, 1865), 11.

²³ Ibid.

²⁴ Ibid.

²⁵ J. W. Finfrock, Diary of Ft. Halleck, Wyoming, February 14, 1864 (Ms. on file, University of Wyoming Archives, American Heritage Center, Laramie).

²⁶ Bryans, Railroads and Coal Mining, 46.

²⁷ Ibid., 46-47.

²⁸ Ibid., 40.

²⁹ Ibid., 48; "Exploration from Fort Riley to Bridger's Pass" in *Report of the Chief of Topographical Engineers, 1856-1857*, 35th Cong., 1st Sess., House Executive Document No. 2. (Washington D.C.: Government Printing Office, 1856-1857), 153-154.

[30] Stewart H. Holbrook, *The Story of American Railroads* (New York: Crown Publishers, 1947), 163.
[31] Robert G. Athearn, *Union Pacific Country* (Lincoln: University of Nebraska Press, 1971), 20.
[32] Ibid., 56.
[33] Keith Wheeler, *The Railroaders* (New York: Time-Life Books, 1973), 27.
[34] Ibid., 36.
[35] Athearn, *Union Pacific Country*, 70.
[36] Ibid., 70-71.
[37] Wheeler, *The Railroaders*, 68.
[38] Everett Dick, *The Sod-House Frontier 1854-1890* (Lincoln: University of Nebraska Press, 1979), 115.
[39] Dena Markoft, *Site Documentation of the Hamilton Homestead Site in Southern Campbell County, Wyoming* (Ms. on file, State Historic Preservation Office, Fort Mead, South Dakota, 1982), 4.
[40] Ibid.; Giezentanner Veda, "In Dugouts and Sod Houses," *The Chronicles of Oklahoma*, 39 (1961): 140-149.
[41]*The Frontier Index*, (Green River City, Wyoming) September 3, 1868.
[42]*History of the Union Pacific Coal Mines 1868 to 1940* (Omaha: The Colonial Press, 1940), 122-123.
[43]Mary E. Hodgson, History of Carbon, Wyoming (Ms. on file, University of Wyoming, American Heritage Center, Carbon File W994+-car., n.d.), 1.
[44]*Union Pacific Coal Mines*, Appendix. Within the text when the term tons is used, it refers to short tons (2000 lb).
[45]Ibid., 29.
[46]Dorothy Schwieder, *Black Diamonds: Life and Work in Iowa's Coal Mining Communities, 1895-1920* (Ames: Iowa State University Press, 1983), 24.
[47]U.S. Department of Census, *Ninth Census of the United States 1870* (Washington, D.C.: U.S. Government Printing Office, 1872); *Tenth Census of the United States 1880* (Washington, D.C.: U.S. Government Printing Office, 1883); *Eleventh Census of the United States 1890* (Washington, D.C.: U.S. Government Printing Office, 1892); *Twelfth Census of the United States 1900* (Washington, D.C.: U.S. Government Printing Office, 1901).
[48]*Union Pacific Coal Mines*, 31-32.
[49]I. Lepponen, Old Carbon, Hanna, and the Coal Mines (Ms. on file, University of Wyoming, American Heritage Center, File No. W994+-car). For census figures, see *Ninth Census of the United States*.
[50]*Union Pacific Coal Mines*, 29.
[51]Hodgson, History of Carbon.
[52]*Union Pacific Coal Mines*, 36.
[53]*The (Cheyenne) Wyoming Tribune*, December 11, 1869.
[54]Ibid.
[55]Silas Reed, *Report of the Surveyor General of Wyoming Territory for the Year 1871* (Washington, D.C.: U.S. Government Printing Office, 1871), 20-21.
[56]Ibid., 20.

[57]*Cheyenne (Wyoming) Daily Leader*, October 5, 1875.

[58]*The Rock Springs (Wyoming) Exposer*, November 10, 1876.

[59]Richard Headlee, An Architectural History of Southern Wyoming, 1867-1887 (Master's thesis, University of Wyoming, 1977), 40.

[60]Wyoming Board of Immigration, *The Territory of Wyoming, Its History, Soil, Climate, Resources, etc.* (Laramie: Daily Sentinel Print, 1874).

[61]*The Rock Springs Exposer*, November 10, 1876.

[62]Taft A. Larson, *History of Wyoming* (Lincoln: University of Nebraska Press, 1978), 113.

[63]*Union Pacific Coal Mines*, 98.

[64]E. A. Stone, *Uinta County: Its Place in History* (Laramie: The Laramie Printing Company, 1924), 122-123.

[65]Ibid.; A. D. Gardner and Robert Rosenberg, *Archaeological and Historical Survey of 26 Mine Reclamation Sites in Uinta and Lincoln Counties, Wyoming.* Cultural Resource Management Report No. 13 (Rock Springs: Archaeological Services of Western Wyoming College, 1984), 14-15.

[66]*Union Pacific Coal Mines*, 98.

[67]Ferdinand V. Hayden, *Fifth Annual Report of the U.S. Geological Survey of Montana and Portions of Adjacent Territories* (Washington, D.C.: U.S. Government Printing Office, 1872), 154.

[68]Veatch, "Geography and Geology," 135; G. Blacker, *Annual Report of the State Coal Mine Inspector of Wyoming, District 1*, (Cheyenne: The Office Company, 1914), 22-24.

[69]F. Shaw, Memories of a Miner (Ms. on file, Wyoming State Archives, Museums, and Historical Department, W.P.A. File No. 1350, Uinta County, Miscellaneous, 1936).

[70]Stone, *Uinta County*, 126-127.

[71]Denise Wheeler, *The Feminine Frontier: Wyoming Women 1850-1900* (Evanston, Wyoming: Denise Wheeler, 1987), 84.

[72]*Ninth Census of the United States.*

[73]Larson, *Wyoming*, 114.

[74]Maury Klein, *The Life and Legend of Jay Gould* (Baltimore: The John Hopkins University Press, 1986), 150-151.

[75]Ibid.

[76]*Laramie Boomerang*, "Annual Edition," November 27, 1891.

[77]Klein, *The Life and Legend of Jay Gould*, 152.

[78]Ibid.

[79]Wyoming Board of Immigration, *The Territory of Wyoming.*

[80]Larson, *Wyoming*, 114.

[81]Ibid.; Dell Isham, *Rock Springs Massacre 1885* (Lincoln City, Oregon: Quality Printing Service, 1985).

2
The Troubled Years,
1875 - 1890

I would say the first job I remember was loading coal in these small cars that would hold about a ton—shoveling by hand into the car in a room neck. . . . For a kid, it's not the easiest thing in the world. But you get toughened into it.[1]

This comment was given years later by a coal miner who started in the mines at the age of fifteen. Getting coal out of the ground was not an easy task during the nineteenth century, but it was straightforward. Men went underground and dug coal with picks, shovels, and blasting powder. Dusty, dirty, and dangerous, coal mining made its mark on the landscape and on the people who mined it.

To make a profit at coal mining, large quantities of coal had to be removed from the ground. This meant a large work force. In the coal industry, there was no equivalent to the solitary, independent miner panning for nuggets of gold. The coal miner might have worked alone underground, but he was dependent on others to get his coal to the surface; and the miner was not paid for his efforts until the coal had reached the surface. The miner's life during the nineteenth century typically involved a complex mix of independence underground and dependence above ground. The dependence of the miner on a not-so-benevolent coal company led to tensions between miners and managers in the 1870s and 1880s.

Nineteenth-century Mining Methods

Throughout the nineteenth century, coal mining in America was strongly influenced by British coal miners. By 1750 coal mining was an established industry in the British Isles. As the coal industry began to expand in America, an ever increasing number of English miners emigrated. These miners brought with them many convictions about the industry and proven mining techniques developed in the Old World. Drawn by the possibility of gaining work in the gold fields of the West, 37,523 miners entered the country between 1851 and 1860. The bulk of this number was made up of British coal miners.[2] Despite their reasons for emigrating, it was only natural that once the coal miners were in America they would become involved in the coal industry.

The British miners brought with them the experience needed to open and operate coal mines. The first step involved in opening a mine was to determine the type of entry needed to reach the coal seam. Following methods adopted in the Old World and taking into consideration local physical conditions, several different methods of underground mining were used to open a mine. The oldest and simplest method of planning the entry was through direct quarrying. Once an outcrop of coal was located, a pit was cut down 20 or 30 feet directly into the deposit. The coal was then hauled to the surface in carts or buckets.[3] This quarrying method was used throughout the West at small mines, especially where coal was extracted for local use rather than commercial distribution. In areas where coal beds lay horizontal and emerged as outcrops in a cut bank or cliff face, the entry was driven directly into the exposed seam. This method formed what is called a drift mine. If the coal seam lay below the ground surface at a distance of less than 100 feet, a sloping tunnel was driven downward from the surface to intersect the seam. This angling tunnel approach is called a slope mine. If the coal was too deep underground to reach through a slope or a drift tunnel, a vertical shaft from the surface was constructed to access the deposit, creating what is called a shaft mine.[4]

Once the coal was reached, the coal mine operators determined whether to use a room-and-pillar method or long-wall method of extracting the coal. These mining methods were developed in the British Isles and found common use in America. With the room-and-pillar method, one left large columns of coal intact to serve as supports. The long-wall method involved removing all the coal and using wooden props and stone and rubble "pack walls" to support the undermined areas. Typically the room-and-pillar method meant opening two parallel entries, or tunnels, from the surface or shaft to the slope bottom. These entries measured about 8 feet in width and 5 to 8 feet in height, depending on the mine. The parallel entries were vital in maintaining good air flow into a mine. Between the two entryways, pillars of coal ranging from 20 feet to 50 feet wide were left.[5] The mine operator designated one shaft the entryway and the other the haulway, or haulageway. The haulway was the route by which the coal extracted underground was transported to the surface.

Providing cross entries was an important part of opening a mine. Cross entries are tunnels that branch off the main entries. The continual need for

Schematic drawing showing the most common types of mine entries used to reach the coal seams: drift (A), shaft (B), and slope (C). The selection of the type of entry to be used was conditioned by a number of factors, such as the depth and dip of the coal seam.

air circulation in a mine required two cross entries be excavated in parallel rows. One of these tunnels was used for haulage, the other solely for airflow. This idea of two openings providing ventilation was again a reflection of English influence in coal mining technology. As early as the middle of the seventeenth century, British colliers had discovered that in shafts more than 50 or 60 feet deep, two openings were required for ventilation. The concept was relatively simple. The idea was to form a U-shaped tube underground through which air could flow. One arm of the tube served as the intake, and the other served as an exhaust. Later, as mechanization in the mines increased, it was found that natural airflow could be increased by placing a fan atop one of the openings.[6]

Within the depths of the mine, the miner extracted the coal from what was called a room. The room was actually a long narrow tunnel. "Most rooms averaged 30 feet in width and rarely exceeded 150 feet in length." The height of the room depended on how high or how low the coal seam extended. A seam of 3 feet meant long hours of kneeling and stooping, whereas a 20-foot-high seam meant the miner had to do a lot of prop work to keep the roof safe. The wall of the room where the coal had not yet been extracted was called the face, and it was at the face that the miner actually extracted the coal.

Once in his work place, or room, the miner began his day by checking the roof. Tapping it with his pick or a stick, he could determine if the roof was safe or if more props were needed.[7] After checking his room for problems, the miner would begin working. With his miner's lamp in place on his hat, the miner began the process of digging out the coal by lying on his side and undercutting the seam. This undercutting was done with a pick. The miner picked as far back under the bottom of the coal as he could reach. To be successful, the miner had to pick with both his right hand and his left

Prior to the invention of modern machinery, extracting coal from underground mines was done completely by hand. To get the coal into a size that was easily loaded by hand to be hauled to the surface, the working face of the coal seam was undercut with a pick. The face was then drilled and blasted to break up the coal. Once the coal was blasted from the face, it was loaded into small, horse-drawn cars for the trip to the surface. The loading of the car was usually the job of a "green miner." The green miner was often the teenage son of the miner working that section of the face, or room.

hand. Skill with a pick was something to be praised.[8] Since coal miners were paid by the ton, one had to be a good picker and loader to make a living.

Once the coal was undercut, the miner prepared to blast the coal downward from the face. The coal would fall down into the undercut area in nice lumps ready to be loaded into a waiting ore cart and transported to the surface. The actual extraction was a relatively simple operation. The coal was blasted out of the face by the miner and loaded into the car by his helper, often a teenager. To blast the coal, the miner drilled holes, several feet long, in the face. In the nineteenth century, black powder was poured into brown paper, rolled up, and pasted. These 12-inch-long rolls were then impaled on a long, thin iron needle and inserted into the bore holes. The open end of the bore hole was tamped with coal dust or a "powder dummy," a cloth bag filled with sand. The purpose of placing the dummy in the hole was to force the explosion downward or outward rather than letting it come back into the room. Once the powder and dummy were tamped, the needle was removed and a fuse, a "squib," was placed in the hole.[9] Initially it was the miner's responsibility to light the squib, and he and his partner scrambled for cover. Later, as mining practices improved, the blasting was done systematically throughout the mine by a "shot firer," literally, the man who lit the fuses exploding the black powder. By systematically lighting the fuses, dust was reduced and safety improved. Random firing throughout the mines resulted in excessive dust and deaths.

Once the coal was removed from the face, the miner resumed undercutting, and the loader loaded the coal for the trip to the surface. "Miners quickly learned the tricks to loading the maximum amount of coal into each car."[10] Since they were paid by the ton delivered to the surface, it was in their best interests to place as much coal in the ore car as possible. One Wyoming miner who began loading coal cars at the age of fifteen related

The rope rider would give me heck sometimes. The cars would only hold a ton but if you just chunked in say a foot and put chunks around the edges of it, you could put a little more coal in there. Well, some of these foreigners that had been in the mines a long time, they could chunk that coal around there just as beautiful as a brick wall. I was pretty green at that. I just would throw it here and there, and I'd pile it up pretty high. The mine was low, and when they came up out of the mine with those loads with the chunks of coal sticking up too high, it would knock the coal over on top of the rope rider and got him a little scratched a few times. But I learned eventually.[11]

The rope rider's job was to convey the loaded coal cars to the surface.

Often one could identify who loaded the coal car simply by how the load was arranged. Some men took great pride in how much they could load in a car. One miner, in describing how to load a car, claimed the correct way was to load "the car good and square and seeing that you had good chunks on each corner butted against the car so they couldn't get jerked off."[12] After loading the car, a metal check identifying the miners was attached to the car. When the car reached the surface, the weighman took off the metal check and recorded the car tonnage. On payday the miner was paid according to the amount of "clean" coal that had reached the surface. Often miners were docked a certain percentage of their wage if stone, "boney," was found in their cart.

Underground, in the room, the coal miner was independent. As one coal mining historian, Dorothy Schwieder, noted

The coal miner was indeed an independent workman. Although he kept specific hours, within that work day he largely determined the amount of coal he loaded out and hence the amount of money that he made. He worked alone in his room, making his own decisions on how he would proceed during the day and the manner in which he would carry out his individual responsibilities.[13]

This independence compensated somewhat for the dangers and discomforts inherent in mining. Unlike a nineteenth-century factory worker, the miner had no supervisor continually "looking over his shoulder."[14]

In spite of his independence underground, the miner did not work alone. In any coal mine, a support network existed that was essential to the smooth operation of the mine. Men who worked in this support network were called, not so fondly, "company men." Since they worked for the company and received a regular salary, they were not dependent on the amount of coal they mined. Yet hauling the coal to the surface was essential to ensuring a continuous and profitable operation. Haulers, or drivers, handled mules or horses to bring coal to the surface. Timbermen set props and kept the haulway in good repair. In addition, there were a host of craftsmen who worked underground, including blacksmiths, track layers, mule tenders, masons, and pump men. In charge of these underground workers were the fire boss and the mine boss. The fire boss, experienced in mining, checked for fire damp or bad air and also supervised the mine

The process of mining and shipping coal required the labor of many people, not only those men working the coal seam. Working the seam, however, fell to the most experienced and able-bodied men. Older men and young boys were hired to fill other jobs, such as "boney picker" in the tipple. (From an original photograph of the Excelsior Mine, courtesy of the American Heritage Center, Photo Archives, University of Wyoming)

workings. The mine boss, or "inside" boss, dictated how the mine ran underground.[15]

The focus of mining was the underground operation, but the purpose of the mine was to ship coal. Once above ground, the coal had to be sorted, sometimes crushed, and loaded into waiting railroad cars. The surface operation was relatively elaborate. Often there were steam engines, hoisting equipment, and pump houses that required individuals with a certain amount of skill to operate. There were, in addition to the structures needed to house the various equipment, powder houses, machine shops, blacksmith shops, carpenter shops, hoist houses, a boilerhouse, and often a paint shop. Because of the lack of trees near the coal mines, mine owners shipped in a large number of mine props, and this timber was stored in a yard near the mine. Finally, there was the tipple. The tipple was positioned just outside the mine opening and usually extended over railroad tracks. It was here that the coal was sorted and processed for shipment.

The coal was brought into the tipple by mule-powered coal carts or by steam-powered hoists. The coal was dumped into a metal pan that carried the coal to a "picking table." Old men and young boys stood over the picking tables separating the coal from slate or stone and throwing out any material that would not burn. In the tipple, coal was also sorted by size or sometimes broken down to desired dimensions. The sorted coal was given descriptive names that corresponded to the size of the coal: pea, egg, and lump. The coal, once sorted, was then loaded into waiting railroad coal cars through chutes. The process of moving coal inside the tipple was accomplished principally by gravity and back-breaking effort. However, steam-powered shakers were also used, and the shakers were noisy. The moving coal created clouds of black dust that covered everything and everyone inside. Working inside the tipple was not an easy job. Wyoming was not immune to using children as boney pickers. In writing about coal mining in Pennsylvania, historian Anthony Wallace related how a miner might begin and end his career.

> At the bottom of the scale were the slate pickers, who might be as young as four, but the category also included mature men whose injuries or advanced age had made them unfit for more demanding work. Thus a miner's career might begin as slate picker, then progress through all the ranks successively as driver, laborer, and miner, and end up picking slate again.

This progression was not uncommon in Wyoming.[16]

Because of the equipment needed to operate a successful coal mine, large amounts of capital were required to open and successfully run a mine. The need for capital plus the fact that coal had to be shipped outside the area to make mining profitable put the control of successful mining ventures in the hands of big business. Duane Smith, in his history of the Crested Butte coal mines in Colorado, stated it best when he wrote

> Coal is a bulk shipment item and needs the cheapest, year-round transportation available. That translated easily at this time into the railroad. Hence railroads, which obviously were prime customers as well as principal carriers, came early to be associated with coal mining. What better way, in the nineteenth century entrepreneur's mind, to cover all bets than to have the railroad own the coal mines? The profits would roll in uninterrupted.[17]

In the 1870s and into the 1880s, railroads were the big businesses that dominated coal mining. In Wyoming that railroad was the Union Pacific.

Expansion, Profits, and Complications

When Union Pacific took control of the coal mines in 1874, it initiated changes that would strengthen its domination of coal mining in southern Wyoming. Jay Gould, who gained control of the Union Pacific Railroad early in 1874, took his first trip west in October of that year. Following his trip he wrote a letter to Silas H. H. Clark, his general superintendent, claiming, "The only thing I have any solicitude about is the coal business." Gould, with his shrewd business sense, quickly decided to develop the coal industry "to its fullest extent." He instructed Clark, "Take hold of this department and get the mining and selling of coal upon the most economical and efficient basis."[18] At that time, the Union Pacific operated seven mines in Wyoming—two at Carbon, four at Rock Springs, and one at Almy. With these mines, Gould had the resources to make a profit.

Jay Gould and other mine managers of the period often failed to understand the temperament and nature of coal miners. Typically the miners were controlled day in and day out by the mine manager's policies. In some areas, the company fixed the prices of mining equipment the miners had to purchase. They controlled housing and the stores where the miners purchased their food. Although the miners at Carbon, Almy, and Rock Springs could build their own homes, their lives were still dominated by the company. But this domination was above ground and outside the mine. Once underground, the miner was essentially his own boss. The skilled miner controlled everything that took place in his room. His decisions had life and death consequences, and interference often adversely affected the miner. There might have been a foreman who looked over the worker's efforts, but they generally let the miner do his job. The

Jay Gould

incentive of getting paid only for the amount of coal extracted made miners hard workers. Gould, and future railroad executives, underestimated their independent and hard-working spirit. Union Pacific's decisions in 1875 to lower wages and bring in new miners were not made with the workers' interests in mind, nor were they made in consideration of the independent nature of the miner. Labor strife would be a theme of the 1880s.

With labor costs sharply reduced in 1875, steps were taken to perfect Union Pacific's coal operation. "I shall be disappointed," Gould declared, "if we do not reduce the cost of our coal to not much over $1 per ton."[19] This proposed cost per ton was down from the 1874 cost of $2.13 a ton. For years Gould would make $1 a ton a company goal. To attain his goal, Gould wanted the mines managed by a separate department outside the railroad. In spite of a separation of powers, he still wanted the coal company and railroad to work towards dominating the coal market. The ultimate goal was to monopolize the coal trade by driving out competitors with discriminating freight rates on the railroad. "What I want," Gould stressed, "is to gain so large a local trade that we can keep our mines and rolling stock busy all the time."[20]

Eventually Gould's interest in the coal mines would diminish. Meanwhile, the fact that the driving force behind the Union Pacific took an active interest in the coal mines in Wyoming increased their productivity. More importantly for the railroad, the mines had become profitable. Between 1875 and 1885 the tonnage produced from Union Pacific mines in Wyoming increased from 208,222 to 746,753. Not only had production nearly tripled, but between 1875 and 1883 the cost per ton had dropped 65 cents. "Gould's drive and vision laid the foundation for future expansion."[21]

Human Costs

The expansion of Wyoming's coal industry between 1868 and 1885 was not without its human costs. Coal mining deaths began to occur not long after the first mine was opened. Most deaths took place singly as the result of bad roofs and "caves," or rock fall. While deaths could occur anywhere in a mine, they were more prevalent in the rooms; but in addition to the dangers found in the rooms, hauling coal out of the mines was another principal cause of death. Derailed cars, runaway cars, and unforeseen changes in the mine created hazards. Prop pulling, the process of creating controlled cave-ins, was extremely dangerous. Scattered mine accidents were the primary reasons miners lost their lives.

Early statistics for mine accidents are scanty for Wyoming. Mine safety was, however, something that concerned the territorial government, and the 1875 Territorial Legislature took steps to address hazards in coal mines. In that year Leonard Coates, representative from Sweetwater County, authored a bill calling for the protection of the "health and safety of persons employed in the coal mines of Wyoming Territory."[22] The bill was passed in the House on the second reading in November of 1875.[23] It apparently was not very comprehensive, and there are few details of what the actual bill encompassed, how it would be enforced, or even if the territorial governor signed the law. Since the Wyoming statutes for 1875 were not published, what became of this pilot legislation is not known. It was a step in the right direction. Prior to 1875, only four states had enacted safety and coal mine inspection laws. The fact that Wyoming at least attempted to introduce some sort of safety measures in 1875 is commendable. Unfortunately, as evidenced in the mine disasters of the 1880s, some form of legislation was needed to help improve safety in the coal mines.[24]

In 1881 the first major coal mine explosion rocked Central Pacific's mines at Almy. On March 4, the Rocky Mountain Coal and Iron Company No. 2 mine exploded and killed thirty-eight miners. Of this number, thirty-five were Chinese and three were what the newspapers of that time called "white men." In addition to the thirty-eight men killed, fifteen were trapped by the explosion, and one was seriously injured. The fifteen trapped were later rescued without loss of additional lives.[25] The explosion had apparently been the result of gas being ignited underground.

The problem of an underground explosion was compounded by the presence of both coal dust and gas. The gases in a mine could easily be ignited by a spark or a flame from a miner's candle. The resulting explosion was made more serious by suspended coal dust particles in the shafts and tunnels. Powdered coal is extremely volatile if an adequate amount of heat is applied. Once the gases exploded, the coal dust was ignited and an underground fireball resulted. The explosions at the Almy mine in 1881 threw "flames many hundreds of feet out of the main slope carrying away the buildings around the mouth of the shaft and setting the machinery and buildings on fire."[26]

Central Pacific opened its No. 2 mine at Almy in 1869. It proved to be a profitable mine, and in 1881 the company "employed a day force of 200 men and a night gang of 75 men." Chinese miners made up nearly the entire crew. "There had been a fire raging in this mine for five years, but it had been walled in by stone walls." Although the cause of the explosion is not known, at least some people felt that gas had accumulated and in some way come in contact with the fire behind the wall. "It was the first explosion of this kind that had ever occurred west of the Mississippi River." Wyoming had the unfortunate distinction of being the first western territory to experience a tragedy of this nature.[27]

Labor Strife

In addition to the dangers in mining, labor strife began to take on menacing overtones in the 1880s. Jay Gould's policies of reducing the cost of coal production in Union Pacific mines resulted in the hiring of miners for lower wages than had previously been paid. Tensions escalated when disgruntled miners were replaced primarily by one ethnic group, the Chinese. Gould's practice of hiring Chinese miners was calculated. As early as 1874 when striking miners were first replaced with Chinese workers, Gould had instructed S. H. H. Clark to employ only Chinese laborers in a new mine at Almy. "With Chinese at Almy and native miners at the other point," Gould pointedly observed, "you can play one against the other and thus keep master of the situation." The replacement of white miners with Chinese miners in Wyoming Territory after 1874 brought protests throughout the territory. At the 1876 Republican convention in Rawlins, the party resolved, "The introduction of Chinese labor into this country is fraught with serious and dangerous consequences." In spite of this resolution, Union Pacific continued to bring in Chinese miners until Chinese outnumbered whites in the Wyoming coal mines.[28]

Throughout Wyoming, misgivings about Union Pacific's hiring of Chinese had been expressed as early as 1868. The *Frontier Index* decried the use of Chinese labor on the Central Pacific Railroad and elsewhere in the West. The *Wyoming Tribune*, in 1870, ran an editorial claiming twelve hundred more "China men" had arrived in California and complained that they would soon be taking "white men's" jobs. The paper went on to say,

Every day a suicide, some poor devil of a white man out of money, too proud to beg, too honest to steal, too noble to starve, blows his brains out. All right white blood is at a discount and coffins are cheap. The potter's field is large; starving white people are welcome to its gates.

The writer of the editorial, in an appeal to the reader's patriotism, concluded the article by imploring workers, "By every consideration of honor and of manhood; by every impulse of justice and patriotism, I conjure you to rise as one man in the majesty of your power as freemen, and throw back the tide of heathen paupers from our shores."[29]

Growing anti-Chinese sentiment, coupled with Union Pacific's wage-cutting policies, led to a volatile situation. Warnings were given to the management of the Union Pacific, but they went unheeded. Seemingly, little was done to avoid events that would eventually erupt in violence.

One of the contributing factors that led to the anti-Chinese movement in the coal mines was a perception that Chinese miners were treated better than their white counterparts. From the outset it was felt that the Union Pacific granted the Chinese extra privileges.[30] The major complaints of the white miners in the 1880s included the feeling "Chinese miners were favored in the assignment of rooms in the mines." The coal miners in Rock Springs felt the Chinese miners were given the easiest "workings" where they could easily extract coal and make more money each day. To this end, they accused J. M. Tisdel, mine superintendent in Rock Springs, of selling "privileges to Chinamen." Adding to their discontent was the fact that Union Pacific coal miners were "compelled to trade at the Beckwith, Quinn and Company store."[31] Being forced to trade at Beckwith and Quinn was especially objectionable to the white miners since this company was the firm that had brought the Chinese miners into Wyoming.

At Rock Springs, the Chinese miners were provided with homes built by Union Pacific. Miners of other nationalities had to make do with less. Dugouts were still evident along Bitter Creek at this time, and many were inhabited by white miners and their families. Although white miners also had homes outside the banks of Bitter Creek, the perception that they were not doing as well as their Chinese counterparts created mounting tensions that accelerated between 1875 and 1885. Not finding the Union Pacific management open to listening to their problems, the workers turned to other avenues to vent their frustrations, notably to the Knights of Labor. British miners, who brought with them the skills needed to mine coal, also brought ideas and values fostered in England. As early as 1850, "British miners had become strong advocates of trade unions, a conviction that they continued to support in the United States." When the British miners emigrated to America, they carried with them the fight for shorter hours, better working conditions, and increased pay.[32] The British influenced other nationalities, and soon coal miners were looking to labor unions as a means of addressing problems they faced in the mines. The Knights of Labor was the major labor organization in the 1880s, and it was to this organization that coal miners in Wyoming turned for help. The miners wanted to increase wages and improve working conditions. The Chinese, seemingly, stood in their way.

The Knights of Labor was very active in Rock Springs after 1883. It was successful not only in organizing miners in Rock Springs but also in enlisting railroad workers throughout the territory. Sweetwater County became one of the union's strongholds in the territory. Initially the Knights of Labor in Rock Springs tried to recruit Chinese workers. This was contrary to its anti-Chinese labor policy, but it showed good faith in trying to bring all coal miners into the union. "Considering the union strictly a 'White Man's Organization,' the Chinese refused to join." This refusal of the Chinese miners to join the union embittered the white

Charles F. Adams, Jr.

miners. The proverbial die was cast, and the union began advocating the removal of all Chinese from Wyoming.[33]

In 1884 the newly appointed president of the Union Pacific Railroad, Charles F. Adams, Jr., was made aware of labor problems in the West. A member of the distinguished Adams family, which had produced two American Presidents, Charles Adams was seen by some people as a possible warrior for the common man. A man in Cheyenne wrote to Adams in 1884 asking for relief from Union Pacific's reduction in wages. The writer told Adams, "I am a member of the Knights of Labor, an organization which comprises many many thousands in the United States." Hoping that Adams could help, he continued, "the name of Charles Francis Adams suggests reminiscences and historic memories, which are entwined around the hearts of every American." Claiming that the Adams "name is identical with Patriotism and the Peoples' rights," the writer asked for help in solving labor problems in Wyoming.[34] Letters to Charles Adams came not only from members of the Knights of Labor but also from Union Pacific managers concerned with the running of the mines.

On January 16, 1885, Adams was told of labor strife brewing in the coal mines. S. R. Callaway, the general manager for Union Pacific Railroad at Omaha, became concerned about possible coal shortages. Callaway wrote Adams on that date:

During my railroad career I have had a good many hard nuts to crack, but the labor question here beats anything I ever tackled. The men are in such a temper that they will only do their work as they please and when they please, and are apparently intent upon having some kind of a row with the company. I have temporized with them until patience ceases to be a virtue.

[At] Carbon, the men were all out on a strike because we will not discharge the foreman and every one else who does not suit them. They claim that before they will go to work they are going to compel us to discharge all Finlanders and Chinese.[35]

Callaway went on to say, if the "Knights of Labor order a general strike, I confess I do not see my way out." Yet he pointed out clearly, "I have told the men that we will not discharge the Chinese and have ordered the discharge of the men at North Platte and those engaged in the trouble last night."[36] Union Pacific's position was galvanizing: the Chinese would stay. The Knights of Labor countered, "The Chinese must go."[37]

Faced with two opposing forces, the Chinese were firmly in the middle of a brewing storm. It was obvious to most observers the situation was deteriorating. In Rock Springs the labor problem was at a crisis stage by the summer of 1885. John L. Lewis (not related to the great labor leader) writing on behalf of the miners, notified D. O. Clark, superintendent of the Union Pacific Coal Department,

Although I have been lying sick in my bed for the last four weeks, I have been flooded with correspondence from Wyoming . . . the sum and substance of which is, that the Chinese are having all the work they can do, working night and day, whilst our men at Rock Springs are left out in the cold. I understand that they are now working almost day and night, whilst Carbon men have worked but one day in the last two weeks. This makes the situation terribly aggravating, and in spite of my efforts will undoubtedly result in a severe struggle if longer continued.

For God's sake do what you can to avoid this calamity; the pressure is more than I can bear. See that justice is done to all the men at Carbon, and to the unemployed portion at Rock Springs.[38]

Union Pacific later held that Lewis' letter did not arrive until too late. It is obvious, however, that Union Pacific knew there were labor problems brewing along the Wyoming section of its mainline. On September 2, 1885, in the tiny coal camp of Rock Springs, twenty-eight Chinese were murdered.

The Rock Springs Chinese Massacre. A riot began in a room in Union Pacific No. 6 mine. The idea prevailed that once a miner began working in a room, it was his and off limits to other miners. On September 1 two miners, Whitehouse and Jenkins, were assigned rooms in Entry No. 5. The pit boss assigned them the first marked-off rooms without being clear as to where he wanted them to begin working. As the miners came to the first two rooms where working had not commenced, they began preparing the room for extracting coal. The next day when Whitehouse returned to work, he found "two Chinamen in possession of what he considered his room." Of course, feeling it was his room, he ordered them out. The Chinese miners, who were equally possessive over what they considered had been their assigned room, would not leave. "High words followed, then blows. The Chinese from other rooms came rushing in, as did the whites, and a fight ensued with picks, shovels, drills, and the needles for weapons." The Rock Springs Independent, which stood behind the white miners, claimed the "Chinamen were worsted, four of them being badly wounded, one of whom has since died."[39]

The Chinese workers in Union Pacific No. 6 mine were, like their white counterparts, working as coal miners in an attempt to make a living. They differed from other nationalities in that their ultimate goal was not to stay in America but to return to China. The Chinese held that "falling leaves from trees settle on their roots," and like those leaves, a person residing elsewhere finally returns to his or her ancestral home. Most Chinese made provisions, once they entered America, to have their bones shipped home if they lost their life abroad. The Chinese working in Rock Springs could not, or did not, understand the exact nature of the other miners' problems. They also felt prejudice, but they did not articulate their feelings in the press as the white miners had. To the Chinese, the worse situation they could face would be no work. The concept of a strike meant time without pay and a delay in returning home to China. It was not a matter of not caring about conditions in the mines; it was a deep-seated concern that they might lose their jobs that prevented the Chinese from joining the white miners' labor union. Unfortunately, the white miners did not understand the plight of the Chinese.

The Chinese left No. 6 mine after the incident underground and returned home to company-owned houses on the north side of Bitter Creek. The foreman at No. 6 had ordered work to cease after the riot broke out underground. The white men apparently took refuge in the bars and the Chinese in their homes.[40] The Chinese told officials, "About two o'clock in the afternoon a mob, divided into two gangs, came toward Chinatown." One "gang" crossed Bitter Creek on a plank bridge; the other crossed over the railroad bridge, and they converged on the Chinese. Part of the mob moved to the No. 3 mine, which was north of Chinatown. This meant the Chinese were virtually encircled. Across Bitter Creek and over the ridge north of town were the only directions they could escape. "At that time the

Chinese began to realize that the mob was bent on killing. The Chinese, though greatly alarmed, did not yet begin to flee."[41]

The Chinese account of what took place next depicts a scene of mob violence. Some who were able to run away dispersed on the south side of Bitter Creek. Others ran north over the hills behind Chinatown, but a number were unable to escape. "Between 4 o'clock and a little past 9 o'clock p.m. all the camp houses belonging to the coal company and the Chinese huts [were] burned down completely." The Chinese who witnessed the event reported:

> Some of the Chinese were killed at the bank of Bitter Creek, some near the railroad bridge, and some in 'Chinatown.' After having been killed, the dead bodies of some were carried to the burning buildings and thrown into the flames. Some of the Chinese who had hid themselves in the houses were killed and their bodies burned; some, who on account of sickness could not run, were burned alive in the houses. One Chinese was killed in 'Whitemen's Town' in a laundry house, and his house demolished. The whole number of Chinese killed was twenty-eight and those wounded fifteen.[42]

Most of the surviving Chinese fled westward toward the town of Green River. Taking quick action, Union Pacific told the railroad conductors to pick up any Chinese they found along the railroad line. Any Chinese located on the mainline were given passage to Evanston, where it was felt they could be protected. This was a questionable notion. White miners at Almy, north of Evanston, were unsympathetic. "The native citizens there threatened day and night to burn and kill the Chinese. Fortunately, United States troops had been ordered to come and protect them, and quiet was restored."[43] Company A of the 9th Infantry and Company I from the 21st Infantry, along with a Gatling gun, were stationed in Evanston. Later the Gatling gun and Company I would be moved to Rock Springs.[44]

On September 9 the troops escorted the Chinese from Evanston back to Rock Springs. In 1880 there were 763 residents in Rock Springs; 497 of these were Chinese.[45] This Chinese majority steadily increased until 1885. Therefore, when Chinatown was burned, it destroyed a large segment of the coal town of Rock Springs. When the Chinese arrived on the ninth, they "saw only a burnt tract of ground to mark the site of their former habitations." A number of the dead had been buried by the company, but not all. Survivors, upon returning, found victims still scattered throughout the ashes of Chinatown. The Chinese survivors reported:

> By this time the most of the Chinese have abandoned the desire of resuming their mining work, but inasmuch as the riot has left them each with only the one or two torn articles of clothing they have on their persons, and

as they have not a single cent in their pockets, it is a difficult matter for them to make any change in their location. Fortunately, the company promised to lend them clothing and provisions, and a number of wagons to sleep in. Although protected by Government troops, their sleep is disturbed by frightful dreams, and they cannot obtain peaceful rest.[46]

The Chinese returned to work under the protection of federal troops. The Chinese Massacre had far-reaching effects. It gained national and international attention, and as a result, the Chinese consul investigated the affair. President Grover Cleveland issued a statement claiming, "This outrage upon law and treaty engagements was committed by a lawless mob. None of the aggressors, happily for the national good, appear by the reports to have been citizens of the United States."[47] Cleveland went on to quote Article II of a treaty between China and the United States that had been signed into law November 17, 1880, stating, "If Chinese laborers or Chinese of any other class, now either permanently or temporarily residing in the territory of the United States, meet with ill-treatment at the hands of any other persons, the Government of the United States will exert all its power to devise measures for their protection."[48] To achieve the terms of this treaty, Territorial Governor F. E. Warren requested federal troops be deployed from Fort Steele, near Rawlins (Wyoming), to Rock Springs. The

Most of the Chinese fleeing Rock Springs were picked up by train crews and taken to Evanston. The Chinese were returned to Rock Springs on September 9, 1885, under the protection of federal troops. (Courtesy of the Sweetwater County Museum)

governor's goal was to ensure that the mines operated normally and that the Chinese miners were protected.

Governor Warren's interests and those of the Union Pacific Railroad and Coal Company were closely related. Warren's interests were expressed in a telegram to S. R. Callaway. Trying to relieve any fears the Union Pacific might have, Warren wrote

> Allow me to express my earnest wish that your road will under no circumstances, recede in the slightest degree from the stand taken, that Chinese shall work and that criminals shall not. I believe that future law and the good order in this territory as well as discipline of Railroad are at stake . . . you surely have the U.S. behind you and China to aid you now.[49]

Warren was apparently referring, in the last part of the telegram, to the presence of the Chinese consul and federal troops stationed at Rock Springs. A telegram was sent by Warren a day earlier from Rock Springs that stated, "Tsang Hay, interpreter, and Wong Sic Chen, Consul at New York, are here under escort of General McCook, conducting an investigation."[50] Warren was pleased with the development. The fact that a general and consular were in Rock Springs made him rest easier. He felt the labor problem would finally be resolved. With troops stationed permanently in Rock Springs, Warren felt the incident of September 2 would not be repeated. Showing the resolve of the United States to protect the Chinese miners, Camp Pilot Butte was constructed adjacent to where Chinatown had stood. New living quarters for the Chinese were constructed next to the camp. The army would remain in Rock Springs until the Spanish American War, assigned to protect not only the Chinese, but also the railroad and its mines.

Continuing Problems, Partial Solutions. Labor tension in the coal mines did not end with the Chinese Massacre. Instead, it generated additional strife in the mines at Carbon and at the Union Pacific mines at Louisville, Colorado. On October 1, 1885, the miners at Carbon went out on strike after issuing a proclamation to the Union Pacific Coal Department. In part the statement read, "the working men at Carbon will not go to work until every Chinaman along the Union Pacific road [is] discharged." Union Pacific reacted swiftly and closed the mines at Carbon. On October 2 the miners at Louisville issued a similar ultimatum calling for "a general settlement of the grievances at Rock Springs." The Louisville mines were closed immediately.[51]

The Union Pacific was, then, in need of outside help to begin reopening its coal mines. Since the principal fuel used to operate the railroad was coal, something had to be done soon. The first attempt at reopening the mines was made shortly after the return of the Chinese miners to Rock

F.E. Warren, the Chinese Protector.
"Pack the Jury, They Must be Convicted."

Political cartoon appearing in the Evanston Register following the "massacre" and the later reestablishment of Chinese miners in Rock Springs. White miners and their supporters held the view that Governor Warren and the U.S. Army were acting in alliance with the railroad to replace them with the Chinese. (Courtesy of the American Heritage Center, Photo Archives, University of Wyoming)

Springs. On September 12, one hundred reluctant Chinese re-entered the mines. The first attempt to reopen all the mines at Rock Springs was made on September 21. Nearly all the white miners, who ran the surface operations necessary to haul the coal out of the mines and load it onto the trains, refused to return to work. Without their assistance, resuming mine operations was impossible. According to the Union Pacific, it became necessary to replace the operators and other mine employees. "[M]easures were accordingly taken to bring white miners at once from Utah and elsewhere. These were mostly Mormons, and no less objectionable than the Chinese to the men who had been concerned in the outbreak of September 2 and who were now waiting to reap the fruits of it."[52] In spite of protests and attempted work stoppages, the mines resumed producing coal at Rock Springs and elsewhere along the Union Pacific mainline with help brought in from outside Wyoming.

Even though the mines were reopened, it was not without a loss in efficiency. Union Pacific's own communications showed a growing concern about their coal operations. A letter from T. J. Potter to Charles Adams in November 1887 noted, "The present Coal Department as I understand has never been run satisfactorily to you." Potter went on to make several recommendations, including a call for a thorough report by John Kangeley, "a practical miner and coal operator" on ways to improve the Wyoming coal mines.[53] In 1887 Kangeley submitted a report on the conditions of the coal mines of Wyoming. In his summary of the Rock Springs mines he concluded, "I would say as a result of my observations in and out of the mines, that everything shows the effect of a long reign of weak management."[54] His criticisms were primarily directed at creating a firmer labor policy, but he also pointed out that Union Pacific needed to make changes. In the late-1880s, Union Pacific stood at a crossroads.

The event that pushed Union Pacific into making changes was the Chinese Massacre. For some time the company had wanted to experiment with cutting machines to reduce the labor force in its mines. Charles Adams wondered if the work stoppage resulting from the strikes and the Chinese Massacre did not offer the ideal circumstances to install labor-saving machinery. From Boston Adams wrote, the company's interest is to "have Rock Springs worked entirely by Chinese and machinery."[55] These changes would ensure increased production in spite of a reduced labor force and past labor problems. As early as 1882, cutting and drilling machines made their appearance in No. 4 mine at Rock Springs.[56] Equipping other mines with these machines would not be difficult. It was hoped that mechanization, coupled with improved management, would alleviate some of Union Pacific's problems.

Increased mechanization paid dividends for Union Pacific. Despite the human tragedy of the Chinese Massacre, the disruption to mining was minimal. The placement of mining machines in the Rock Springs No. 4 mine in 1882 was but a small forerunner of things to come. In 1884, prior to employing large quantities of equipment underground, Union Pacific mines extracted 306,150 tons of coal. This increased to 328,601 tons in 1885, 359,238 tons in 1886, and 465,445 tons in 1887. In part due to increased mechanization between 1887 and 1892, coal production doubled: 943,943 tons of coal were mined in 1892.[57] By 1892 it appeared Union Pacific Coal Company had weathered the storm. The miners who died on September 2, 1885, did not.

The troubled coal industry, which had witnessed the mine explosion at Almy in 1881 and labor strife at mid-decade, experienced yet another disaster in 1886. On January 12, at about midnight, Union Pacific's Almy No. 4 mine exploded, killing thirteen miners. Included in the thirteen fatalities were "two boys," who were working underground at the time. The Salt Lake City *Deseret Evening News* reported that "for a few seconds, the sky was illuminated for miles like a bright-yellow sunset." The explosion, like the one in 1881, erupted like a cannon shot and blew "all the buildings above ground into kindling wood, sending great timbers and rocks three quarters of a mile. Miners' houses were struck and pierced, but the people in them were not seriously injured." Investigations indicated that the explosion occurred when gas "was ignited by a miner's open lamp."[58] This accumulation of gas was due, in part, to poor ventilation.

The territorial coal mine inspector, writing about conditions in Wyoming coal mines in 1886, pointed out that ventilation was a problem in coal mines throughout the territory. Newell Beeman, the first territorial coal mine inspector, wrote

Until recently very little attention has been paid to ventilation in most of the mines in the Territory, the levels and rooms being worked without lines, and no system of ventilation or drainage, the main object having been to get out the coal at as little cost as possible, regardless of the health and safety of employees, or the future development and operation of the mines. This economical policy resulted last January in an explosion of fire damp in one of the mines, which cost the lives of thirteen men, besides a direct pecuniary loss to the company of a great many thousand dollars.

This circumstance, in connection with the passage of the mining law, has been the means of causing the operators to take steps to improve the ventilation of the mines.[59]

Beeman felt that recent legislation was one of the principal reasons steps were being taken to improve the conditions in the mine.

Wyoming territorial legislatures did not stand idly by in the wake of the Chinese Massacre and the 1886 explosion. Wyoming, in 1886, passed legislation to protect the "lives, health, safety, and welfare" of coal miners. Interestingly, Wyoming was preceded only by Washington Territory, in 1883, in being the first territory to pass such legislation. Elsewhere in America this type of legislation had been enacted by state legislative bodies.[60]

The law enacted by the Territorial Council and House of Representatives went a long way toward improving conditions in the mines. It required mine maps to be drawn of each coal mine. These maps would assist in rescuing workers from cave-ins and also provide a basis for knowing if coal was being mined from areas that actually belonged to a coal company. During the nineteenth century, mine operators often wanted to extract coal not only from their land, but from property that belonged to someone else. Coal under lands still owned by the United States was especially susceptible to this type of underground theft. Mine maps provided a means of checking what areas were actually being mined. In addition to requiring a mine map, the Coal Mine Safety Act required that each mine have two openings and be well ventilated. To enforce these and other safety measures, the office of Territorial Inspector of Coal Mines was established. The inspector was instructed to "make records of all examinations [of mines] . . . showing the condition in which he finds them, especially in reference to ventilation and drainage." The concerns growing out of past mine explosions were reflected in the instructions to the mine inspector that he ensure mines were properly ventilated.[61]

Since "two boys" were killed in the 1886 explosion, the territorial legislature took steps to ban children from working in coal mines. The coal mine safety law prohibited boys under the age of fourteen and "women and girls of any age" from being employed "in or about any coal mine."[62] Even though children were prohibited from working in the mines by law, there were still incidents where boys performed a variety of tasks. Moreover, teenagers did not fall under this law. Since Wyoming's attempts to minimize child labor did not prevent boys under sixteen years of age from entering the mines, a large number of teenagers remained in the mines after 1886. Federal statistics for 1889 indicate that the average number of boys under sixteen years of age working underground in Wyoming coal mines stood at nineteen per mine. By comparison, neighboring Colorado averaged eight boys underground per mine, and Utah averaged twenty-nine.[63]

All too frequently teenagers were killed. In those cases where a teenager was killed while working underground, it was not uncommon for the father to be blamed for the accident.[64] A coal company in nineteenth-century Wyoming would never assume responsibility for a mine accident.

Although Wyoming passed a child labor law in an attempt to keep children out of coal mines, the effort was only marginally successful. Children and teenagers continued to work in the mines. As shown by this R. W. Stone photograph of a small wagon mine, children were an important part of this family business. (Courtesy of United States Geological Survey, Denver)

The annual coal mine inspector's report listed the ages of victims, and into the twentieth century it was not uncommon to find teenagers listed along with adults in the fatality reports. One incident that took place eleven years after the territory passed its first safety laws illustrates the circumstances surrounding a teenage death and the way the death was investigated.

> On last Friday about noon Geo. Dubensky, the fourteen-year-old son of Mr. and Mrs. John Dubensky was killed in [Union Pacific] No. 9 mine by falling coal.
> Thomas Gregory testified: "At 12:30 o'clock, Friday, April 30, 1897, I heard a cry for help from John Dubensky. Ed McCourt and I ran to his room and we found the boy, George, dead. He was lying in a pile of slack. We notified the mine foreman right away and took the boy outside immediately. I should judge there were two or three hundred pounds of coal that fell on him, which in my opinion, caused his death. . . .We, the jury, duly impaneled and sworn to according to law . . . to investigate the death of George Dubensky, do find that he came to his death by a fall of coal. . . . According to the evidence given by the boy's father, John Dubensky, we find he is responsible for the same.[65]

By law the county coroner had to investigate the death of miners, but coroners' inquests commonly fixed blame on the miner; and the coal mine inspectors' reports all too often reported that deaths in the mines were not the fault of the coal company. Changes were slow in coming, especially in the coal mines of the nineteenth century. Until the coal companies were forced to accept the responsibility of mine safety, conditions underground would not improve dramatically.

In the late 1880s Wyoming was about to become a state. The coal industry had passed from its infancy to a point where western markets sought more Wyoming coal. The Anaconda copper mines in Butte, Montana, were expanding, and Anaconda wanted Wyoming coal for its smelters. As Union Pacific projected, "at least 250 tons per day more coal from Rock Springs"[66] would be needed to supply Anaconda's demands. Coal yards in Nebraska and the Central Pacific Railway also wanted more Wyoming coal. As a result, interest in opening new coal fields elsewhere in the territory grew out of the increased demand. The coal industry, which had witnessed both difficulty and growth, was about to expand into northern Wyoming. The hazards associated with coal mining had not been alleviated, nor had the labor problems been addressed, but with the prospects of statehood for Wyoming, the expanding coal markets, and the development of new coal fields came an air of optimism.

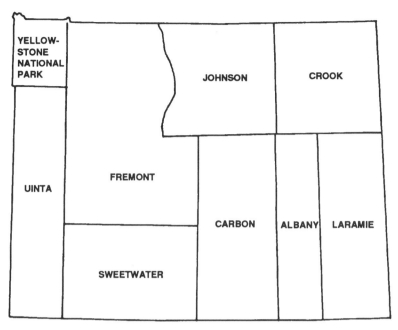

Wyoming Counties in 1884 and prior to statehood in 1890

Notes

[1] Joe Bozovich, interview with author, Rock Springs, Wyoming, December 1987 (Ms. on file, Archaeological Services of Western Wyoming College, Rock Springs), 1, 5.

[2] Dorothy Schwieder, *Black Diamonds: Life and Work in Iowa's Coal Mining Communities, 1895-1920* (Ames: Iowa State University Press, 1983), 7-8.

[3] Anthony F. C. Wallace, *St. Clair, A Nineteenth Century Coal Town's Experience with a Disaster-Prone Industry* (New York: Alfred A. Knopf, 1987), 8.

[4] Schwieder, *Black Diamonds*, 28.

[5] Ibid., 9.

[6] Wallace, *St. Clair*, 39; Schwieder, *Black Diamonds*, 29.

[7] Schwieder, *Black Diamonds*, 35.

[8] Joe Bozovich interview; Schwieder, *Black Diamonds*, 9-10.

[9] Wallace, *St. Clair*, 12.

[10] Schwieder, *Black Diamonds*, 37.

[11] Joe Bozovich interview, 11.

[12] Schwieder, *Black Diamonds*, 37.

[13] Ibid., 57.

[14] Joe Bozovich interview, 6; Schwieder, *Black Diamonds*, 57.

[15] Wallace, *St. Clair*, 20-21.

[16] Ibid., 22; Jack Korogi, personal communication, retired Union Pacific coal miner, Rock Springs, Wyoming, December 1987. Korogi's father picked boney as a child in Rock Springs and retired as a boney picker.

[17] Duane Smith, *When Coal was King, A History of Crested Butte, Colorado, 1880-1952* (Golden: Colorado School of Mines Press, 1984), 9.

[18] Maury Klein, *Union Pacific, Birth of a Railroad 1862-1893*, (Garden City: Doubleday and Company, 1987), 330.

[19] Ibid., 332.

[20] Ibid.

[21] Ibid., 333-334; *History of the Union Pacific Coal Mines 1868 to 1940* (Omaha: The Colonial Press, 1940), XLIV.

[22] *House Journal of the Fourth Legislative Assembly of the Territory of Wyoming* (Cheyenne, Wyoming Territory: Leader Steam Book and Job Printing House, 1875), 105, 132.

[23] *Cheyenne Daily Leader*, November 26, 1875.

[24] *State Coal Mine Inspector's Report 1886; Carbon County Journal* (July 31, 1886):4. Newell Beeman stated, "Until recently very little attention has been paid to ventilation.... This economical policy resulted last January in an explosion of fire damage in one of the mines, which cost the lives of thirteen miners."

[25] *Cheyenne Weekly Leader*, March 10, 1881. The problem of gas in the underground mines at Almy is discussed in both the 1895 and 1896 state coal mine inspector reports.

[26] *Salt Lake Herald*, March 5, 1881; Walter R. Jones, "Coal Mine Explosions at Almy, Wyoming. Their Influence on Wyoming's First Coal Mining Safety Laws," *Annals of Wyoming* 56(Spring 1984):7.

[27] *Cheyenne Daily Leader*, March 5, 1881; H. B. Humphrey, *Historical Summary of Coal Mine Explosions in the United States, 1810-1958* (Washington, D.C.: United States Government Printing Office, 1960), 5.

[28] Klein, *Union Pacific*, 331-332; Taft A. Larson, *History of Wyoming* (Lincoln: University of Nebraska Press, 1978), 115.

[29] *Wyoming Tribune*, May 14, 1870.

[30] Arlen Ray Wilson, The Rock Springs, Wyoming, Chinese Massacre, 1885. (Master's thesis, University of Wyoming, 1967), 28; Isaac Hill Bromely, *The Chinese Massacre at Rock Springs Wyoming Territory* (Boston: Franklin Press, Rand, Avery, and Company, 1886), 30, in University of Utah Special Collections, Salt Lake City. This particular document was compiled to present Union Pacific's viewpoint of the Massacre and is quoted copiously in the company's *Union Pacific Coal Mines*.

[31] Bromely, *The Chinese Massacre*, 34.

[32] Schwieder, *Black Diamonds*, 7-9.

[33] Dell Isham, *Rock Springs Massacre 1885* (Lincoln City, Oregon: Quality Printing Service, 1985), 19; *House Reports, 49th Congress, 1885-1886, No. 2044* (Washington D.C.: Government Printing Office), 23, 28.

[34] Fred J. Stanton to the Honorable Charles F. Adams, president of the Union Pacific Railway Company, Boston, September 1, 1884. Nebraska State Museum and Archives, Lincoln (UPRR Co. MS3761, SG2 Pres.).

[35] S. R. Callaway to Charles F. Adams, January 16, 1885. Nebraska State Museums and Archives, Lincoln (UPRR Co. MS3761).

[36] Ibid.

[37] This quote was posted the night of September 26, 1885, after the Chinese Massacre. Wilson, The Rock Springs Massacre, 58; *House Report No. 2044*, 28.

[38] Bromely, *The Chinese Massacre*, 46-47.

[39] *Rock Springs Independent*, September 3, 1885, contained in *House Report No. 2044*, 21.

[40] In the House report the Chinese and white miners differ on this point. The Chinese claimed the whites became drunk, whereas the *Rock Springs Independent* mentions nothing of this. *House Report No. 2044*.

[41] *House Report No. 2044*, 28.

[42] Ibid., 29.

[43] Ibid.

[44] Special Orders No. 103, Headquarter Department of the Platte, Omaha, Nebraska, October 15, 1885. Microfilm, United States National Archives. Letters received by the Office of Adjactant General 1881-1889.

[45] *Tenth Census of the United States 1880* (Washington, D.C.: U.S. Government Printing Office, 1892).

[46] *House Report No. 2044*, 30.

[47] Ibid., 16.

[48] Ibid., 17.

[49] Francis E. Warren to S. R. Callaway, general manager of the Union Pacific Railway, September 18, 1885. Microfilm National Archives, Denver, Colorado, Territorial Communications.

[50] Bromely, *The Chinese Massacre*, 87-88.

[51] Ibid., 88-89.

[52] Ibid., 72-73.

[53] T. J. Potter to Union Pacific President Charles F. Adams, November 29, 1887. Nebraska State Museum and Archives, Lincoln (UPRR Co. MS3761).

[54] Report of John Kangley, an experienced coal miner, on the UP Coal Department mines in Wyoming and Colorado 1887. Nebraska State Museum and Archives, Lincoln (UPRR Co. MS3761).

[55] Klein, *Union Pacific*, 487; Wilson, Chinese Massacre, 53.

[56] *Union Pacific Coal Mines*, 166.

[57] Ibid., Appendix.

[58] Humphrey, *Coal Mine Explosions*, 13. The Deseret Evening News articles for January 14, 15, and 19, 1886, are reprinted in this publication.

[59] "Office of Territorial Inspector of Mines, June 20, 1886." *Carbon County Journal* (July 31, 1886):4.

[60] Humphrey, *Coal Mine Explosions*; Jones, "Coal Mine Explosions at Almy." For the history of 1886 legislation in Wyoming Territory, 12-13.

[61] *Session Laws of Wyoming Territory, passed by the Ninth Legislative Assembly* (Cheyenne: Vaughn Montgomery Printers and Binders, Democratic Leader Office, 1886), 44-55.

[62] Ibid., 55.

[63] David T. Day, *Mineral Resources of the United States, Calendar Years 1889, 1890.* (Washington, D.C.: Government Printing Office, 1892), 171.

[64] *Rock Springs Miner,* May 6, 1897.

[65] Ibid.

[66] Union Pacific Railway Company Coal Department Report for 1887. Nebraska State Museum and Archives, Lincoln, (UPRR Co. MS3761).

3

Statewide Expansion,
1880 - 1900

As it is, [Wyoming coal] ranks with the best coals in the world. Compare it to England, which has been used for generating motive power for machinery, which aggregates more power than all the man power on the globe, and [Wyoming coal] contains more carbon by fifteen percent. . . . It staggers the human mind to comprehend the power lying hidden and dormant in these boundless and endless mountain depositories.[1]

Wyoming territorial newspapers boasted of the potential of Wyoming's coal reserves. This potential was quickly proven in the 1860s, but these mining efforts were confined to the Union Pacific corridor. Ranchers in eastern Wyoming were beginning to find coal beds on their land, but their mining efforts were small in comparison to what was to come. These small mines opened by ranchers and homesteaders did demonstrate the potential for mining north of the Union Pacific mainline.[2] Coal awaited the ring of the miner's pick. But more than picks and shovels were needed: railroads were needed to ship the coal from Wyoming to markets throughout the region. Without railroads, expansion could not begin. Moreover, the northern part of the state still belonged to the land's first inhabitants, the Native Americans. Things were about to change.

The expansion of the coal industry in Wyoming between the years 1880 and 1890 contributed to the largest single rise in population the territory and state would experience to the present day. In ten years Wyoming's population would triple.[3] In 1887, when the territory first began to keep detailed records of the coal mines, 1501 men were employed in the coal mining industry. In 1889 this number had risen to 3564.[4] In two years Wyoming more than doubled its work force in the mines. Between 1880 and 1890, coal production more than tripled—rising from 527,811 tons to 1,870,366 tons. By 1890 in the western states, only Colorado exceeded Wyoming in the number of men employed in coal mining.[5] The increase in mining activity coupled with the building of new railroads played a role in making the decade of the 1880s one of unparalleled growth. In 1880

Wyoming's population was 20,789. This number jumped to 62,555 by 1890. This slightly more than 200 percent increase over the preceding decade is the largest single population gain in the history of the state.[6] Wyoming's growth was made possible by an expanding economy, and coal was the cornerstone.

The enormous coal fields of the Powder River Basin in northeastern Wyoming remained untapped in the years preceding 1877. This was due to the fact that the Powder River Basin lay within lands belonging to the Sioux, Cheyenne, and Arapahoe Indians. The Fort Laramie Treaty of April 1868 designated lands north of the North Platte River and east of the Big Horn Mountains as "unceded Indian territory." It also stipulated "that no white person or persons shall be permitted to settle upon or accept any portion of the same." Unfortunately, the treaty did not prevent white settlers from moving into the area, especially after reports of gold in the Black Hills circulated in 1874. With prospectors swarming into Indian sacred lands, hostilities soon erupted between the U.S. Army and groups of Sioux and Cheyenne. During the summer of 1876, the army suffered defeat at the battles of the Rosebud and Little Bighorn. Despite these victories, the Indians could not hope to halt the advance of gold miners. The army was bent on placing the Indians on reservations outside Wyoming, and it was only a matter of time before the Sioux and their Arapahoe and Cheyenne allies were defeated. Crazy Horse, the able leader of the Sioux, surrendered by the spring of 1877, and the federal government removed the Indians from northeastern Wyoming. The Powder River Basin was open to development by white settlers.[7]

Indians, explorers, and, later, homesteaders contributed much towards knowing where coal was actually located. Some of the largest coal fields in Wyoming were first developed by homesteaders. The principal value of coal to these miners was to use as fuel for heating their homes. Their mines were simple ventures designed to extract coal cheaply and efficiently; however, the value of these small mines came not only from the fuel they provided but also from the knowledge gained about the extent of Wyoming's coal deposits.

Wagon Mines

The lack of rail service in large areas of Wyoming did not prevent small coal mines from being opened. Throughout much of rural Wyoming wood was not readily available, and it was too valuable to be used as fuel on the plains and basins. Coal provided an excellent means of heating and cooking at remote homesteads. Cold weather lasts for nine months in the

The McDonald mine in the Big Horn Basin was a small coal mining operation. Mines such as these are called wagon mines because wagons were used to transport the coal. (Courtesy of the Wyoming State Archives, Museums, and Historical Department, Stimson Collection)

Intermountain West, and the process of providing cooking fuel continued year round. Wagon mines, literally mines serviced by wagons instead of railroads, were a common sight wherever coal was available.

The seams of coal used for wagon mines were visible on the surface and did not require elaborate mining methods. Cora Ellis, who grew up on a ranch south of Medicine Bow, related that most of the coal from small mines in the area was sold "to some of the ranchers . . . but never went any farther than just local consumption."[8] In some instances, neighbors would barter for fuel. They would trade cream, butter, eggs, or meat for a load of coal.[9] Because these mines were independent ventures, various methods were used to extract the coal. Some mines had no bracing for the walls or ceilings; some had bracing from locally available cottonwood, juniper, or pine trees. Often when mine openings became unsafe or a shaft or portal became too dangerous, it was abandoned and a new mine opened elsewhere in the coal bank. Simply put, mining for the homesteader was an expedient process. Homesteaders turned miners simply went after the easiest diggings. They did not intend their mines to be long-term ventures and since coal was abundant on public lands, homesteaders and ranchers usually opened mines without obtaining legal title to the minerals.[10]

Wagon mines were often hazardous. The state coal mine inspector wrote in 1894, "During the past year several accidents have occurred in the small country banks, supplying local trade, one of which was fatal. These mines," he added, "are situated all over the state and employ anywhere from one to seven men." The problems facing a miner employed in these small mines were numerous. There was "no attention . . . paid to ventilation or to ordinary safety of any kind." In most cases "they were opened in a primitive manner" and the danger of solitary miners being trapped underground with little chance of escape was always a possibility since most mines did not have a second entry.[11]

Some of these wagon mines would develop into major endeavors, but most would be abandoned after a short time. These mines, however, provided valuable information to geologists and mining interests alike. For example, the first coal mines in present-day Fremont and Lincoln counties were small endeavors initiated by private investors. Ten miles northeast of Lander, mines were opened in 1888. The coal, it was felt, was "very similar to the Rock Springs coal at the same distance from the surface."[12] As early as 1875 small mines were opened at Sage, in Lincoln County. These early mining efforts, though small in scope, paved the way for future development. Statewide, major coal fields were generally first developed by small mine operators. Yet railroads were needed before mines could be enlarged and profits realized. When the railroads finally reached remote regions with proven coal reserves, mining expanded rapidly.

Expansion of the Railroads

The opening of northeastern Wyoming after 1877 meant almost the entire territory of Wyoming was opened for settlement. Only Yellowstone National Park and the Shoshoni and Arapahoe Indian reservations were closed to developers. Railroad investors saw potential opportunities and were quick to build into the newly opened areas. Nationwide the railroad industry was expanding; over 70,000 miles of railroads were constructed between 1881 and 1890.[13] Wyoming would benefit from this expansion, and the coal industry would reap the benefits of this growth.

As long as the northeastern portions of Wyoming Territory remained Indian lands, the Union Pacific Railroad was able to maintain its status as the only major railroad in the territory. This monopoly lasted for 17 years, from 1869 to 1886. In spite of the monopoly, Union Pacific felt expansion was necessary for it to continue as a profit-making corporation. What the

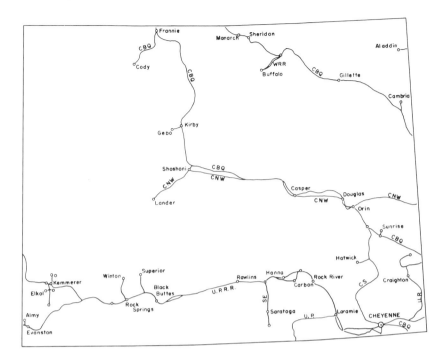

CBQ	Chicago, Burlington and Quincy
CNW	Chicago and Northwestern
CS	Colorado and Southern
UP	Union Pacific
WRR	Wyoming

Principal railroads serving the Wyoming coal fields. Railroads, especially the Union Pacific, led to the intensive development of the extensive coal deposits throughout the state. (After Waldo Neilson 1974)

Union Pacific attempted to create in the 1880s and the years prior to 1893 was a system which tied sources of revenue, such as mines, mills, factories, and farms, with markets where products could be sold and income from freight received.

In its early years, the Union Pacific wasted little time in expanding into new markets. Between 1870 and 1881, it laid branch lines from Cheyenne to Denver, the center of the Rocky Mountain gold and silver mining region, and to Butte, Montana, where a large copper mining industry had been established. Both regions offered potentially rich markets for Wyoming coal. And in 1880 Union Pacific bought the Kansas Pacific Railroad, which connected Kansas City and Denver, further increasing the markets for its freight and commodities.

Throughout the 1880s the Union Pacific continued to develop its rail system. Between 1881 and 1884 it built the Oregon Short Line between Granger, Wyoming, and Portland, Oregon, to counter the movement of the Northern Pacific Railroad into the Pacific Northwest.[14] Another branch line, known as the Cheyenne and Northern, was built northward from Cheyenne to Orin Junction, enabling freight and passengers to reach destinations in central Wyoming. By 1893 the Union Pacific system extended from Omaha, Nebraska, to Portland, Oregon, and from Butte, Montana, to Fort Worth, Texas.[15] But it was not the only system.

In the 1880s, other railroads began competing with the Union Pacific for the same markets. Two railroads, the Chicago and Northwestern and the Chicago, Burlington, and Quincy, extended westward from Chicago and entered Wyoming. The Northwestern reached the Nebraska border in 1886. Within two years it laid tracks across eastern Wyoming, reaching Douglas by the end of 1886, Glenrock in 1887, and Casper in 1888. Casper remained the Wyoming terminus of the Northwestern until 1906 when the road was extended to Lander.[16]

The Chicago, Burlington, and Quincy Railroad arrived in Wyoming shortly after the Northwestern. Between 1887 and 1915, the Burlington built or purchased a network of rail lines which connected Denver and Cheyenne with the coal fields of northern Wyoming. Coal towns which grew up along the Burlington tracks include Sheridan, Gillette, Cambria, and Gebo. The Burlington Railroad ultimately developed a rail system that connected Denver, Billings, and Chicago. The extensive network of Burlington tracks permitted northern Wyoming coal to be shipped not only to Denver but also to major midwestern markets as well as to the Pacific Northwest.[17]

Unprecedented Growth in the Coal Industry

The building of new railroads throughout Wyoming during the 1880s created unprecedented growth in Wyoming's coal industry. The Oregon Short Line opened new coal lands for development in western Wyoming. In northeastern Wyoming the railroads found almost an inexhaustible supply of coal. Some of the coal, like that found in the Black Hills of Wyoming, was extremely high in British Thermal Units (BTUs). Coal in the Powder River Basin west of the Black Hills was not as high in BTUs, but coal seams in the Powder River Basin were thick enough to attract investments from both railroad and mining companies. The combination of capital and transportation provided by the railroads led to the creation of coal mining ventures throughout northern and eastern Wyoming.

Expansion into the Northeast

In 1883 mines were opened near Glenrock and Douglas, but these experienced only limited activity until the arrival of the railroad in 1887. Then mining began in earnest when "Governor J. D. [sic] Richards and Messrs. Chamberlain and Vosbergh," opened the Inez mine in 1888. More than likely the governor was DeForest Richards who organized the First National Bank of Douglas in 1886. He was also involved in the mercantile and cattle business. In 1888 the Inez mine produced 12,986 tons of coal. About the same time the nearby Deer Creek No. 1 mine, owned by separate interests, opened at Glenrock and produced 13,000 tons in 1888. Together the Inez and Deer Creek mines employed 114 men, and they pushed to expand their operations.[18] With transportation readily available, the mine operators hoped to increase productivity and profits. Along with the opening of the Inez and Deer Creek mines, a small coal mine was opened near the site of Buffalo. Called the Buffalo Fuel Company No. 1 mine, it hired 12 employees in 1888. These three mines produced the majority of Wyoming coal mined outside the southern corridor. The *Territorial Coal Mine Inspector's Report of 1888* reported only three mines operating in areas outside the Union Pacific mainline. Two of these mines were located adjacent to the newly created Chicago and Northwestern line. But in 1888 not all mines were listed by the mine inspector. The reports included only mines with "sufficient number of men." Of those operating in Wyoming Territory, 82 percent were along the Union Pacific mainline. For Albany, Converse, and Johnson counties, the total production was listed at 27,986 tons. This would soon change.[19]

With the arrival of the Burlington Railroad at Newcastle in 1888, the coal in the Wyoming Black Hills became accessible. A spur line was built north from Newcastle in 1889 to an infant coal camp called Cambria. The mines developed rapidly because the coal was of extremely high quality and could be coked for use in the gold smelters at nearby Deadwood and Lead, South Dakota. Moreover, it made excellent fuel for steam locomotives. The territorial mine inspector warned, "Rock Springs will have to look well to her laurels, actively on the alert to maintain her reputation in and out of the Territory as the producer of the best Wyoming Coals." By 1892

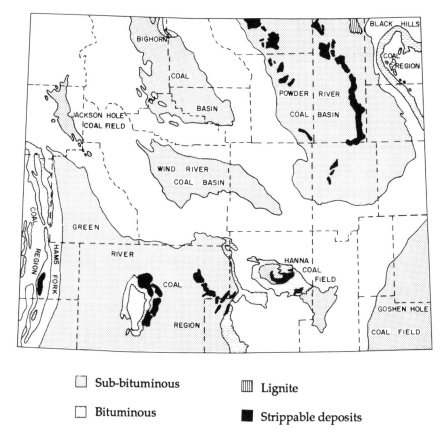

| ⬜ Sub-bituminous | ▦ Lignite |
| ⬜ Bituminous | ⬛ Strippable deposits |

Wyoming Coal-Bearing Areas

Cambria coal production had risen to 366,944 tons. The Antelope and Jumbo mines, the main sources of fuel for Cambria Coal Company, were together producing 1000 tons of black diamonds per ten-hour shift.[20]

Cambria was unique in the fact that there was gold in the coal deposits. It was in the coking facilities that gold was the most obvious. "A peculiar feature in connection with the coke was the fact it carried gold." The coal was checked often for gold content and "assays made on 31 railroad cars showed the coke to have an average gold content of $2.74 per ton, some of the assays showing as high as $5.60 per ton." Cambria was located on the southwestern edge of the Black Hills Uplift where it was held "gold is universally distributed throughout that section. This geological fact probably has a bearing upon the occurrence of gold in this coal."[21]

Located in a well-watered area of Wyoming, the coal mining camp of Cambria was a pleasant place to live. Neat, orderly buildings lined the canyons. Pine trees dotted the hillsides. Many miners and their families had gardens adjacent to their homes. Cambria was, however, a company town. Everything from the water system to the houses were owned by the company. Along with the expansion of the coal mining frontier into northeastern Wyoming came the company town.

As the Chicago, Burlington, and Quincy pressed northwestward towards Billings, Montana, in the late 1880s, it crossed through what would become the largest developed coal fields in Wyoming. The beginnings of development were not impressive, but they were small-scale examples of things to come. In the Powder River Basin surrounding Gillette, wagon mines were attempted near the railroad mainline, but mining was not very extensive until the twentieth century.

Farther west, near Sheridan, mining began as early as 1888. The mines near Sheridan began initially as wagon mines. In 1890 the first ventures at Dietz were initiated by James and John Birchby. These brothers did not own the land, but they are credited with initiating one of the earliest commercial mines north of Sheridan. The Birchbys hired several men to expand their mine. These men, along with their families, lived in dugouts and tents until more substantial structures could be built. In 1892 C. N. Dietz formed the Sheridan Fuel Company and began to develop the mines on a larger scale. The town and mines were named after this entrepreneur. As demand for coal increased, Dietz expanded and grew into a fairly sizeable community.[22] At the turn of the century it could boast of all the facilities and services of any respectable company town.

By 1892 the annual production from Sheridan County had reached 2000 tons. The state geologist, whose job it was to record the state's mineral wealth, commented in 1893, "To enumerate all the coal banks in Sheridan County would be an endless task for they are almost as numerous as the farms." He went on to offer the opinion that the coal in Sheridan County was not high enough in BTUs to be used for "locomotive work, unless their present method of consumption be discarded."[23] Eventually steam locomotives would alter their engines to burn the coal found near Sheridan, and the mines would expand. But for the time being, the Chicago, Burlington, and Quincy would rely principally on coal mined at Cambria.

Expansion in the Southwest

Meanwhile in southwestern Wyoming, new coal mines were rapidly being developed and old ones expanded as Union Pacific intensified its

efforts. Along the Ham's Fork River, in
Lincoln County, the Union Pacific Railroad began to explore for coal to fuel its
Oregon Short Line. In 1881 they developed the Twin Creek mines just west of
the Continental Divide, between the
Green River and the Great Basin. The
first effort at opening the Twin Creek
mines had been made by the Smith and
Bell brothers in 1876. Although the Twin
Creek mines were failures, they introduced into the region a man named
Patrick J. Quealy.

Patrick J. Quealy began his career
with the Union Pacific Railroad as the
superintendent of the Grass Creek mines
in Utah. Because he was experienced in
coal mining, Union Pacific felt that Quealy
was the right person to open its new
mines and in April 1881 directed him to
examine and report on the coal deposits

Patrick J. Quealy

at Twin Creek. When Quealy arrived at Twin Creek, he found the field
already occupied by other interests led by a man named Negus. Negus had
jumped the Bell brothers' claim. After discussing the matter, the Bell
brothers agreed to sell their interests to Quealy and the Union Pacific
Railroad for $10,000. Feeling that the property was safely in his hands,
Quealy went to Evanston to wire the railroad company. In his absence,
however, the Bell brothers decided to renegotiate with Negus. Quealy,
accompanied with a labor force armed with picks and rifles, returned to
open what he thought were Union Pacific mines. When he learned of the
double-cross, he offered the Bell brothers $25,000. The increase in the
amount offered for the mines, plus the fact that Quealy's men were armed,
put the mines in the control of Union Pacific.[24] The Twin Creek mines only
operated from 1881 to 1885, but they provided the impetus for further
mining in the area. Union Pacific's expansion in southwestern Wyoming
coupled with the opening of the Powder River Basin led to a coal mining
boom. The impact on the future state was felt immediately.

Between 1880 and 1890 coal mining spread throughout the territory. By
1890, when Wyoming became a state, all of its thirteen counties had
demonstrated the potential for developing coal mines. Admittedly, Laramie County and Albany County showed little potential, but coal was
present. As W. C. Knight noted in 1893, "Every county in the state with the

exception of Laramie has an abundance of coal land. Even in Laramie County," he went on, "coal does exist in the southwest corner."[25]

Slowed Development and Other Problems

With mines opened at Cambria and initial ventures beginning at Sheridan, the coal industry across Wyoming seemed destined for unparalleled growth. In 1893, however, a nationwide depression slowed development in Wyoming's coal fields. The Panic of 1893, the worst economic downturn in American history prior to the Great Depression, continued through 1897, and it affected all segments of American industry. The coal industry, which depended on railroads as a steady market, was victimized by bankrupt railroads. On August 15, 1893, the Northern Pacific went bankrupt; the Union Pacific Railroad followed in October of the same year. Union Pacific, in spite of competition from other railroad lines in northern Wyoming, was, at the time, still the chief source of revenue for the Wyoming coal industry, especially in terms of wages paid to miners. In 1893 Union Pacific mines accounted for 63 percent of the state's total

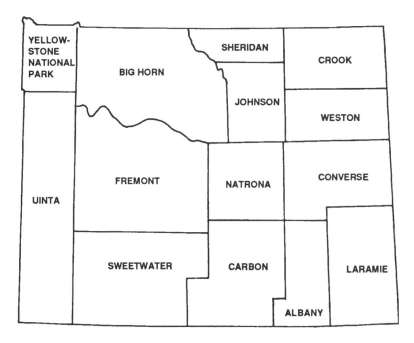

Wyoming Counties in 1890

output of coal.[26] Failure of a company so important to the state's well-being impacted all aspects of the Wyoming economy. Moreover, the Wyoming coal industry was dependent on outside capital for expansion. Without investments from the eastern United States, there was little possibility for growth. It would take major reorganization of the Union Pacific for the company to continue. Time was needed for the railroad company to correct the errors that had led to its failure. Union Pacific would survive under the direction of its receivers, but for a time, the coal industry was relegated to a slower pace of development.

The effects of the 1893 Panic were felt statewide. In 1889, 2,818,283 tons of coal had been mined in Wyoming. Thereafter coal production fell off, and not until 1898 would it surpass the 1889 total.[27] This statewide decrease in production occurred in spite of increased production at Cambria and the opening of new mines at Sheridan in 1893, at Diamondville in 1894, and at Kemmerer in 1897. While new mines were opening, Union Pacific moved to reduce production and cut wages.

Wages and Pay Periods

Miners' wages at the Union Pacific Almy mines were cut by ten cents per ton in 1894. This reduction was preceded by a change in pay periods. In October of 1893, Union Pacific began paying monthly instead of every two weeks. This was in violation of state laws. The miners at Almy decried this change as "robbery."[28] The state laws of Wyoming, approved in 1891, required all coal companies to pay "semi-monthly . . . in lawful money of the United States, or by a good and valid check or draft, payable . . . in lawful money."[29] This law was designed to protect miners from company scrip and the company store.

Paying wages once a month was a widespread coal mining practice. Also, coal companies usually paid in scrip, which was usable only in company stores. Often this scrip could not be converted into cash. The state law of 1891 was designed to keep companies from using a nonexchangeable scrip for wages. The law also attempted to address problems associated with receiving pay at irregular intervals. Too often coal companies paid wages sporadically, or at best, once a month. Since housing often belonged to the coal company, rent was automatically deducted from the miner's wage. If the miner owed for supplies or food purchased at the company store, this was also deducted. At times a miner might go months living on credit extended to him by the company store. The liberal credit policies of the company store led many families into debt for amounts they could not easily repay. When Union Pacific changed its policy of paying wages twice a month to once a month, the miners feared going into debt. One retired miner recalled,

> Lot of times we only worked one day a week. Lot of times some of them would get so much in the grocery store that they would get more groceries than they had on their check. So down on the bottom of the check would be two lines. That is what they called ribs [or rails]; you wouldn't get nothing. You owed it to the company.[30]

The check was a list of wages and a list of debts. The rails indicated the miner owed the company more than he had earned.

The miners at Almy notified their fellow miners at Rock Springs of their plight in the form of an editorial published in October 1893. The anonymous writer claimed that the miners had first been asked to take a ten cent per ton reduction on the coal they extracted. This wage reduction was followed by a notice that they would be paid monthly. On August 10, 1894, the miners at Almy had their wages reduced by ten cents a ton.[31] The bankruptcy of Union Pacific, brought on by the Panic of 1893, necessitated changes in the company's financial structure and led to wage reductions.

A miners' supply and general merchandise store in Carbon. The company store was seen by coal companies as an important element in the mining business. Not only was it an additional source of income, it was also a means of keeping miners working by keeping them in debt. (Courtesy of Sweetwater County Museum)

It also began the eventual demise of the Almy coal mines. In 1893 the Union Pacific and Rocky Mountain Coal and Iron Company mines combined to produce 311,380 tons of coal at Almy. The Almy mines would never again reach this level of production. In 1894 production plummeted to 145,213 tons.[32] The Panic of 1893 contributed to Almy's sharp decline in production, but it was not the only contributing factor.

The Explosion of 1895

David G. Thomas

The mines at Almy were "gassy." Explosions in 1881 and 1886 had served notice of this problem. On March 20, 1895, the third worst mine explosion in Wyoming history ripped Rocky Mountain Coal and Iron Company's Red Canon No. 5 mine, killing sixty-one men.[33] The man who investigated this disaster was David G. Thomas, the state coal mine inspector at the time. A sensitive man who enjoyed writing poetry, Thomas had become involved in coal mining at the age of ten. He worked in Missouri mines until 1878 when his health failed. In 1878 he secured a position with Union Pacific at Rock Springs.[34] Then in 1891, at Union Pacific's request, Thomas assumed the position of state mine inspector.[35] Thomas brought to the position of state coal mine inspector a rare combination of sensitivity and knowledge of mine operations. He held that the "most dangerous mines in the state are the ones at Hanna, Red Canon, and Almy."[36] Red Canon, located adjacent to the Union Pacific mines at Almy, contained the deadly mix of methane gas and coal dust. This volatile mixture was something Thomas clearly understood.

For four years Thomas had warned of the dangerous conditions existing at Red Canon No. 5. In describing the events that led to the 1895 explosion, Thomas related that a pocket of gas accumulated underground in an area where the roof had caved. The gas in this area was not displaced, and when another small cave-in occurred, "gas was forced down onto the men and ignited the dust, and from that point extended to every portion of the mine." According to Thomas,

Devastation caused by the explosion of gas and dust at the Rocky Mountain Coal and Iron Company's Red Canon No. 5 mine at Almy, Wyoming, in 1895. (Courtesy of the American Heritage Center Photo Archives, University of Wyoming)

The mine was fearfully dusty, and the miners had been working all day, firing heavy shots, the mules tramping all day with loaded and empty trips. At every shot fired and steps of the mules and movement of ore cars, the impalpable dust was raised into the current of air, which averaged more than a thousand cubic feet per minute per man, was carried forward to every nook and crook in the mine, and all it needed was a strong flame to start it on its course of destruction. The explosion would have never occurred had the mine been regularly sprinkled to keep down the dust, the gas in this room might have burned just the same, but when it ran out into a clear atmosphere it would have soon expended itself with hardly any damage to life and property.[37]

The small particles of suspended dust led to the worst explosion Wyoming experienced in the nineteenth century.

Thomas perceptively pointed out another problem. Dust as fuel for an explosion was his primary concern, yet Thomas was also concerned with dust as a potential health hazard. "It is obvious," he claimed, "that this dust, consisting of minute particles of carbon, must exert a deleterious effect upon the health of the miners, and that, therefore, it will have to be taken into account when estimating the requirements of the ventilation."[38] He knew, as all miners did, that in the work space, dust was hard on the lungs. The term "black lung" was not yet used, but "miners asthma" was something coal miners feared.

Coal dust was a class leveling factor underground. Everyone, mine foremen included, had to contend with dust. One miner recalled, "Heck you used to go in some of those mines when they was cutting rock, and you couldn't see your neighbors light up on the face."[39] Conditions in the tipple, although outside the mine, were little better. When "picking boney, there was six feet of cloud. You couldn't even see the person standing right by you."[40] Black lung usually did not affect people until after they had been in the mines for some time. Often miners would leave the mines, hoping for a better job in another trade, or they might retire from the mines only to find the years of working followed them in the form of black lung. One miner's son described this disease from personal experience. "It's a terrible death. My dad was a guy about my size, a lot huskier, stronger; and when he finally passed away, he was just nothing but a skeleton."[41] Coal dust was, and still is, part of coal mining. Thomas, in 1895, understood dust was one of coal mining's greatest hazards. Unfortunately, little was done at the time to minimize the dust that caused black lung.

Coming Out of the Downturn

By 1898, some of the problems associated with the Panic of 1893 had passed. One of the first signs that the coal industry was recovering came in 1897 when the Kemmerer coal mines opened. These mines were opened by Patrick J. Quealy with Mahlon S. Kemmerer providing the financial backing. Quealy understood Wyoming coal mining; in addition to his work for Union Pacific and his stint as territorial coal mine inspector, he and two other men had formed the Rock Springs Coal Company in 1887. By 1894 Quealy had sold his interests in the Rock Springs company. He then turned his energies toward opening mines in the Ham's Fork Valley. Quealy's experience in mining had provided him with a modest cash surplus but not enough to initiate the enterprise of opening the mines he envisioned. For financing he turned to M. S. Kemmerer. Kemmerer was a pioneer Pennsylvania coal man. He was chairman of the Carbon Iron and Steel Company in Pennsylvania and served as treasurer of the Virginia Coal and Iron Company. After negotiating by mail for some time, Kemmerer and Quealy met in Chicago in 1895 and drafted a document called the Ham's Fork Coal Land Proposition. This document would serve as the basis for the partnership that led to the creation of the town of Kemmerer.[42]

Quealy encountered keen competition at the Kemmerer site. The Diamondville mines, opened in 1894, were but a few short miles south of his proposed venture. Familiar with obtaining coal lands, Quealy tied up the coal properties directly north of the Diamond Coal and Coke mines. By December 1895, Quealy was able to inform Kemmerer that he had "carefully endeavored to secure an option on the Diamond Coal Company's property or a control of the stock."[43] Buying out the competition before they ever started their own mines was something the partners had contemplated. Kemmerer advised caution in January 1896. In a letter to Quealy he warned, "It might be better to have them as competitors than a more formidable party. Undoubtedly territory could be obtained by other outside parties who might give us more trouble than the Diamondville people . . . [who] are not good managers . . . [and not] very strong financially."[44] The formidable party Kemmerer feared came in the guise of Anaconda Copper. Anaconda decided it would be in its best interests to own its own mines in order to supply its smelters with coal for coking. To secure this end, it purchased the mines at Diamondville in 1898.[45] Kemmerer and Quealy found themselves competing for coal with one of the most powerful mining interests in the West.

From the outset, Kemmerer and Quealy organized their company to make profits. Like most coal companies in the late nineteenth century,

Kemmerer Coal controlled more than just the mines. In addition to Kemmerer Coal, Quealy and Kemmerer formed the Frontier Supply Company, the Ham's Fork Cattle Company, and the Uinta Improvement Company. The supply company provided goods to the company stores, and the improvement company conducted land transactions and developed land. Behind these ventures, Quealy was the driving force, M. S. Kemmerer was the financier, and his son, John L. Kemmerer, of Scranton, Pennsylvania, served as legal counsel. Controlling everything from land to coal, profits would naturally follow.

Two towns were initiated by Quealy in 1897. One was Kemmerer, where land could be privately owned; the other was Frontier. Frontier was a company town. Following patterns used in other Wyoming towns, such as Hanna and Cambria, Quealy constructed company housing at Frontier. Tenements were occupied as quickly as they were completed; however, more men were employed in opening the mine and completing the mine facilities than could possibly be housed in the new rentals. Even though the tenements were being built as fast as possible, there was not enough housing available. In spite of an initial decision not to allow men to build their own houses on company land, an acute housing shortage forced a change in policy.[46] Along with housing, railroad tracks were laid, an office building was erected, and surface mining facilities were constructed. Where a sage flat had stood, a town appeared.[47] A mining boom had hit the Ham's Fork Valley.

Company Towns

Mining companies, such as Kemmerer Coal, attempted to control as much of the surrounding mining community as possible. Everything from water and food to housing was provided by the company. This created a somewhat unique experience in a previously uninhabited area. In 1897, southwest Wyoming was sparsely populated. The total population for the state stood at 62,555 in 1890 and only 92,531 in 1900. In 1900 there was still less than one person per square mile. Just to open the mines at Kemmerer, 250 "men and boys" were employed.[48] Since there was not a large enough urban or rural population from which to draw, miners had to be recruited outside Wyoming.

European and Asian immigrants proved to be willing recruits. Of course, these newly hired workers would need a place to live and, more important, food to eat. Housing and feeding these men and their families on a semi-arid steppe required shipping in food and building materials. The coal company gladly built housing and provided the stores. Unless poorly managed, there was no way to lose money since the wages the miners earned digging out the coal were spent at the company stores and on rent for company housing. Prior to the turn of the century, it was held that renting company houses generated a large profit, and some contended there was more to be made in renting houses than in mining.[49] However, it was also contended that coal company profits from housing were modest, "But 5 percent is a bonanza for many bituminous coal operators. If only they [mine operators] could do as well at mining coal, they would be wondrous glad. We should not be surprised when we hear them say that the house saved the day." Defending the practice of making profits from the company houses, coal industry spokesmen added, "We should not necessarily infer that the day had been saved, as ordinary business would view it, or that in saving it the houses and store had yielded an unfair profit."[50]

Company towns and big coal corporations became synonymous in Wyoming. Some independent coal towns had privately owned homes, but the big mines near Sheridan, Kemmerer, and Cambria all provided company housing. Rock Springs started out with very few company-owned buildings, but as the twentieth century approached, company houses and the company store became a fixture. In 1899 Union Pacific reported they had 160 company houses in Rock Springs alone. Another 30 Union Pacific employee families were reported to be living in dugouts in the banks of Bitter Creek.[51] Other communities, such as Hanna, were designed as company towns. Small, independent communities like Elmo, near Hanna, took pride in their autonomy, but they understood they owed their existence to the nearby coal companies.

In the 1890s more than one miner complained of conditions in Wyoming's company-owned towns. One Almy miner in a letter to the editor of the *Union Pacific Employees Magazine* complained in 1890, "the miners are in miserable hovels and have to pay $7 to $10 per month for rent." He went on to say, "Supplies for mining the coal average $10 a month, while the average adult in 1889 only makes $60.25 per month in the Almy mines."[52] This average monthly pay was for good months when the mines were working full shifts. The Almy miner went on to add:

> [B]efore the miner . . . [has] the blessed privilege of inhabiting one of these shanties he must sign a contract to the effect that he will vacate the same upon five days notice, or less if they [Union Pacific] wish it. No doubt you will say the miners have the privilege of building their own houses. Are you aware that the company will not even permit this, as they have every inch of ground here cornered, and they will not sell or lease enough to build a small shanty on.[53]

The author of this letter simply signed his name as Miner. Complaining was one thing. Signing your name to a letter such as this would have meant finding employment elsewhere.

The company housing constructed at Frontier in 1897 followed patterns used previously at Almy, Hanna, and Cambria. Hanna and Cambria had the distinction of being the first completely company-built coal towns in Wyoming. At Hanna, which had its beginnings in 1889, great attention was paid to community planning. The Union Pacific Coal Company took pride in Hanna, claiming, "the streets were laid out at the opening of the town with somewhat more consideration than had been given them in the majority of other coal towns." Builders, the company boasted, "laid out an orderly scheme of streets and alleys."[54] Order was the norm in company towns. Although tents and dugouts might appear outside of town, they were not permitted within the company towns. Company towns were planned communities.

Company towns were, moreover, distinctive in appearance. James B. Allen, who has focused on the company town in the American West, pointed out that these communities were strikingly similar throughout the region.

> If a person suddenly found himself in the middle of a company-owned town, he would have little difficulty identifying it as such, for certain general features usually stood out. First to be noted would be the standard, uniform architecture of the company-owned houses. In a prominent location, however, would stand a larger, more imposing structure: the home of the company manager or superintendent. It would be observed that the town seemed to center around a focal point where a store, community hall, school, and other public buildings were located. The company store usually dominated the group. It would be noted that the settlement had no "suburbs," or no gradual building up from a few scattered homes to a center of population. Rather, one would note the complete isolation of the community and the definiteness of its boundaries. Finally, it would be apparent that the existence of the community was completely dependent upon a single enterprise, because a mine, mill, or smelter would seem to dominate the entire scene.[55]

Allen went on to point out that it was difficult to find a "typical" company town, but they were all similar in the fact that they centered around a single industry.[56] Whether it was a copper town in Montana or a coal mining town in Wyoming, company towns were constructed to serve one industry.

Nice neat rows of houses did not necessarily mean comfort. Women who lived in the coal camps often complained of poorly built homes. One

Hanna No. 1 Town is an example of the planned company towns that were built throughout Wyoming beginning in the 1890s. Company towns were built by smaller companies, such as the town of Frontier built by Kemmerer and Quealy, and by large companies, such as the town of Hanna built by the Union Pacific. (Courtesy of the Union Pacific Railroad Museum Collection, 8-117)

Polish immigrant's daughter who lived at a mining camp near Sheridan
recalled,

> Everybody was poor. The houses were old. We had a little three-room
> house, and it was pretty cold in the wintertime 'cause the houses were made
> out of ... boards. There was no insulation or anything like that. When it got
> really cold, [the walls] frosted. Then they'd drip when it would warm up in
> there 'cause you had a coal stove in the kitchen and a little heater in the living
> room.[57]

Cold houses were a common complaint. One young black woman, whose
husband moved from southern Illinois to work in the mines near Rock
Springs, never forgot her first winter. "It was really cold," she recalled. "I
didn't stay but three months. I didn't think I would ever come back. I said
I'd never be back, but I did."[58] Another black woman, who lived in the
same mining camp, described the structures as being unfinished. "This
house we lived in, we could lay in bed and see people passing by."[59] Most
women took note of the lack of insulation and the dust that came in through
the cracks, covering floors, tables, and beds. Whenever the wind blew,
there was little to hold back the dust or snow.

Recruitment Policies and Ethnic Diversity

As the effects of the 1893 Panic finally wore off, there was a rise in the
demand for Wyoming coal. Between 1898 and 1899 output jumped by
almost one million tons. In 1900 Wyoming ranked thirteenth in the union
in total coal production.[60] In the West, only Colorado exceeded Wyoming
in tonnage. To accomplish this jump in production, more miners had to be
hired. In 1896, when production declined to its lowest point during the
decade, 2949 men were employed. This number increased to 4697 in 1899
and 5332 in 1900.[61] In order to find enough workers to increase production,
the coal companies once again recruited immigrants.

Examples of coal companies actively recruiting immigrants are found
throughout the West. In Utah, for instance, the territory, and after 1896 the
state, "engaged in advertising in eastern metropolitan areas in order to lure
immigrant labor to Utah's growing industrial, mining, and smelting centers."[62] At Butte, Anaconda welcomed, and even brought, Italians and
Slovenians into their mines under contract.[63] Union Pacific Coal Company
hired a variety of nationalities. In 1899 a notice was published in the *Carbon
County Journal* stating

The Union Pacific is now trying Japanese miners at Rock Springs. If they prove a success, several hundred will be employed. The company claims it cannot get sufficient employees from other nationalities to get out the amount of coal that they desire.[64]

Active recruitment of diverse nationalities resulted in a variety of ethnic groups in Wyoming. In 1880 most of the immigrants in the mining communities of Sweetwater and Uinta counties came from China, England, Ireland, Scotland, Sweden, and Germany. These nationalities continued to dominate coal mining into the early 1890s, but Finnish miners also began immigrating to southern Wyoming in significant numbers.[65] In 1886 an official for the Union Pacific reported that Finnish miners should be hired because they did not "fraternize with other miners" and were not prone to organizing labor unions.[66] Union Pacific's policy of hiring Finnish immigrants caused one Almy miner to comment, "A practical miner comes along and applies for work and he is refused, a Finnlander comes right after him and gets work."[67] French, Austrians, Slovenians, and Italians began arriving in increasing numbers after 1890. These immigrants not only went to the newly established mining camps but also found work in some of the older towns, such as Rock Springs and Carbon.[68] After the turn of the century, Union Pacific claimed to have 32 different nationalities working in its coal mines at Rock Springs.[69] Foreign-born residents outnumbered native-born Americans by more than two to one.[70] This ethnic diversity reflected the coal company's desire to hire immigrants, a policy that would continue well into the twentieth century. The policy grew from a desire to keep union organizations out of the mines, and for a time, the practice succeeded in keeping unions out of Wyoming coal fields.

Within the Union Pacific Coal Company, the task of keeping unions from forming fell to a formidable man named Dyer O. Clark. D. O. Clark was no newcomer to Wyoming coal mining. He entered the industry under the employ of the Wyoming Coal and Mining Company in 1868 and climbed through the ranks to affect Union Pacific Coal Company policy for almost four decades. After he was promoted to superintendent of the coal department in 1874, he quickly moved to increase coal production. In ten years Clark would lead the coal department to a point where coal production more than doubled. D. O. Clark was always looking for ways to increase production and at the same time reduce labor tensions. Hiring immigrants was, to Clark, a means of accomplishing both. In the late 1890s Union Pacific actively looked to hire a variety of nationalities.

A letter from Clark to Horace G. Burt, president of the Union Pacific Railroad, illustrates the policy of hiring a variety of ethnic groups as a means of keeping down labor agitation as well as a means of supplying needed labor. Clark wrote, "We have been short of men all winter but it was impossible to induce good men to come to us."[71] Written in 1899, this letter reflected an increased demand for coal. Although on the surface it would seem otherwise, the policy of hiring various nationalities was mixed with some prejudice on the part of the company. D. O. Clark clearly pointed this out when he wrote about the miners in Rock Springs.

> Our 155 colored miners are not better than half the number of the men we had in 1897. Many of them are good miners, the others are practically worthless. These will be weeded out and good men substituted as fast as we can get them. Do not understand we consider the colored miners a bad investment. We were simply unfortunate in wanting men at a time of the year when work was plenty. Good men all had work and we could offer them but little inducement to move, so we had to take what we could get. The colored miners as a rule, do not care for six days a week full work; all they care for is a living, but I consider them necessary to equalize our nationalities and keep down labor agitations.[72]

D. O. Clark pointed out earlier in his letter that the men had been working twelve hours per day. To modern readers there is seemingly a contradiction in saying the men worked twelve hours per day and in claiming they do not "care for . . . full work." But a twelve-hour work day was not uncommon at this period of time. When the demand for coal lessened and layoffs occurred, the men were weeded out; and often immigrants and blacks were the first to lose their jobs.[73]

Adjusting to a New Life

Upon their arrival in America, many immigrants had little idea of what Wyoming was like. The daughter of a Japanese immigrant said, when "my mother came there . . . she thought she'd reached the end of the world. Well, you can imagine what Superior [Wyoming] looked like in those days. It was just no trees." When the immigrants first arrived, they often faced social isolation. This was especially true for the Japanese. Instead of being placed in company housing next to the rest of the immigrants, they were placed in separate, isolated towns, not so kindly called "Jap Towns." The isolation was especially hard on the women, since most coal towns were dominated by males. Edith Sunada, in talking about her mother's first days at Superior, pointed out, there were "not any women for her to talk to. Just very few of them. . . . She came from a place where there was trees and flowers and everything to come out to Superior where there's nothing but

Dyer O. Clark

sagebrush."[74] The town of Superior had its beginnings in the first decade of the twentieth century, but it was not the only Wyoming coal town to have a separate Japanese community. Rock Springs (twelve miles southwest of Superior), Hanna, Frontier, and Acme (north of Sheridan), all had Japanese "towns" next to the coal mines. Possibly due to lingering prejudices against Asians, Japanese miners were segregated from other miners and their families. At the turn of the century they alone were given quarters away from other immigrants, separated from the rest of the community, like the Chinese immigrants before them.

Unlike the British coal miners who preceded them, the new arrivals around the turn of the century had little experience in coal mining. Some had been miners in their homeland, but most, like the Slovenians, were farmers or underemployed urban dwellers.[75] Coming from areas where industrialization was in its infancy, Slovenian immigrants had to make the transition from a society where manpower, not steampower, dominated industry. Working in mines that were increasingly dependent on machines, the immigrants adjusted not only to a new homeland but also to mining techniques that were ever-changing and that reflected America's growing industrial strength. Formal training was often minimal, but most of the immigrants gained knowledge quickly from experienced miners. Accidents, however, all too frequently were part of the learning experience. For the immigrants, adjusting to the conditions found in the mines proved easier than eliminating the dangers.

As a reflection of the number of immigrants working in Wyoming during the 1890s, most fatal underground accidents struck foreign-born miners. From 1891 to 1894, 88 percent of all fatal accidents involved immigrants. At Hanna, Finnish miners initially had the most dangerous jobs. In 1892 there were four fatal accidents in Union Pacific's Hanna No. 1 mine. Three of the men killed were Finnish, the other was a black man. In the same year, thirteen non-fatal accidents were reported. All but three of these accidents involved "Finnlanders."[76] From 1897 to 1900, 81 percent of those killed underground were foreign born.

In Wyoming for 1897, six deaths were recorded; 83 percent were foreign born. Foreign-born fatalities for 1898 were 90 percent; in 1899, 84 percent; and in 1900, 79 percent.[77] In 1900 there were twenty-four miners killed in the state, nineteen of whom were foreign born. Fatalities primarily befell Finnish emigrants in 1900, but fatal accidents also involved Japanese, Chinese, French, Italian, Slovenian, English, Scottish, and Polish miners. Between 1897 and 1900, eleven different nationalities were listed as casualties in Wyoming coal mines.[78] Often the state coal mine inspector listed these deaths as "accidental" with "no one being to blame." As in the case of a young Italian miner killed in 1897 at the Jumbo Mine at Cambria, the state mine inspector reported "that no responsibility was attached to the . . . company or any of its employees on account of the accident."[79] This statement was not a reflection of prejudice against foreigners; companies were never found at fault in the case of fatalities. If the inspector felt the company was in error, he might point out problems, but he rarely found the coal company at fault. Immigrants seeking opportunities in Wyoming coal mining found work; unfortunately these opportunities were accompanied with the risk of injury or death.

Immigrant miners were more likely than native miners to face serious injury because recently hired miners were unaware of safety measures to be taken. Two of the three Japanese miners who died in 1900 at Rock Springs had worked in the mines less than four months.[80] Length of service for the third Japanese miner was not given; however, since Japanese were first employed in 1899, it is doubtful he had worked in the mine for more than a year. One forty-year-old Finnish miner who died in Carbon No. 2 in 1899 had been in the "employ of the company four months." According to the report, "John Runama was killed by a fall of rock. . . . The rock under which he was working gave a sudden crack and the deceased's partner called to him to run, but he became confused and ran underneath the rock which fell."[81]

Language barriers contributed to deaths underground. Most foremen were either American or English. They informed translators about assignments who in turn passed on the instructions to their countrymen. When translators were not available, disaster could be the result. An example of this problem is seen at Cambria in 1897. "Employed by the company twelve months prior to the accident," Phillip Mediati, a twenty-four-year-old Italian, fell victim to an accident November 9. The accident report stated,

> Mediati was standing on the track of the main south entry, when a loaded car ran away. . . . He was struck by the car and killed, the car running over him. At the point where the accident occurred, a trapper boy is stationed

whose duty it is to look out for runaway cars; keep tracks clear, and throw switches in case of danger. This boy was warned by the driver of the runaway car, he in turn called to Mediati to move off the track; in fact told him three times to move; but he did not move and the car struck him.[82]

The trapper boy possibly did not speak the same language as the miner. Facing language barriers and unfamiliar with mining operations, foreign-born miners were at risk of being injured or killed.

It was a widely held assumption that immigrant miners would be involved in more accidents than English-speaking miners.[83] Dorothy Schwieder, in writing about Iowa coal mines in the 1890s, pointed out that

Most mine operators [held] that since most eastern and southern Europeans were unable to speak or read English, they could not be counted on to read mining procedures or safety regulations. Mine inspectors in particular believed that the miners' lack of English-language capability resulted in carelessness. Mining officials also regarded southern and eastern European miners as less intelligent than English-speaking miners. One corporation executive, asked about the high number of mining accidents, replied: 'Yes, but after all, it's not so serious, because most of the men killed are ignorant foreigners who can be easily replaced.'[84]

These immigrants were not ignorant; simply, they could not understand English.

Even immigrants, Union Pacific soon found, would not tolerate harsh and unsafe labor conditions. In 1893 the Finnish miners decided that changes had to be made at Hanna. Dissatisfied with working conditions, they petitioned the company to remove the mine boss. The petition, which was submitted to the assistant general superintendent of the Union Pacific Coal Department at Rock Springs, gave the impression that the miners would no longer tolerate conditions at Hanna. Unfortunately, the area supervisor in Rock Springs decided to retain the mine boss.[85] Conse-quently, on September 1, 1893, the Finnish miners decided to settle their grievances against the mine boss. That night two hundred "Finns" marched on the company's office in Hanna. They notified "the local superintendent that they would give the mine boss twenty-four hours to leave the camp. If found after that time, they would hang him." The mine boss fled Hanna. Even though "county officers . . . pledged him safe protection, nothing would induce him to remain." The state coal mine inspector, who investigated the affair, reported that the men rebelled because "the boss was very overbearing towards his men, refusing to give them necessary material for their rooms, such as ties and rails." He was also accused of "using language not becoming to any man in dealing with others." Union Pacific "wisely concluded not to make any effort to get the boss back and since then," the report concluded, "everything has been moving along smoothly."[86]

In addition to the hazards associated with the mines, immigrants and native-born workers alike had to deal with the fact that mining jobs were not permanent. When the coal ran out in a particular seam, another mine had to be opened elsewhere if the coal company wanted to continue production from a field. When a field was finally exhausted, the mines were completely shut down and the miners had to find employment at another mine or outside the industry. While companies often took good workers with them, others were displaced. Other than Wyoming, the coal mines in Montana, Utah, and Colorado provided possible employment for miners. For example, during one work slowdown, Finnish miners from Rock Springs moved to the coal fields surrounding Red Lodge, Montana.[87] Then when prosperity returned, the displaced miners might once again enter Wyoming mines, especially in cases where higher pay induced them to return.

Mines closed either because of changing economic conditions or because they ran out of coal. Regardless of how thick a seam was, it would eventually "pinch" and become too thin to mine. The closure of mines often resulted in the abandonment of entire towns. Yet the abundance of coal in Wyoming ensured that new towns would replace the older communities. Initially there were some concerns that mine closures would result in coal shortages for the Union Pacific Railroad, but this fear proved unfounded as newly opened mines created increased production. In 1900 Union Pacific's Almy mines produced coal for the last time. To offset the loss of these mines, Spring Valley, east of Evanston, began producing that same year. More importantly, the Union Pacific's coal mines at Cumberland, south of Kemmerer, began producing coal in 1901. During the first year, Union Pacific's Cumberland mines produced 177,715 tons of coal. This production offset the loss of the Carbon mines, which closed in 1902. The short-lived Spring Valley mines closed in 1905, but this had little impact on Union Pacific because in 1906 the Superior mines were opened. The opening of the Superior and Cumberland mines more than adequately offset the loss of Almy and Carbon.[88]

Carbon was the first mine opened along the Union Pacific mainline; when it closed, an era in Wyoming coal mining had passed. Carbon miners had to find work elsewhere, and a number moved to the Union Pacific mines in Rock Springs and Hanna. The "Finn-Hall" and other buildings, including 35 homes from Carbon, were moved to Hanna.[89] Other structures were slowly dismantled through the years and eventually only tailings from the mine, stone foundations, and scattered debris remained. The situation at Carbon set the precedent for Spring Valley and other communities operated by Union Pacific. Once the mine closed, the buildings were moved or dismantled for reuse in nearby towns or at newly opened mining communities. Without activity, foundations and debris were once again covered with sage. Closing old mines and opening new mines was a cycle common to coal mining.

Early in the twentieth century, Wyoming coal found ready markets. In 1902 P. J. Quealy, who had watched the Wyoming coal industry pass through some of its most tumultuous and most prosperous periods, tried to place the industry into historical perspective and project its future. In a speech delivered to a convention in Cheyenne, he proclaimed, "The early history and indeed the more recent comparatively large development of the mines is so closely connected with the early history and development of the Union Pacific and its branches that the one may be said to be the largest factor in the success and development of the other." Prior to 1887, Quealy observed, "the Union Pacific coal department monopolized the coal business of the state." This development was made possible from "the coal mines of Carbon, Sweetwater, and Uinta counties." As of 1902 these mines had been the largest producers in the state and dependent "entirely on the Union Pacific and its branches for transportation, as well as the consumption of about 33.3 percent of the output."[90]

Quealy went on to attribute northern Wyoming's growth to the railroad expansion. He held that, "The Burlington railroad since coming into our state has made it possible to develop mines of Weston, Sheridan, and Big Horn counties" while the construction of the Elkhorn railroad has "made it possible to develop the mines of Converse County by its branch to Casper and of Crook County by . . . M. S. Kemmerer of Pennsylvania building a branch from Belle Fourche to Aladdin." Confirming what others had said before him, Quealy added, "Having no navigable rivers or lakes to facilitate transportation, it will be seen that the commercial development of our coal and iron mines must depend solely on the development of our railroad system." Moreover, "without railroads we can never rank with our sister states in population or industrial development."[91]

Why Wyoming had not developed its coal resources to its fullest potential was a subject that troubled Quealy. He felt, "It might be urged or suggested that the policy and practice indulged in up-to-date by our present railroad system has to a certain extent retarded the greater and further development of our mines and industries, which to a certain extent may be true from the general public point of view."[92] Understanding that his mines were dependent on the Union Pacific railroad, he very diplomatically pointed out that the railroad deserved to make a profit. He also added,

> The writer is one of those individual coal operators who has struggled along even in competition with the railroads who have their own coal mines, and while we have at times been made sensible of our total dependence on them, and fought personal battles with their management, when we compare the condition of the individual coal operators of Wyoming with those of our sister state of Utah, who boasts of her four different and independent railroad systems, we are forced to congratulate ourselves as being treated more liberally than the Utah railroads treat their individual coal land owner, for in Utah today there is but one coal company worthy of mention, while we have at least six individual companies who have no connection whatever with our railroad system.[93]

The development of the Wyoming coal industry was inexorably linked to the growth and expansion of the railroads. Quealy advocated building more railroads to increase the wealth and population of the state. "In order to show the importance of the coal industry to this state as a wealth producer," Quealy compiled figures of how many people were directly and indirectly supported by coal mining. For the year 1900, "statistics show the average number of employees . . . to be 5332 . . . supported by the labor necessary in the production of coal." When adding in the number of railroad employees required to load and transport the coal, Quealy estimated that "26,728 people out of a total population of 92,531," were involved in the coal industry.[94] Then in a statement intended to emphasize the significance of coal, he claimed, "It would be safe then, to estimate that at least 50 percent of the present population, of the State of Wyoming is supported directly or indirectly from our coal mining industry, which at present time is only in its infancy."[95] Labor statistics at the turn of the century indicate Quealy was correct in the number of men he claimed worked in Wyoming coal mines.[96] It is more difficult to substantiate the estimate that 50 percent of the state's population owed support directly to the coal industry. But clearly, coal mining was among the leading industries in the state.

Men like Quealy were quick to promote railroads as a means to prosperity. Wyoming newspapers during the 1890s and early 1900s editorialized about the benefits of expanding the railroads. Prosperity would surely follow the railroad.[97] Who cared if there were no population centers needing rail service. The transcontinental railroad had preceded civilization across Wyoming, surely all that was needed were more railroads. Quealy himself said, "[E]ncourage and develop your coal and iron mines and apply yourselves rigorously to the extension of our railroad system, work for the establishment of reservoirs and irrigation systems, and Wyoming will stand well up in the list with its neighboring states in prosperity, population, and enterprise."[98] Wyoming was entering what one twentieth-century publication called the Coal Age.[99]

Notes

[1] *Cheyenne Daily Leader,* November 24, 1869.

[2] *Cheyenne Daily Leader,* April 24, 1874.

[3] Robert H. Brown, *Wyoming, A Geography* (Boulder, Colorado: Westview Press, 1980), 39.

[4] *Territorial Coal Mine Inspector's Report* 1887 and 1889. (All territorial and state coal mine inspector's reports are on file Wyoming State Archives, Cheyenne.) Throughout this work, production figures are taken from the reports of the territorial coal mine inspector and, later, the state coal mine inspector of Wyoming. There are certain inconsistencies between the state reports and federal reports, such as those given in the *Mineral Resources of the United States.* Why total coal production in Wyoming does not agree in federal and state documents might be due to types of reporting methods. For example, coal consumed by railroads that came from railroad mines might not have been reported to the federal government. Yet another possibility is human error. By the early part of the twentieth century, the federal government began to rely more on the state of Wyoming for statistics. At this point in time the inconsistencies in total tons of coal produced diminish.

[5] David T. Day, *Mineral Resources of the United States, 1889 and 1890,* (Washington D.C.: Government Printing Office, 1892), 170-171.

[6] Brown, *Wyoming, A Geography,* 40.

[7] Taft A. Larson, *History of Wyoming,* (Lincoln: University of Nebraska Press, 1978), 32, 106.

[8] Cora Ellis, interview with author, Medicine Bow, Wyoming, 1984 (Ms. on file, Archaeological Services of Western Wyoming College, Rock Springs), 10.

[9] A. Dudley Gardner, David E. Johnson, and Marilyn Christiansen, *Archaeological and Historical Survey of 31 Mine Reclamation Sites in Carbon and Albany County, Wyoming.* Cultural Resource Management Report No. 14 (Rock Springs: Archaeological Services of Western Wyoming College, 1985), 49.

[10] A. Dudley Gardner and David E. Johnson, Mining and Homesteading in the Intermountain West. Paper presented at the 42nd Annual Plains Conference, Lincoln, Nebraska. (Ms. on file, Archaeological Services of Western Wyoming College, Rock Springs).

[11] *State Coal Mine Inspector's Report 1894,* 5.

[12] *Fremont Clipper,* November 21, 1890 (Ms. on file, Fremont County Museum, Lander); W. C. Knight, *Geology of the Wyoming Experimental Farms and Notes on the*

Mineral Resources of the State (Laramie: University of Wyoming Agricultural Department Bulletin No. 14, 1893).

[13] Robert A. Divine, T. H. Breen, George M. Fredrickson, and R. Hal Williams, *America, Past and Present* (Glenview, Illinois: Scott, Foresman, and Co., 1987), 520.

[14] Robert G. Athearn, *Union Pacific Country* (Lincoln: University of Nebraska Press, 1971), 253, 262, 312, 316.

[15] Ibid., 300.

[16] William H. Stennett, *Yesterday and Today: A History of the Chicago and Northwestern Railway System* (Chicago: Chicago and Northwestern Railway Company, 1910), 132, 137, 168.

[17] W. W. Baldwin, ed., "Chicago, Burlington, and Quincy Railroad Company," *Documentary History: Volume Three, Lines West of the Missouri River* (Chicago: Chicago, Burlington, and Quincy Railroad Company, 1929), 172-183.

[18] E. Wesley Shaw, "The Glenrock Coal Field, Wyoming," *Contributions to Economic Geology 1907*, (Washington D.C.: Government Printing Office 1909), 157; Virginia Cole Trenholm, *Wyoming Blue Book*, vol. 2 (Cheyenne: Pioneer Printing, 1974); *Territorial Coal Mine Inspector's Report* 1888 and 1889.

[19] *Territorial Coal Mine Inspector's Report 1888*.

[20] *Territorial Coal Mine Inspector's Report 1889*, 34; Knight, *Geology of Wyoming*, 150-151.

[21] Jesse Simmons, "The Cambria Coal Field in Wyoming," *Coal Age* 1 (March 23, 1912): 766.

[22] *The Sheridan Post*, January 12, 1906.

[23] R. W. Stone and C. T. Lupton, "The Powder River Coal Field, Wyoming, Adjacent to the Burlington Railroad," *Contributions to Economic Geology 1908*, (Washington D.C.: Government Printing Office, 1910); Knight, *Geology of Wyoming*, 152-153.

[24] *History of the Union Pacific Coal Mines 1868 to 1940* (Omaha: The Colonial Press, 1940), 104-107; A. D. Gardner and Robert Rosenburg, *Archaeological and Historical Survey of 26 Mine Reclamation Sites in Uinta and Lincoln Counties, Wyoming*. Cultural Resource Management Report No. 13 (Rock Springs: Archaeological Services of Western Wyoming College, 1984), 30.

[25] Knight, *Geology of Wyoming*, 137-138.

[26] *State Coal Mine Inspector's Report 1893; Union Pacific Coal Mines*, Appendix.

[27] *State Coal Mine Inspector's Report* 1889-1898.

[28] *Rock Springs Miner*, October 26, 1893, and January 11, 1894. In the October 26 article, the exact words are "thus robbed."

[29] *Session Laws of the State of Wyoming, First State Legislature*, (Cheyenne: The Daily Sun Publishing House, 1891), 356.

[30] Henry Zampedri, interview with author, Rock Springs, Wyoming, 1984 (Ms. on file, Archaeological Services of Western Wyoming College, Rock Springs), 101.

[31] *Rock Springs Miner*, October 26, 1893, and January 11, 1894.

[32] *State Coal Mine Inspector's Report* 1893, 1894. In 1894 the state coal mine inspector notes labor strife at two places, Almy and Rock Springs.

[33] *State Coal Mine Inspector's Report 1895*. The total of 61 seems most accurate;

but a later report (1941) lists the fatalities at 60. Humphrey in *Historical Summary of Coal Mine Explosions in the United States* claims 62 men were killed.
  [34] Frances Birkhead Beard, *Wyoming: From Territorial Days to the Present* (New York: The American Historical Society, 1933), 185.
  [35] D. O. Clark to H. G. Burt, March 12, 1900. Nebraska State Historical Society, Lincoln (UPRR Co., MS3761, SG2, Series 1, Box 128, Folder 334), 1.
  [36] Walter R. Jones, "Coal Mine Explosions at Almy, Their Influence on Wyoming's First Coal Mining Safety Laws," *Annals of Wyoming* 56 (Spring 1984):56.
  [37] *State Coal Mine Inspector's Report 1895.*
  [38] Ibid.
  [39] Frank Dernovich, Mike Duzik, Eugene Paoli, Norma Paoli, Antone (Tony) Pivik, and Amy Pivik, interview with author, Rock Springs, Wyoming, 1984 (Ms. on file, Archaeological Services of Western Wyoming College, Rock Springs) 44.
  [40] Ibid.
  [41] Ibid., 45.
  [42] Glen Barrett, *Kemmerer, Wyoming: The Founding of an Independent Coal Town 1897-1902* (Kemmerer, Wyoming: Quealy Services Inc., 1975), 4-9.
  [43] Ibid., 8.
  [44] Ibid., 8-9.
  [45] Ibid., 26; Michael P. Malone, *The Battle for Butte: Mining and Politics on the Northern Frontier, 1864-1906* (Seattle: University of Washington Press, 1981), 42.
  [46] Barrett, *Kemmerer, Wyoming*, 10-12.
  [47] Ibid., 13-16.
  [48] Brown, *Wyoming, A Geography*, 40-41; *State Coal Mine Inspector's Report 1897*.
  [49] "Housing and Coal Miners," *The Coal Age* 8 (July 24, 1915): 137-138.
  [50] Ibid.
  [51] D. O. Clark to H. G. Burt, February 22, 1899. Nebraska State Historical Society, Lincoln (UPRR Co. MS3761, SG2, Series 1, Box 136, Folder 329), 1-2.
  [52] *Union Pacific Employees Magazine* 1 (February 1890):61.
  [53] Ibid.
  [54] *Union Pacific Coal Mines*, 115.
  [55] James B. Allen, *The Company Town in the American West*, (Norman: University of Oklahoma Press, 1966), 79-80.
  [56] Ibid.
  [57] Mary Wolney, interview with author, Dayton, Wyoming, July 1987 (Ms. on file, Archaeological Services of Western Wyoming College, Rock Springs), 6.
  [58] Lola Carter, interview with author, Rock Springs, Wyoming, (Ms. on file, Archaeological Services of Western Wyoming College, Rock Springs), 86-87.
  [59] Elizabeth Crouch, interview with David Kathka, Green River, Wyoming, 1975 (Ms. on file, Archaeological Services of Western Wyoming College, Rock Springs), 70.
  [60] *State Coal Mine Inspector's Report 1899*. The data for coal mine production varies from source to source. This report lists 1899 tonnage at 3,774,487, whereas the *Mineral Resources of the United States 1905* lists it at 3,837,392. Both reports, however, confirm a jump in production of almost a million tons.

[61] David T. Day, *Mineral Resources of the United States, Calendar Year 1900,* (Washington D.C: Government Printing Office, 1901), 456. Statistics are expressed as "Average number of employees."

[62] Joseph Stipanovich, *The South Slavs in Utah: A Social History* (Saratoga, California: R. and E. Research Associates, 1975), 35.

[63] Malone, *The Battle for Butte,* 69.

[64] *Carbon County (Wyoming) Journal,* April 22, 1899.

[65] *Tenth and Eleventh Census of the United States.* Since Finland was part of Russia at this time, Finnish miners were counted as Russian in the census.

[66] Maury Klein, *Union Pacific, Birth of a Railroad 1862-1893* (Garden City: Doubleday and Company, 1987), 516.

[67] *Union Pacific Employees Magazine* 4 (February 1889): 31. Nebraska State Museum and Archives, Lincoln (UPRR Co. MS3761, Box 3).

[68] Gordon Olaf Hendrickson, ed., *Peopling the High Plains, Wyoming's European Heritage* (Cheyenne: Wyoming State Archives, 1977).

[69] *Union Pacific Coal Mines,* 163-164. The actual date Union Pacific gives for this number is 1912.

[70] *Eleventh Census of the United States.*

[71] D. O. Clark to Horace G. Burt, president of the Union Pacific Coal Company, February 15, 1899. Nebraska State Museum and Archives, Lincoln (UPRR Co. MS3761, SG2, Box 127, Folder 330). The letter cited here refers to hiring more miners at Hanna and Rock Springs.

[72] Ibid.

[73] Ibid.

[74] Edith Sunada, interview with author, Green River, Wyoming, 1986. (Ms. on file, Archaeological Services of Western Wyoming College, Rock Springs), 1, 2, 6.

[75] Stipanovich, *The South Slavs,* 24-25.

[76] *State Coal Mine Inspector's Report 1892.*

[77] *State Coal Mine Inspector's Report 1897 to 1900.*

[78] *State Coal Mine Inspector's Report 1899 and 1900.*

[79] *State Coal Mine Inspector's Report 1897.*

[80] *State Coal Mine Inspector's Report 1900.*

[81] Ibid.

[82] *State Coal Mine Inspector's Report 1897.*

[83] Dorothy Schwieder, *Black Diamonds: Life and Work in Iowa's Coal Mining Communities, 1895-1920* (Ames: Iowa State University Press, 1983), 20.

[84] Ibid; Howard I. Smith, "Accident Frequency among English-Speaking Men and Others," *Coal Age* 5 (Jan.-June 1914): 686-687.

[85] *State Coal Mine Inspector's Report 1893.*

[86] Ibid.

[87] Leona Lampi, "Red Lodge From a Frantic Past of Crows, Coal, and Boom and Bust Emerges a Unique Festival of Diverse National Groups," *Montana, the Magazine of Western History* (Summer 1961): 21.

[88] *Union Pacific Coal Mines,* Appendix.

[89] Alexander Biggs to George L. Black, assistant superintendent Union Pacific Coal Company, March 14, 1899. Nebraska State Museum and Archives, Lincoln (UPRR Co. MS3761, SG2, Box 127, Folder 330).

[90] Patrick J. Quealy, Coal Miners and Mining. (Ms. on file, Wyoming State Archives, Cheyenne, W.P.A. Subject File 1169).

[91] Ibid.

[92] Ibid.

[93] Ibid.

[94] Ibid. Quealy, in the original manuscript, rounds the census figures to 92,000. Here it was corrected to reflect the actual figures. Brown, *Wyoming, A Geography*, 40.

[95] Ibid.

[96] Day, *Mineral Resources 1900*, 455.

[97] Some examples of this are seen in the following articles. *Rock Springs Miner*, "Opening a New Country," February 14, 1895, and "Railroads and Mines," *Rock Springs Miner*, November 27, 1902.

[98] Quealy, Coal Miners and Mining.

[99] The *Coal Age* was a magazine devoted to coal mining. It began publication in the early twentieth century.

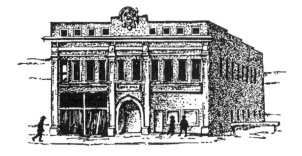

4
The Coal Age, 1900 - 1920

All night women and children walked the streets or hovered around the entrance to the mine. Many were inconsolable and their cries of grief filled the air until a late hour. It was a pitiful sight to see women wheeling babies back and forth, carrying them in their arms, or leading small children by the hand.

Hanna had witnessed the worst mining disaster in Wyoming history on June 30, 1903, and the entire coal camp waited for news of those trapped below. The news was not good; 169 miners died in the explosion of Hanna No. 1. One newspaper estimated that two-thirds of these men had been married and left behind large families.[1]

A build-up of gases underground caused the explosion that tore through Hanna No. 1. It had been known that the mine contained an excessive amount of gas, and precautions had been taken to provide adequate ventilation. In spite of the precautionary measures, at 10:30 a.m., when the work force was at its peak, the mine exploded. The reports as to where and why the explosion actually took place are vague, but newspapers throughout the region were quick to detail the human tragedy surrounding the explosion. The *Denver Times* held that inadequate safety measures had caused the explosion in Hanna No. 1 and reported that the men who died were "Martyrs not to our civilization, but to our ignorance, thoughtlessness, and greed." One hundred fifty women lost their husband, and 600 children lost their father as a result of the explosion.[2] The Rock Springs paper stated, "100 were Finlanders, 50 were colored, and the balance Americans."[3] The explosion still stands as Wyoming's worst underground mining disaster.

After the explosion in Hanna No. 1, several months passed before access to the lower reaches of the mine could be gained. It took five months to recover all of the bodies. Although the ages of the deceased were not listed, several "boys were found at the edge of the 'manway'" (the access route in and out of the mine). The force of the explosion was so great that loaded cars were "overturned along the mainslope." While the state coal mine inspector, A. M. Bradbury, could not precisely state where the explosion originated, he speculated the explosion possibly resulted "from a series of rapid shot-firing from the solid and several concussions [that] created a fog dust."[4] This dust came in contact with another shot fired underground, and as a result, the coal dust exploded. Shooting off the solid, referred to by Bradbury, means the coal was drilled and blasted without first undercutting the coal. By shooting off the solid, the blast would have a tendency to be carried out into the working space instead of downward, thus creating more coal dust and increasing the potential for an explosion. Fearing that explosions such as the 1903 disaster might reoccur, Bradbury recommended that "in the future, all mine operators should observe the mining laws strictly and use all precautions they possibly can in regulatin[g] shot firing in dusty or gaseous mines and if possible, to introduce some other kind of explosives than black powder."[5]

Unfortunately, the explosion in Hanna mine was not the only one to mar the decade between 1900 and 1910. In all, five major explosions rocked Wyoming coal mines during the first decade of the twentieth century. For the decade, 448 men were killed in coal mines, making it the most disastrous decade in the history of Wyoming coal mining. In February 1901, Diamondville No. 1 exploded, killing twenty-eight men. On October 26 of that year, another twenty-two men died in Diamondville mines. In 1905, Diamondville No. 1 once again exploded, this time killing eighteen people.

Wyoming was not alone in suffering mine disasters. "The year 1907 has the dubious distinction of having the highest recorded number of mine deaths in American mining history—about 3000 lives lost."[6] The following year, on March 28, 1908, disaster struck Hanna No. 1 for the last time. On that day, fifty-nine miners were trapped by two separate explosions. All fifty-nine died.[7]

The first explosion in Hanna No. 1 in 1908 took place at about 3 p.m., killing eighteen men. David M. Elias, who was the state coal mine inspector at the time, led a rescue party underground in an attempt to save any survivors. Caught in a second explosion, these rescuers were also entombed. Forty-one men in the rescue party died.[8] The second explosion was so devastating that further rescue attempts were halted. In all, fifty-nine men lost their lives in the two separate explosions.

These mine disasters were costly in human terms. Coming as they did at No. 1 less than five years apart, the impact on Hanna was overwhelming. As one miner so aptly put it, "the effects on the surviving family members are felt for years."[9] Edith A. Erickson remembered the second explosion in Hanna No. 1 mine and told how she lost her family.

There were several people at our house that day. Father, Andrew, Uncle Johnny, Uncle Andrew, myself, and the baby, as we called her, and also two young fellows that were friends of Uncle Andrew. [When they heard the explosion] they all jumped up and put on their coats and left to see what had happened. . . . Father stayed home to fix some things and then left to join the others.

The men had asked me to leave the dominoes and drafts out so they could finish the game when they got back, so that's what I did. But they stayed so long I got the next meal ready for all of them, and waited and waited. At 10:15 that night it blew up again.

Quite a number of men had volunteered to try to rescue those caught in the mine after the first explosion, including all six that had left our house. They did get five out when the mine blew up again, killing all my family.

The next morning was Sunday. I put the game away and the dishes of food I had cooked. You see, it was up to me to do these things. I didn't have a relative nearer than England. I was alone, if you understand what that is.[10]

As a result of the two separate explosions on March 28, 1908, 33 wives lost their husband and 103 children lost their father. In spite of further efforts to recover the bodies of men trapped below, Hanna No. 1 mine was eventually closed forever with twenty-seven men entombed.

To Joseph Bird and Noah Young, who replaced David Elias as mine inspectors, fell the job of determining why Hanna No. 1 had exploded for a second time. Noah Young, providing a thorough description of the rescue attempt, implied that Union Pacific Coal Company at Hanna had been "lax in obeying laws regulating coal mines."[11] Bird and Young made extensive recommendations in an effort to prevent future disasters. Their report called for improved roadways, improved ventilation, improved escape routes, and a change in blasting powders. Young noted that "safety explosives" were in general use in Europe. Readily admitting that the term "safety powder" was somewhat of a contradiction, Young pointed out that if carbonite or nyalite was used in place of black powder, the mines would be made safer. To add credence to his argument, he wrote

Within the past few years these powders have been introduced to some extent into the coal mines of this country while in England, Belgium, Germany, Austria, and France, there are strict regulations requiring the use of [safety] powders. And it is a pregnant fact that in these countries the loss of lives through mine explosions is fully 40 percent less than in the United States, in spite of the fact that the mines are far more dangerous creating as they do a far greater volume of gas.[12]

Noah Young did not attribute the explosion of No. 1 mine to black powder, but he took the opportunity to point out the hazards associated with using it. He noted that only in Wyoming was black powder used in blasting underground. Citing tests made at Diamondville in 1906, he said nyalite "proved highly satisfactory, the charges giving off much less smoke than black powder and practically no flame." At the time, however, miners bought their own powder, and nyalite cost $3.50 more per 100 pounds than black powder. The inspectors held that the miners "prefer[red] the additional risk to the extra cost." Young and Bird felt that miners would change only if legislation required safety powder to be used in the mines.[13] Other recommendations proposed by Bird and Young also suggested that new laws were needed to protect coal miners.

Young and Bird's recommendations did not fall on deaf ears. In 1909 the state legislature passed six bills relating to coal mining. Half of these bills related to mine safety, and they clearly followed the 1908 state mine inspectors' suggestions. The primary concerns raised by Young and Bird were poor ventilation, excessive coal dust, use of black powder, and loose coal on underground roadways. They also pointed out a need for examining boards to test fire bosses and a need to increase the jurisdiction of the state mine inspector over small coal mines. With the deadly explosion in Hanna No. 1 fresh in the minds of most lawmakers, the Tenth State Legislature passed laws to rectify the problems noted by Young and Bird. Most significant was the passage of House Bill No. 57. This bill stated that when an "inspector, or deputy, or deputies" found unsafe conditions underground, they had the "power to stop immediately the working and operation of any mine or any part thereof where any dangerous or unlawful conditions are found."[14] This bill also gave state mine inspectors the authority to quickly address potentially dangerous situations underground. Whereas 296 men died in underground explosions between 1901 and 1908, only 14 men were killed in explosions between 1909 and 1923.[15] The changes initiated in 1909, in addition to subsequent improvements, resulted in safer conditions in Wyoming mines.

Early Twentieth-century Coal Towns

In spite of the devastation wrought by the mine disasters during the first decade of the twentieth century, coal production in Wyoming doubled. In 1900, 3,774,487 tons of coal were produced. This rose to 7,583,088 tons in 1910.[16] The increased production resulted from a healthy national economy that demanded coal. Throughout the state, mines were opened to supply the regional markets, which included railroads, smelters, and domestic consumers. The largest mines opened during this period were located near Sheridan, Kemmerer, and Rock Springs. However, because these new mines were situated away from the established towns, it became necessary to construct new towns to house the miners. At Cumberland (south of Kemmerer), Superior (northeast of Rock Springs), and Monarch (north of Sheridan), large communities were constructed, seemingly overnight. All of these new towns were company built and controlled by the mine owners.

In 1900 Superior and Cumberland were little more than sagebrush flats. With the increased demand for coal in the early 1900s, interest in these areas and the Sheridan area grew. Since little development had previously taken place, there was a need to construct mining facilities, homes, and commercial buildings. The company town was seen as a quick and easy way to develop previously unsettled areas. Superior, Cumberland, and Monarch were all constructed by coal companies on lands obtained for the purpose of building towns.

The construction of a coal town in the early twentieth century was fairly systematic. Most coal companies entered into an agreement with a railroad to construct a spur to their mine. If a railroad owned the coal company, getting tracks built to the mine was simplified. Once the tracks were completed, mine operators shipped heavy equipment to the mine site. Hoists, electric generators, coal cars, fans, and a variety of mining equipment too heavy to haul by wagon were brought to the mine by rail. While the mine was being cut into the ground, the surface structures were built to house generators, hoists, and sorters. A tipple for loading the coal into waiting railroad hoppers or boxcars was also constructed. Employee homes were built after the other mining facilities were operational. Other

This tipple and power plant at Cumberland No. 2 were typical of the coal mining support facilities built in the early 1900s. The surface support facilities, including housing, a school, and a company store, were built as the shafts were dug to reach the coal seams. (Courtesy of American Heritage Center, Photo Archives, University of Wyoming)

Materials, equipment, and machinery for the new mines were brought in on rail. If the spur line to the mine was yet to be completed, materials were shipped to the nearest depot. This large generator was destined for the powerhouse of one of the local mines in the Rock Springs mining district. (Courtesy of Bud Tebedo, New Studio, Rock Springs)

common features in company towns were barracks, boarding houses, pool rooms, schools, hospitals, and even opera houses. Of course, the opera houses and hospitals were not large, but they represented an attempt to make company towns more liveable and were usually built last. The mining office, from which company operations were directed, and the store, which enhanced company profits, were built first. Still, once the decision was made to open a coal mine, everything was built in a hurry.

Company towns were self-contained in the sense that everything a person needed could be obtained from the company. This even included water. At Superior, water had to be hauled in by tank cars until a good source of water was found locally. Union Pacific owned the water cars. At Cumberland, a reservoir was built. Constructed like a large outdoor amphitheater, bricks lined the entire reservoir. Water for the camps was piped to the reservoir and distributed through a system constructed and managed by Union Pacific. Water was readily available at Monarch, but the company owned the utilities. Because coal camps were often built in semi-arid regions, bringing water to a town was no small feat, and it was an effort the companies controlled. Some renters were permitted to grow gardens, even where water was scarce, but the company dictated how water was to be used. Company towns could be abandoned as quickly as they appeared. If a company decided to abandon a mine, an eviction notice followed by cutting off the water supply meant people quickly moved elsewhere.

Dyer Clark was instrumental in the growth and development of Union Pacific coal towns in Wyoming. Signing his letters simply D. O. Clark, he would, throughout his working life, pour out volumes of letters referring to the Wyoming coal industry. When Jay Gould seized control of the Wyoming Coal and Mining Company in 1874, he ousted Wardell and made D. O. Clark "Superintendent of the Coal Department of the Union Pacific Railroad." Clark remained in this position until 1890. Between 1890 and 1895, Clark was given a special assignment and spent much of his time in Washington, D.C. Completing his assignment in the nation's capitol, he resumed his duties as superintendent of the coal company, a position he held until 1904. In 1904 he was promoted to vice president and general manager within the Union Pacific organization. Clark would remain in this position until his retirement in 1911. On November 21, 1921, D. O. Clark passed away at his retirement home in Towanda, Pennsylvania. Throughout his 43-year tenure with Union Pacific in various capacities, Clark took Wyoming's coal industry from its infancy into the Coal Age.[17] Knowing how to build a company town was something D. O. Clark clearly understood.

When coal companies constructed company towns in the twentieth century, they usually had a clear idea of what they wanted to build and how they wanted to run the camp. Each company took a different view of how they wanted to open and operate their mines. They also viewed management of the towns differently. A letter from Clark to the president of the Union Pacific Railroad shows Union Pacific attitudes in Wyoming. In describing the mining operation and the coal camp the company planned to build in 1899 at Spring Valley, Clark wrote

I would strongly recommend that we own the entire town site and control the entire business, building such buildings as necessary. The miners as a class, will have liquors, and if we do not arrange for them to get it in town, low grogeries will start up just out of town.

I would build up a good saloon, rent it to [a] responsible party who should be under absolute control. Would also as a counterbalance put in a good reading room and furnish it with some books, papers, and writing desks— and would also build and rent any other business house that might be necessary. This would give us absolute control of the town in case of trouble with employees. To mine 1000 tons per day we will need about 300 men— 100 should be married men with families. More families would be better, but I have estimated for only 100. I know this absolute control will be more profitable to the coal company than selling of town lots. If the company prefer[s] to sell lots and have an open town, we can reduce the estimate for tenements one-half, but this will destroy revenue of the store, place the town out of control, and [we would] be compelled to support a town organization. I have also estimated for a school house. We would have to pay for this even if built by [a] school district. We own the school house at Hanna, and all the town lots, so have no town organization to support.[18]

Following Clark's advice, Union Pacific constructed a company town and began operations at Spring Valley in 1900. According to the Union Pacific Coal Company history, "Everything that was done indicated that they were building a town that would last for many years. Here was no fly-by-night camp of tents and clapboard shanties, but the beginning of a permanent settlement, it would seem." The mines at Spring Valley, however, would prove to be short-lived.

The reason Spring Valley had to be abandoned came from an unexpected source. Oil from underground deposits began seeping into the mine workings, causing dangerous conditions underground. Soon oil began collecting at low points in the mine, and in 1905 Union Pacific abandoned the town. The equipment and houses were moved north to the mines at Cumberland.[19]

Whether the company town was Monarch, Spring Valley, or Rock Springs, building a company store was a matter of prime importance. D. O. Clark talked about company stores in terms of making a profit. To him, they were money-making ventures and should be perpetuated as such. Several letters written to Union Pacific headquarters in Omaha reflect Clark's managerial philosophy. At the turn of the century, Clark felt that recruiting family men to work in the mines was a good investment; they were more stable and more dependable than their unmarried counterparts. To this end, Clark actively recruited miners with families and encouraged the company to build and rent housing for families. In Rock Springs, for example, he informed the president of Union Pacific that having men with families "is a good investment" as it gives the company a "better class of men and more mouths to feed, so the company is a gainer all around."[20] Not only would the families live in company houses, but as Clark stated, they would buy groceries in the company store. Purely and simply, this was a very profitable business venture. For the year 1889, Clark projected sales from the stores in Rock Springs would reach "one hundred thousand dollars."[21] In 1900 he estimated that just one of the Union Pacific company stores in Rock Springs would "pay a clean profit of from eighteen to twenty thousand per year."[22] Although Union Pacific was not completely successful in having only company stores at Rock Springs,

Company housing at the newly constructed coal towns during the early 1900s, although improved from the 1890s, was considered by the United States Government to be unfit for habitation. The coal companies countered that the housing was like that of most American small towns. This R. W. Stone photograph of a street in Cambria records fairly typical housing of the period. (Courtesy of United States Geological Survey, Denver)

requiring the miners to shop at Union Pacific stores proved profitable. In those places where the company store was the only one in town, business was even better.

Once a coal company decided to invest in constructing a town, it was built post-haste. Profits were only realized once the town and mining equipment were in place; therefore, companies spared little effort in beginning their operations. An example of this is seen at the Monarch mines north of Sheridan. In 1903 the Wyoming Coal Mining Company built forty houses for residents, four boarding houses, a company store, a schoolhouse, and the support facilities for its Monarch mines. The houses were purchased from the American Portable House Company of Seattle, Washington, built in sections there, and then shipped and set up at Monarch. "These buildings were erected at a cost ranging from $65 to $350 each." The cost varied according to how many rooms each building contained. Those with one to four rooms, according to one writer, were "neat in appearance and reasonably substantial and durable."[23] These portable, prefabricated buildings went up quickly; but lacking insulation, they proved hot in the summer and cold in the winter. The portable structures did provide the means for constructing a town quickly.

Quickly-built homes did not lend themselves to comfort. As early as 1915 the United States Government took an active interest in industrial housing nationwide. Discussing both urban and rural housing for working men, one government report noted, "Not only are the houses and tenements which are available for workers largely insanitary [sic] and unfit for habitation, but they are inadequate."[24] The United States Coal Commission attested to the fact that nationwide, housing was generally poor in coal camps. A Coal Commission report, conducted in the 1920s, is important in that it compared company housing to housing in towns that were "self-governing." The commission concluded that three-fourths of the company-owned towns had populations of less than 2500 people. Nearly nine out of every ten of the company towns, according to the report, were "more than five miles from the resources of community life and the institutions of civil liberty that characterize the ordinary American urban center." They went on to add that, "it is evident that available facilities for family and group life often depend upon the coal operator and reflect the standards which he sets up for the men—and for the wives and children of the men— who dig his coal."[25] Ninety-five percent of the houses were made from wood. Two-thirds of the "71,000 family dwellings" included in the survey "were finished on the outside with weather board usually nailed directly to the frame with no sheathing other than paper, and sometimes not even that. . . . The houses usually rest on post foundations with no cellars, though the double houses—particularly those in more rigorous climates— often rest on solid foundations and occasionally are provided with excavated cellars."[26]

The Coal Commission attempted to be fair and gave its report in terms that presented coal company views as well as comparing coal towns to other small towns in America. They noted that most small towns in the nation did not have adequate sewage disposal systems. Yet, they also felt that "There can be no question as to the general backwardness of the bituminous coal patches as regards satisfactory disposing of human excreta. In many mining camps and towns, too, it is apparent that the importance of the subject is but partially realized." The problems present in these towns were attributed to "careless planning, failure to enlist the services of experts, and inadequate knowledge of health safeguarding."[27] The report went on to add that while the company stores "are maintained in good order," and relatively clean, the protection of foodstuffs in the separate homes was of a point of concern. Overall, "the general sanitation of coal patches is relatively low." Similar unsanitary conditions existed in small towns throughout the country, but coal towns were perceived as being among the worst.[28]

In the early decades of the twentieth century, the coal camps of the Intermountain West were not immune to the problems found in coal camps elsewhere in America. J. Kier Harding, a member of the British Parliament and a national Socialist campaign speaker, decried conditions in Colorado's southern coal fields saying,

> Had I not seen them with my own eyes I should not have believed that such conditions could have existed as are the case among the miners in the southern Colorado coal fields. The men not only receive starvation wages but they live in company houses, buy what they want from company stores, and are completely under the domination of the coal companies. It is terrible.[29]

In describing similar conditions in an unnamed, isolated community, the *Coal Age* reported, "The houses were all built on a hillside and no garden patches were available. Moreover, there were no fences around the individual houses. Livestock of all descriptions roamed at will." The author went on to note that the town had no coal houses. (Coal houses were used to store coal during the winter months.) Coal for cooking and heating was dumped on the ground, at least whenever the coal wagon "had time to deliver coal; otherwise the tenant carried his own fuel."[30] Conditions varied from place to place, but there was a consensus among miners that houses needed to be better built and that sanitary conditions needed to be improved in company towns.[31]

The people moving into Sweetwater County mining towns after the turn of the century had little choice but to live in company housing. In 1905 only 4 percent of Sweetwater County residents owned their own homes. By 1915, this had increased only to 8 percent of the total population.[32] As a point of comparison, in Laramie County in 1905, 11 percent owned their own homes; and in 1915, 15 percent of the total population owned their homes.[33] Laramie County, with Cheyenne as its largest city, was dependent on agriculture and the railroad. Sweetwater County owed its existence to coal mining. Where coal mining was the principal industry and company towns the norm, single miners lived in company-built boarding houses or bunkhouses and families lived in two- or three-room frame structures.

In Sweetwater County and elsewhere in Wyoming, company houses dominated well into the twentieth century. Elizabeth Crouch, who lived in company housing owned by Colony Coal at Dines, gave a description of what these houses were like:

The quality and type of housing varied from company town to company town and, in some cases, with the intended residents. Housing for the Japanese families at Superior in 1906 was barracks-type buildings typically used for housing single men. These units were generally less attractive than housing provided for white families.

[W]hen we first started housekeeping, we went to the store out there and bought what we could. Powder used to come in sticks in boxes. He [Mr. Crouch] brought enough of these powder boxes home to build me a kitchen cabinet. Then my refrigerator was a box in the window; and we had a few chairs, but not enough. Some people that were already there were nice enough to us when we moved out to give us different pieces, like a chair or something that they weren't using. They were very nice to us out there in Dines. But those houses, if you didn't keep the repairs up yourselves, it was too bad. . . .

[We rented them for] $10 to $15 a month. Then we had to buy our own coal, and we had to carry water. They had these hand pumps in different spots, and you had to carry water.

Before my husband had time to repair it [the company house], we could lay in bed and see people passing by. Of course, if you didn't repair those things, why you just didn't get it done. They did have one carpenter out there, but he kept pretty busy. He did mostly company work. As far as houses were concerned where people lived, the men had to take care of that themselves.[34]

The quality of houses varied, but the fact remained that miners generally had to live in company housing. For the immigrants and others moving to the various coal camps in Wyoming, moving into company housing was not an option but something mandated by the company.

The fact that immigrants and those moving into coal towns were assigned houses led to a mixing of nationalities. People were not allowed to choose where they lived. Company housing and company control of the camps had a melting pot effect. In describing the Italian settlers of Wyoming, David Kathka stated

> [C]ompany housing encouraged a mixing of nationalities. Sheridan, Sunrise, and Rock Springs never developed the 'Little Italies' that sprang up at other areas of the United States. Housing assigned on the basis of availability prevented the development of exclusive ethnic neighborhoods, although some areas might have had heavier concentrations . . . than others.[35]

Indeed, during the early twentieth century, it appears there was little racial tension in the mining camps. In reflection, miners often state that "everyone was in the same boat" and that it was better in "them days."[36] In spite of this general mixing of nationalities at coal camps, there was some

Residents of the company towns were represented by a variety of nationalities, and company housing generally encouraged their mixing. As evidenced by the creation of a separate area in Superior for the Japanese, there was still some segregation. This photograph of a Japanese family occupying a house previously reserved for other nationalities indicates that the segregation of the Japanese, at least for some, was lessening. (Courtesy of Sweetwater County Museum and Edith Sunada)

segregation. The Japanese lived in a separate part of town, as evidenced by the early town maps of Superior. Moreover, "When members of the Dillingham Commission surveyed 1751 miners in Sweetwater and Uinta Counties in 1908, they found that few of the newcomers could communicate with their fellow workers." Employers thought "Italians, Greeks, and Montenegrins [from what is now Yugoslavia] 'tricky,' undependable, and unsuited for supervisors or other responsible positions."[37] Even though the company-run towns brought diverse ethnic groups together, there was discrimination. This discrimination too often was strongest among the mine managers. Immigrants living next door to nationalities different from themselves had little choice but to interact with their neighbors. Mine managers, who always lived in bigger houses away from the miners, did not have to interact.

Labor Relations

Unsafe working conditions, the perceived paternalistic nature of coal companies, and substandard living conditions at many coal camps made Wyoming coal fields ripe for labor trouble in the first decade of the twentieth century. Poor wages added fuel to simmering fires. Unionization grew out of real and perceived problems facing coal miners throughout Wyoming and the West.

A miner's wage was based upon how much coal he mined. When company men, who managed the mines and were responsible for hauling and weighing the coal, failed to do their jobs, the individual miner suffered while the company men continued to earn a salary. The problem was especially acute when the miner could not get empty cars in which to load his coal. No matter how much coal he dug, if the miner could not get the coal to the surface, he received no pay. It was even worse when the miner was not credited for the coal he mined. Crediting the miner for coal extracted fell to the "checkman." The checkman, also called weighman, recorded how many tons of coal a miner loaded. The miner placed a brass check on the outside of the ore cart. This circular piece of brass had the miner's number stamped in the center. On the surface, the checkman weighed the coal, noted the weight, kept the check, and informed the miner of his output at the end of the shift or on payday. Miners, once they gained experience, knew how much coal they had loaded. Judging from their own experience, they were very accurate at predicting their daily or weekly output. Problems arose when the checkman recorded production well below what the miner knew to be the true weight.

Weighmen deducted weight, and thus wages, for several reasons. The most common deduction was for stone or slate found in the ore cart. Good miners were careful not to give the checkman a reason to deduct weight from their load, but some checkmen were corrupt. A corrupt weighman was not beneath changing checks or altering weights to help a miner who had paid him for just such a service. Checkmen might also alter weights to serve the company needs, but most companies attempted to avoid this practice because shorting a miner on loads was a sure means of creating a walkout. Corrupt checkmen were often cited as the reason miners went out on strike.

An example of work stoppage precipitated by a weighman was noted at Carbon. In a coded message sent from D. O. Clark to H. G. Burt, the mine superintendent informed the president of the Union Pacific that the miners walked out of the mine without giving a reason for the "work stoppage." The coded telegram was then deciphered in Omaha, and it indicated the miners stopped work in early December 1900 demanding a new checkman. D. O. Clark complied with this demand, only to have the men refuse to return to work unless the prices for black powder and oil were reduced.[38] In response to he telegram received by Clark, Burt wrote

> Your cipher message in regard to Carbon mine received. Would give the best men a chance to return to work before making any further concessions, failing in which, would issue time checks. Would rather close the mine than accede to unreasonable demands which would certainly affect our other mines.[39]

Burt had little to lose in making this statement since Union Pacific intended to close the Carbon mines in the near future. Cooler heads prevailed. D. O. Clark, upon investigating the miners' grievances, found the weighman "was surly and ugly with the men," so he removed him from his position. The miners also asked for a "check weighman" of their own choosing. The miners would pay for his services. The check weighman was a man who checked the weighman to ensure the coal was accurately weighed. Clark reinstated all the men and summed up the incident by saying "These men are not all bad men, they are more like a lot of children and very sensitive."[40]

Union Pacific was not the only company to experience labor unrest growing out of dissatisfaction with a weighman. In early January 1901, the miners at Sweetwater Coal Company No. 1 mine, located south of Rock Springs, walked out of the mines protesting the fact that their check weighman was fired. Even though these mines were not owned by Union Pacific, U.P. officials feared their men would walk out in sympathy with the plight of the other miners. D. O. Clark, while having Union Pacific's men watched, decided to support Sweetwater Coal Company. Writing in confidence, Clark told H. G. Burt not to worry as he "felt the situation could be controlled." His confidence was not unfounded. On January 8, 1901, three of the four strike leaders were sent to jail. Threatened with eviction from their homes and with their leaders in prison, the miners returned to work. As tensions mounted in Rock Springs, the miners in Hanna (who were called "young Finns") ordered the mine superintendent, E. S. Brooks, and the weighman to leave town. Brooks, one of Union Pacific's prized employees, discharged the men. Turning the tables, he was able to force the disgruntled workers to leave. D. O. Clark, very much abreast of the situation in Hanna, once again told H. G. Burt not to worry as, "I have a Pen Kinton [sic] man among them so will keep posted."[41] Pinkerton agents were often employed by Union Pacific to help quell potential labor problems.

Aborted strikes were nothing new in the Wyoming coal fields. As quickly as the miners organized, the companies found workers to replace the strikers. In company towns, the fact that the strikers could be evicted from their homes made the miners painfully aware of the risk they would run in trying to change their conditions. For example, at Diamondville, in December 1899, a strike was broken when the company brought in mounted patrols to protect strike breakers and ensure eviction notices were carried out. The deputies, as the mounted patrols were called, gave "a most formidable appearance and the strikers well know that it will cost them heavily if any attempt is made to interfere with the mines."[42] Most efforts to settle strikes or prevent labor unions from forming were more subtle.

Union Pacific Coal Company had several different ideas on how to keep down labor disputes. One of their policies, initiated after the Chinese Massacre, was to bring in mining equipment to replace miners and increase productivity. In defending the use of more equipment in No. 8 mine at Rock Springs, one mine official told D. O. Clark that machinery would help "handle and head off labor troubles much better [since] we are not entirely dependent upon the miner."[43] Another policy that the company found successful was hiring spies to disrupt labor meetings and determine what the labor organizers were planning. For instance, in July 1900 George L. Black, the assistant mine superintendent for Union Pacific, informed D. O. Clark of a planned union meeting at Swanson's Hall in Rock Springs. Having knowledge of the meeting's proposed agenda, he "quietly started [a] counter move to make [the] meeting a failure." Not only was he successful in keeping attendance at the meeting "small," he also reported it to be a "failure" in that he felt no union was organized.[44]

These policies were coupled with the continuing policy of hiring a diverse group of immigrants that would, in the minds of the company officials, frustrate organizers from creating effective labor unions.

The practice of recruiting a variety of ethnic groups was designed to prevent labor unions from forming, but it also had the effect of creating a diverse population in remote areas—an unusual situation. Cumberland, Superior, and Monarch from the outset were inhabited by immigrants from southern and eastern Europe. Where Union Pacific was the principal employer, the ethnic mix was extremely diverse. During the early years of the twentieth century, Union Pacific employed thirty-six different nationalities in the mines of Wyoming.[45] In 1900, 53 percent of the population of Rock Springs was foreign born.[46] The coal mining counties of Wyoming all had a high percentage of foreign-born residents; however, none compared to Sweetwater County where the principal industry was coal mining. In 1905 Sweetwater County, with 47 percent foreign-born residents, was the highest in the state. Weston County, where Cambria was located, was a distant second with 27 percent. Statewide in 1905 the percentage of foreign-born residents stood at 18 percent, whereas the nationwide percentage stood at 23 percent in 1900.[47]

In 1912 Union Pacific employed 2680 miners at its various mines in central and southwestern Wyoming; of this number, only 438 were Americans.[48] The rest of the coal mining workforce were immigrants. Miners came from a variety of countries, but certain areas, such as southern Europe, Finland, and the British Isles, were the principal sources of immigration into southwestern Wyoming coal fields. Polish and Italian miners dominated the Sheridan coal fields. Weston County had many Polish and Italian immigrants living at Cambria. Uinta County, and later the newly formed Lincoln County, had a variety of immigrants from southern Europe living and working in the mining camps around Kemmerer. All of the major coal fields continued to employ Japanese miners, but their numbers never equalled that of European immigrants in Wyoming. Sweetwater County's high percentage of foreign-born residents reflected Union Pacific's conscious policy of keeping labor unions out of the mines through hiring diverse ethnic groups. As the largest employer in the county, Union Pacific was successful not only in keeping out the unions but also in creating an area where foreigners were in the majority.

The tendency to hire immigrants as miners continued to be a nationwide trend. Immigrants also continued to represent the highest number of fatalities in the mines. In Pennsylvania, where accurate statistics are available from 1899 to 1911, 81.58 percent of all fatalities in the mines befell "foreigners." In West Virginia from 1907 to 1911, 64.23 percent of the fatalities were foreign-born miners. In 1914 in the eastern and central coal

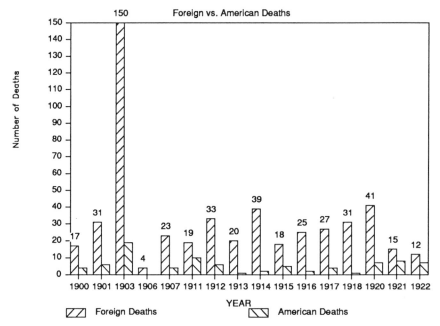

Frequency histogram of Wyoming coal mining deaths during the period 1900 - 1922. The graph shows the relationship between the number of deaths of foreign versus American miners. No data are available for missing years.

fields of America, 61.91 percent of the coal miners "were of foreign birth and 9.5 percent were of native birth but with a foreign [born] father." Of particular interest and one that probably contributed to the number of immigrants dying in the coal mines was the fact that "only 20.7 percent of the foreign-born employed had had any experience in bituminous coal mining before coming to this country."[49]   Most of those who came to America with mining experience were from Great Britain.

Some mine managers contended that it was impossible to hire American coal miners. In 1915 some mine superintendents held "Americans would rather earn $1.50 a day at some 'clean collar' occupation than twice as much in the mines." Contributing to this, managers felt, was an attitude of "false pride" that looked "down on manual labor." The hiring problem also stemmed from a negative perception of coal mining. Prior to World War I, mine managers complained "American young men seem to imagine that some sort of social stigma attaches to coal dust."[50] For whatever reason, whether it was a lack of American-born miners or active recruitment of immigrants by mine managers, coal miners were predominantly foreign born.

Superintendent Clark was influential in developing the policy that called for hiring various ethnic groups to keep labor unions out of the coal mines of Wyoming. For example, worried that labor strife in Diamondville might spread to Rock Springs, he wrote, "There are no signs of organization among the Rock Springs men and I think we can head off any attempt at organization by gradually increasing [the] number of Japanese and negro miners."[51] The plans to prevent labor unions from forming went beyond just bringing in foreign-born miners. In a letter to H. G. Burt, Clark further defined his plans to keep out labor organizers.

> Our labor question is easing up a little for miners here. Hiring some men daily. Saturday we sent out 80 German miners from Pennsylvania with eleven families. Stopped eleven men at Hanna—balance went to Rock Springs. These men were selected by one of our own men, and each one signed [an] agreement to withdraw from all labor organizations and not join one while in our employ. While this may not be any good legally, it has a moral effect. Every possible care is taken to keep nationalities mixed, and not allow any nationality to predominate, and no member of a labor organization is knowingly employed. If by accident we get one, he is dropped on first indication. The organizers who were trying to organize the miners at Rock Springs made a failure. Their last meeting was held under name of "Bryan Silver Club" and was attended by four men—the two organizers, and two outsiders.[52]

At the turn of the century, labor unions were seen as one of the major problems facing coal mine owners.

Fear of union organizations forming in coal towns affected coal companies nationwide. In some areas, mine owners met the challenge quietly but firmly. In Colorado, for example, strikes were violent, and owners and miners suffered alike. The Illinois Coal Operators Association in 1903 contended that "There is today only one cloud in the commercial heavens and that is the labor cloud."[53] Coal companies reacted to labor organizations in several different ways. In Wyoming the coal companies chose to join in an alliance against labor unions.

In addition to Union Pacific's active policies to discourage labor unions, the company also quietly supported the Citizens' Alliance. This association, a secret society, pledged "To promote the stability of business and the steady employment of labor, whether organized or unorganized, by encouraging friendly relations between employers and employees, and to discourage lockouts, strikes, and boycotts and all kindred movement which savor of persecution." The by-laws of the alliance, which was in operation throughout the West, also stipulated that "its members" would be protected "from unlawful interference and the evil effects of strikes, lockouts, and boycotts." To be a member of the alliance, a person had to own property or be a part of a "firm, association, or corporation, owning property, employed in or engaged in business." An employee who was not a member of a labor organization that supported strikes could also be part of the alliance. However, the Citizens' Alliance was designed to include corporations and businessmen; it was not designed to include employees.[54]

A number of notables joined the Wyoming Citizens' Alliance. "About three hundred of the most prominent businessmen attended" the charter meeting of the alliance, including Senator F. E. Warren and Governor Fenimore Chatterton.[55] The main points argued were "the rights of the employer to do exactly as he saw fit in the management of his business." Doing whatever management saw fit included, "the employment of whoever [sic] he wished at wages satisfactory to both." The alliance also upheld "the rights of the workmen to work for whoever [sic] he wished."[56] While not wanting to be directly aligned with the alliance, Union Pacific was very supportive of the effort. With the establishment of the Cheyenne Alliance, a confident D. O. Clark once again wrote H. G. Burt, "I am of the opinion that they [the alliance] have absolute control of the situation from now on."[57] This time D. O. Clark was overly optimistic. Before the decade was over, miners would walk out of the coal mines across the state.

United Mine Workers of America

In 1890 the United Mine Workers of America formed a national labor organization that would prove attractive to coal miners throughout Wyoming. The United Mine Workers of America, or UMWA as they were most commonly called, formed as a coalition allying portions of the old Knights of Labor and the Miners' Progressive Union. It was not until 1903, however, that the UMWA began organizational activities in Wyoming.[58] The first attempts at organizing took place in the northern coal districts, specifically in the area around Sheridan. "The first local was organized in Sheridan County at . . . Dietz, despite considerable opposition on the part of the employers."[59] Then the miners at Dietz helped labor organizers establish locals in neighboring coal camps. With the northern fields successfully organized, attention turned to southern Wyoming. By the spring of 1907, the UMWA had organized coal miners along the Union Pacific Railroad in what was called the southern Wyoming coal field.

Union Pacific strenuously objected to the UMWA, but to no avail. On May 26, 1907, all the mines in Rock Springs closed. The *Rock Springs Miner* reported the strike was peaceable and the coal company did not want any

Workers and their families of Japanese ancestry at Superior ca. 1910-1920. The Japanese coal miners in the Rock Springs mining district were instrumental in the successful establishment of the union in the mines of the district. (Courtesy of Sweetwater County Museum and Edith Sunada)

trouble; however, the coal company moved to dismiss all the miners. Even with the threat of being thrown out of their homes, the miners did not buckle.[60] Speeches, delivered in four different languages, were received enthusiastically. The UMWA in Rock Springs also moved to admit Japanese miners into the union. Previously unheard of, the move to accept Japanese miners proved pivotal. Union Pacific had counted on the Japanese remaining in the mines. Without the Japanese miners to break the strike, the union won the day.[61]

The *Sheridan Post* questioned the wisdom of admitting Japanese into the union. Calling it "but another phase of the yellow peril," the paper conceded that the Japanese had helped the union to succeed. The paper reported

> The men at Rock Springs asked for a union, which the company refused to recognize, stating in addition that no union man would be employed in any capacity about the works. Upon this flat-footed refusal the men immediately walked out from their work and with them three hundred Japanese. After three weeks of a lockout the company agreed to recognize the union, provided every miner, then idle, would immediately commence work. Then it was that the leaders faced the gravest problem in the history of organized

labor. The question was, shall we refuse to resume work with the Japanese and lose the fruits of the victory already within our grasp or shall we accept the Japanese on equal terms and thereby receive recognition of the union? The question had never been presented before. It was an entirely new situation. The wise counsel of John Mitchell was sought. His advice was that it would be better to receive the Japanese miners to membership in the union and gain better conditions for all than to refuse them admission and lose everything that had been striven for. Thereupon the Japanese were admitted. The die was cast, and the result upon union labor is in the dim and distant future.[62]

The union's decision to accept all nationalities in Rock Springs ensured success. Union Pacific was forced to negotiate, and its mines in southern Wyoming became unionized.

The miners returned to work in early June 1907. Union Pacific chose to negotiate with the union. It was a good time for the coal industry in the West; there were more orders than they could fill. With orders up and profits assured, Union Pacific agreed to "the eight-hour day, effective September 1, 1907, [and a] wage increase of approximately 20 percent more for eight hours than formerly paid for ten hours work." In addition, improved working conditions were guaranteed, and a union check weighman was to be employed at each mine. With these concessions from Union Pacific, the entire state of Wyoming was organized.[63]

For several reasons, the nation experienced a financial slump in late 1907 and early 1908. While the need for coal remained strong, the recession threatened the hard-won gains of the UMWA. In 1908 Wyoming miners were once again on the picket lines. "The controversy [was] simply a matter of dollars and cents." The coal companies contended, "The business of coal mining is not what it was a year ago and we must reduce expenses slightly."[64] The coal companies wanted wage reductions. On September 1, 7000 Wyoming coal miners walked out of the mines. It was a statewide strike that included not only the large mining companies but the independent mines as well.[65] By the end of September, the UMWA settled with Union Pacific and the coal companies at Kemmerer. By the end of October, the union reached an agreement with the various operators at Sheridan. The miners were successful in keeping their wages at 1907 levels.[66] More important, the union solidified the gains achieved in 1907. The UMWA would continue to be a factor in Wyoming coal mining.

Good news greeted the miners from other quarters. The eventful Tenth State Legislature followed the union's lead and enacted legislation in 1909 stipulating "the period of employment of working men in all underground mines or workings shall be eight (8) hours per day."[67] Although already mentioned in the State Constitution of 1890, additional legislation was needed to enforce the law; thus, this legislation was heralded as a major accomplishment. When Labor Day parades were held celebrating hard-won gains, they were truly international festivals in Rock Springs. The union was just that, a joining together of members of diverse nationalities to accomplish a single goal. Problems did not vanish overnight, but there had been progress.

Land Frauds

While coal companies continued to make profits in the early years of the twentieth century, there were also numerous problems. Labor strife, a major source of trouble, was not the only problem facing the coal companies. The federal government was about to bring suit against Wyoming's major coal producers. Charged with theft of federal land and coal reserves, the coal companies were faced with a formidable opponent in the form of the United States Government.

In 1901 Theodore Roosevelt became President of the United States. A lover of nature and the wilderness, some of his most lasting accomplishments came in the conservation of the nation's resources. Working closely with Gifford Pinchot, a personal friend and chief of the Forest Service, Roosevelt established the country's first comprehensive national conservation policy. During his administration, Roosevelt "undertook a major reclamation program, created the Federal Reclamation Service, and strengthened the forest preserve program in the Department of Agriculture." Not content with these measures, Roosevelt also broadened the concept of conservation by placing power sites, coal lands, oil reserves, and national forests in the public domain. "When Roosevelt took office in 1901 there were 45 million acres in government preserves. In 1908 there were almost 195 million."[68]

To accomplish the task of conserving national resources, Roosevelt gave attention to land frauds of all kinds. In his search for land fraud, he "did not spare the coal mining companies in Wyoming." As early as 1873, coal lands could be purchased outside the original railroad land grant. The process was somewhat cumbersome but permitted lands to "be bought at no less than twenty dollars an acre if within fifteen miles of a completed railroad and not less than ten dollars an acre if more than fifteen miles from a railroad." There was a catch. In purchasing coal lands, an individual could purchase only 160 acres while a corporation could obtain up to 640 acres.[69] This policy limited the amount of land available for mining. Even though the Union Pacific Railroad obtained much coal land in its original land grant, it felt there was a need to round out its holdings. To simplify the mining process and obtain enough fuel for railroads, Union Pacific sought to acquire some sections still owned by the government. "Unable to buy lands in the quantities desired, the Union Pacific Coal Company used dummies, vagrants, and respectable citizens much as the cattlemen used their cowboys." The process involved having a person either homestead or purchase the land; then Union Pacific obtained the land for costs and "considerations." In most instances, "the land was fraudulently acquired by assorted individuals and then transferred to the coal company."[70] Union Pacific Coal Company was not alone in this practice.

In October 1906, Roosevelt directed the Department of Justice to begin legal proceedings against the Union Pacific Railroad. The purpose of this action was to restore illegally obtained coal lands to the public domain. The Union Pacific's holdings were extensive. Similar charges of fraudulently obtaining coal lands were levied against the Wyoming Coal Mining Company in Sheridan County, the Diamond Coal and Coke Company near Kemmerer, and the Owl Creek Coal Company at the newly opened Gebo Mines north of Thermopolis.[71] Eventually, all the fraudulently obtained lands were returned to the federal government, but not without first going through the federal courts.

The investigations of fraud implicated a number of leading citizens. T. A. Larson provided an excellent insight into how far-reaching the federal investigation went.

> Government land agents testified before the Interstate Commerce Commission at Salt Lake City in November, 1906, that they had been compelled to see Senator Francis E. Warren regarding official business of the General Land Office. Warren could not avoid suspicion whenever land frauds were aired in this period because he was considered mainly responsible for the appointment of Wyoming's William A. Richards as Commissioner of the General Land Office and the appointment of Wyoming's Willis Van Devanter as Assistant Attorney General for the Interior Department, in which position he was "the legal conscience of the land department" during the years 1897-1903.
>
> Like Warren, Senator C. D. Clark and Representative Frank W. Mondell were much interested in furthering the Wyoming economy, which included, prominently, the Union Pacific Railroad and its subsidiary coal companies. Clark and Mondell probably understood coal problems even better than Warren did. Clark had worked for the Union Pacific Coal Department in territorial days. His older brother, Dyer O. Clark, was vice-president and general manager of the Union Pacific Coal Company from 1904 to 1911 and had worked for the Union Pacific in various capacities since 1868. Mondell knew the coal business first-hand, having developed coal properties at Cambria in the late 1880s.[72]

Union Pacific kept good records detailing correspondence between the various principals of the company. These first-hand accounts provide an excellent source of information regarding the coal land issue. Union Pacific was no different from other Wyoming coal companies of the period. They needed more land to carry out their mining operations profitably. Deprived of legal means to obtain the land, they felt compelled to move outside federal regulations.

An example of Union Pacific's close ties with the U.S. Land Department in Wyoming is seen in a letter from D. O. Clark to H. G. Burt. Describing the need to obtain land near their proposed Spring Valley coal mine, Clark wrote in 1899,

> Now, as to securing title to the land we want to purchase: Under a strict construction of the wording of the law we cannot get title to it, and our Legal Department rules against it, but we must have the land, and a little stretch of some man's conscience will enable us to get it, and three hundred dollars per entry of 160 acres or less is sufficient to cover the stretching process. Of course it is not absolutely safe, but we have the U. S. Land Department officials in Wyoming with us. So if our papers are in proper form, no questions will be asked, and we do not need to implicate our Legal Department in any way.[73]

Stretching "some man's conscience" was not the only means of obtaining additional lands.

Coal companies unable to obtain land through other means often turned to outside sources. An example is seen in the area south of Kemmerer. Unable to get the coal land needed, D. O. Clark advised Union Pacific to use soldier's additional homestead scrip, "which would cost $10.00 per acre and land office fees to obtain the property." Soldier's scrip was supposed to help veterans obtain lands in the West. Clark felt purchasing this scrip, "would give us good title to the land and keep it off the tax books as coal land, as it would come under the head of agricultural lands..." Clark went on to add that this type of scrip was scarce, two-thirds of it being "held by a syndicate in Washington." He felt he could obtain this scrip in Washington and use it to gain clear title to the land. This title, in his opinion, "would be one that cannot be attached after the patent is issued."[74]

Where coal was plentiful, coal companies often played a game of chess with the playing board being sections of land. Coal companies tried to block other companies and individuals from gaining coal lands near their holdings. Kemmerer Coal, with P. J. Quealy as the leader, controlled most lands north of Kemmerer. Anaconda, with its Diamondville mines, sat between Kemmerer on the north and Union Pacific's Cumberland mines to the south. The Diamond Coal and Coke Company felt compelled to block encroachment by both companies. D. O. Clark, always looking out for Union Pacific, quietly leveled accusations as early as 1900 "that nearly all the [land] purchases from the government by the Diamond Company, were fraudulently made, many of them made as Homestead and Desert entries."[75] Clark was correct in his accusations; however, he had to be careful since he lived in the proverbial glass house. Soon, both Diamond Coal and Coke Company and Union Pacific Coal Company would be investigated for attempts to grab federal lands.

In 1906 both the Department of Interior and Interstate Commerce Commission investigated Union Pacific's land holdings adjacent to the railroad right-of-way. Of the two agencies, the Interstate Commerce Commission pursued the investigation with the most vigor. The local Rock Springs paper ran an article stating "Coal Filings of U.P. Declared Honest." The article claimed

> [The Interior Department] long ago proved to its own satisfaction that these lands were secured by the Union Pacific and its subsidiary corporations the Union Pacific Coal company and the Superior Coal company, in legitimate fashion and it manifests small sympathy for any investigation that now threatens to bring its conclusion into question and besides, it was explained there is nothing new to be gained by pursuing the matter, because these lands have been patented more than six years, and patents outstanding that long cannot be assailed.[76]

At least temporarily the local paper stood behind the town's major employer. This support would change as it became evident Union Pacific and its subsidiary, Superior Coal, were guilty of land fraud.[77] Union Pacific was forced to surrender "vast tracks of valuable coal lands in Wyoming obtained by fraud."[78]

The year 1907 was an eventful one in terms of the number of fraud cases brought against coal companies. Turning their attention to Superior Coal, "a Union Pacific concern," the federal government filed suit over 27 fraudulent entries with a total value of $600,000.[79] In a number of cases, the federal courts decided that Union Pacific would have to relinquish illegally obtained land, but Union Pacific was not alone. During the summer of 1907, federal authorities brought suit against Diamond Coal and Coke and Wyoming Coal Mining Company. Diamond Coal and Coke had obtained land near Kemmerer through securing "transfer of soldiers additional homestead claims." This meant that Diamond Coal and Coke had used "soldiers scrip" to obtain land. The value of the 2760 acres filed under these claims was set at $1,000,000. At Monarch, Wyoming Coal Mining Company fraudulently obtained 1200 acres. Federal coffers had been deprived of revenue; now through its courts, the federal government was attempting to regain millions. In July 1907 the various owners of Wyoming Coal Mining Company were found guilty of conspiring to defraud the government.[80] Federal authorities also continued to press their case against Union Pacific. In July 1909 the case was finally settled and Union Pacific was forced to give up its claims at Superior and pay $40,000 for coal already extracted.[81]

In October 1907 yet another Wyoming railroad company was implicated in coal land fraud. Government officials charged that the Chicago, Burlington, and Quincy Railway was behind the land grab at Gebo. While not being mined by the Burlington, the coal was hauled over its lines; and the government felt this land was secured for Burlington's benefit. Three men, specifically Samuel W. Gebo, for whom the mines were named, and New York millionaires George Dally and Alfred Sully, were brought before the Federal Grand Jury in Cheyenne on charges of land fraud.

> They [would] be charged with the downright theft of 2000 acres of the most valuable coal lands owned by the government in the west, through the means of sixty-four dummy entrymen, most of whom were bartenders, waitresses, and members of New York's lower stratum.[82]

The charges held that Sully, Dally, and other members of a New York-controlled syndicate had spent upwards of $150,000 in obtaining the coal entries. Their principal expense included "the expense of filing by the entrymen." Once the "dummy entrymen got hold of the land at $10 an acre, it was immediately transferred to the corporation formed by the syndicates." The *Sheridan Post* reported the government "will demand the recovery of the land and its immediate transfer." The article went on to say, "Bowery waitresses, saloon hangers-on, and others will not be allowed to lounge in their resorts and sign papers to land they never saw. Some of them do not even know where Wyoming is."[83]

Samuel Gebo was optimistic about the pending court case. Feeling he would not be found guilty of land fraud, he took a trip to Europe in 1910. Returning home to Wyoming in February 1910, he learned his mines were closed by court order and had been since December 1909.[84] The restraining order against mining at Gebo would stay in force until mid-February. Even then, mining was only resumed in areas not affected by the fraud charges. Only coal found under private lands could be mined.[85] The federal lands in question were off limits to further mining until the court case could be settled. The effect of the court battle was layoffs. Two hundred miners lost jobs; "two-thirds of the miners had families." The *Sheridan Post* sympathized with the miners claiming, "To be thrown out of employment" hurt "these sturdy men and they felt it keenly."[86]

The criminal trial against Gebo and the fraudulent coal entrymen finally began in Cheyenne in May 1913. Forty witnesses were subpoenaed, some from as far away as New York. Gebo's previous optimism proved false as the federal court in Cheyenne ruled against Owl Creek Coal Company. Samuel Gebo and his partners paid fines of $7500 plus court costs. The federal land office cancelled all leases. Once the lease was cancelled, however, the land was then opened for leasing to Owl Creek Coal on a royalty basis.[87] This lease was made possible through a recently passed coal lease law. A few years earlier, Wyoming State Representative Frank W. Mondell had introduced legislation into Congress establishing a separation of mineral rights from surface rights. The legislation became law in March 1909.[88] Under this new law, Gebo could lease land legally. Other coal companies eventually leased lands, ending the decades-long practice of obtaining land fraudulently.

Political Activism

Possibly encouraged by their successes in forming unions and the fact that the federal government had successfully prosecuted some of the largest companies in Wyoming, the miners in Wyoming became more politically active. To some extent, coal miners had been active in politics in the nineteenth century. Some miners had served in territorial and state legislatures and were influential in obtaining mine safety laws.[89] The State Constitution even called for the eight-hour work day for miners laboring underground. However, the eight-hour day did not become a reality until the twentieth century. With the unions serving as a catalyst, the miners organized not only as a labor organization but as a political force. Often the political parties to which the miners belonged differed, but they had similar goals. Specifically, the miners wanted better and safer working conditions and shorter hours underground. To the immigrants, the union's political strength made joining a labor organization attractive. Even before the immigrant gained citizenship, the union offered a political voice. Once the immigrant became a citizen and could vote, he remembered the union had helped him voice his concerns. Often the new citizen followed the politics of the union, but some voted for parties imported from Europe. Whatever politics they followed, the goals the miners supported were similar.

To accomplish their goals, miners in Wyoming supported a variety of political parties, including the Socialist party. The Socialist party was not unique to Wyoming coal fields. It had gained strength in Colorado coal camps and in the hardrock mines surrounding Butte, Montana. The strength of the party lay in its pro-worker platform. Because of this, it was successful in mining towns and registered successes in local elections. In 1911 Butte elected a Socialist mayor.[90] In Rock Springs and Sheridan, the party had enough strength to garner votes and notices in the local newspapers. The goals of the party were modest, and most miners in the early twentieth century viewed Socialism in a positive light.

In 1908 the Socialist party held its statewide convention in Rock Springs. Representatives from Sheridan, Evanston, Kemmerer, and Laramie attended. The platform for 1908 called for the eight-hour day, "state insurance and old age pensions," and asked "that coal mine inspectors be elected only by the miners."[91] Locally the Socialist party, which met in the Finn Hall in Rock Springs, nominated candidates for mayor and councilman.[92] The Socialist platform included reforms that were addressed by the 1909 State Legislature when six pieces of coal legislation became law. Included were two bills that reflected Socialist concerns. While not gaining everything asked for, the party did see reforms initiated in the state coal mine inspector's office and the passage of the eight-hour day law for coal miners.[93]

The Socialists continued to press for labor-related legislation. Their goal was to improve working conditions for miners and other laborers.[94] In 1910 the Sweetwater County Socialists did not send any representatives to Cheyenne, but they did garner 13 percent of the vote in the governor's race. Some voting districts, such as Superior, gave 25 percent of the votes to the Socialist candidate for governor. At Quealy, voters also gave 25 percent of their vote to the Socialist party.[95] Superior and Quealy voting districts were both in coal camps. To elicit support for their party, the Socialists brought in activists. The UMWA hall in Rock Springs sponsored speeches by such notable Socialists as Ida Crouch Hazlett. The papers reported that "everyone that attended was more than pleased" with her speech in Rock Springs.[96] The local paper gave ample space to Socialist topics, possibly because the UMWA gave its tacit approval to the party.

Although the Socialist party was never a major party in the coal towns of Wyoming, it continued to function until World War I. The party conducted lecture courses in the Grand Opera House in Rock Springs, and Socialists held conventions in the Finn Hall. The party began to lose followers as early as 1912 when only Superior showed repeated strong support. Part of the reason was the splintered nature of the 1912 election when five parties were represented on the ballot. Of the five parties, the Socialists typically tallied third behind the Republicans and the Democrats. In the race for Wyoming's lone seat in the United States House of

Representatives, Superior voters gave the Republicans 50 votes, the Democrats 65, the Socialists 39, and the Progressive Party 14.[97] The Socialist's share of the vote totalled only 23 percent, a decline from 1910. The Socialist's share of the vote continued stable until World War I. Then, with the Russian Revolution fresh in the minds of many, the party lost support. Although the party continued, it would never quite recover. Miners continued their support for labor issues through political activities, but their votes were cast for candidates in the more traditional parties.

Mechanization and Labor Shortages

The decade between 1910 and 1919 proved to be one of growth for the Wyoming coal industry. Coal was in demand throughout the nation. Used in steamships, factories, and locomotives, the need for coal proved great. In 1913 Union Pacific ran an advertisement in the *Rocket Miner* calling for "1000 Miners and Laborers." The ad went on to say, "The Union Pacific and Superior Coal companies want for their mines at Rock Springs, Superior, and Reliance, 1000 miners and laborers. The mines are safe and free [from] gas, work is steady, and wages are good."[98]

The demand for workers reflected the strong coal market. The mines at Gebo, Sheridan, and Kemmerer experienced similar growth. The increased demand for coal was partially met through mechanization, which helped to increase productivity. Initially in coal mining, everything from picking the coal off the face to shoveling, loading, and unloading the mine cars was done by hand. Mules were used to haul the loaded cars from the workings to the tipple. Even though mules hauled coal well into the twentieth century, this method of hauling was slow. Even with good miners, only a limited amount of coal could be extracted by hand methods. Mechanization, which had its beginnings in the late nineteenth century, eventually sped up the mining process and increased productivity.

The mines at Rock Springs began to mechanize at a relatively early date. One of the first innovations used was the newly invented telephone; it was installed in Union Pacific No. 1 and No. 2 mines in 1881. A year later, air-driven cutting and drilling machines were installed in Union Pacific No. 4. A great improvement over the hand-mining methods, this equipment led to a rise in production. In the early 1890s, air-driven puncher machines were introduced into the Rock Springs No. 8 mine. Then by the turn of the century, air operated cutting, drilling, and hoisting machinery was being replaced by electrically operated machinery in the Wyoming mines. About 1902, a short-wall automatic miner was installed in the Rock Springs Union Pacific No. 8 mine. This was a forerunner of the more modern short-wall machinery. When the Superior mines were fully opened in 1906, they were entirely equipped with electric undercutting machines. Up to 90 percent of the coal was recovered mechanically from the Superior mines. When the mines opened in Reliance in 1910, they too were equipped with electric undercutters.[99] Union Pacific claimed

> One of the real advantages that has come out of mechanization of the Coal Company's mines is that of the increased extraction secured per acre, of mineral in place. In 1900 the extraction did not exceed forty per cent; today [1940] it averages in excess of eighty per cent, a clear gain of one hundred per cent.[100]

Mechanization clearly increased productivity for the Sweetwater County coal mines.

In 1912, Sweetwater County mines produced 40 percent of the state's total output. Statewide for the same period, 32 percent of the coal produced was extracted by machinery. According to a 1913 government report, it was held that "The labor efficiency in Wyoming is among the highest in the country, usually showing an average production per man per year of over 900 tons."[101] This efficiency was due to increased mechanization.

Overall the years between 1900 and 1917 had been prosperous years for the coal industry. During the war years between 1917 and 1919 production would rise dramatically. The increase in coal production brought about by the development of new coal mines and mechanization of the mines accelerated rapidly during World War I. Due to increased demand for coal, additional coal camps came into being during this period. One miner stated that during this time, "People would buy anything that came out of the ground and was black."[102] In 1917 the coal town of Winton, located north of Rock Springs, came into existence. Another camp located north of Rock Springs, called Dines, began production in 1918. These two coal camps became substantial settlements and continued production into the 1950s. The stage was set in the early years of the twentieth century. As the industry grew statewide, new technology allowed men to mine more coal. From 1915 to 1920, coal production climbed steadily to a point where 9,580,274 tons were extracted in 1920.[103] The results of the Coal Age were high levels of production that would not be duplicated again until World War II.

Notes

[1] *Rock Springs Miner,* July 2, 1903.

[2] Taft A. Larson, *History of Wyoming* (Lincoln: University of Nebraska Press, 1978), 33. *The State Coal Mine Inspector's Report 1903* lists the fatalities at 169 and continued to do so in subsequent publications. The Bureau of Mines Coal Mine Explosions also lists the fatalities at 169.

[3] *Rock Springs Miner,* July 2, 1903.

[4] *State Coal Mine Inspector's Report 1903,* 13. (All state coal mine inspector's reports are on file Wyoming State Archives, Cheyenne.)

[5] Ibid.

[6] *State Coal Mine Inspector's Report* 1901-1908; *America 200, The Legacy of our Lands* (Washington: U.S. Department of the Interior, 1976), 99. The State of Wyoming was divided into two inspection districts. State coal mine inspectors filed reports for both areas but discussed the two districts separately. The two districts consisted of the northern and southern districts.

[7] Ibid.

[8] P. A. Kalish, "The Woebegone Miners of Wyoming: A History of Coal Mine Disasters in the Equality State," *Annals of Wyoming* 42(2):237-242; *History of the Union Pacific Coal Mines 1868 to 1940* (Omaha: The Colonial Press, 1940), 118.

[9] Eric Margolis, *Coal Mining as a Way of Life: An Oral History of the Western Coal Miners* (Boulder, Colorado: University of Colorado Institute of Behavioral Science, 1984).

[10] Miners Monument Pamphlet, Hanna, Wyoming (Ms. on file, Union Pacific Railroad Company, Omaha, Nebraska).

[11] Larson, *Wyoming,* 337, cf Mr. Bird was accompanied in his efforts by Noah Young of District 2. The *State Coal Mine Inspector's Report 1908* was apparently co-authored with Bird serving as the principal author.

[12] *State Coal Mine Inspector's Report 1908,* 26.

[13] Ibid.

[14] *Session Laws of the State of Wyoming passed by the Tenth State Legislature* (Sheridan, Wyoming: Post Printing Co., 1909), 104.

[15] *State Coal Mine Inspector's Report* 1901-1923.

[16] *State Coal Mine Inspector's Report* 1900-1910. Statistics for coal output are not complete in 1910. The federal government records also disagree with the SCMI. The figure of 7,583,088 tons comes from federal compilation of the *State Coal Mine Inspector's Report 1910.* Specifically, these figures are in *Mineral Resources of the United States 1912* (Washington, D.C.: Government Printing Office, 1913), 227.

[17] *Union Pacific Coal Mines,* 179-180.

[18] D. O. Clark to H. G. Burt, November 20, 1899. Nebraska State Museum and Archives, Lincoln (UPRR Co. MS3761, SG2, Series 1, Box 127, Folder 333), 3-4.

[19] *Union Pacific Coal Mines,* 127.

[20] D. O. Clark to H. G. Burt, April 28, 1899. Nebraska State Museum and Archives, Lincoln (UPRR Co. MS3761, SG2, Series 1, Box 127, Folder 330).

[21] D. O. Clark to H. G. Burt, February 22, 1899. Nebraska State Museum and Archives, Lincoln (UPRR Co. MS3761, SG2, Series 1, Box 130, Folder 329).

[22] D. O. Clark to H. G. Burt, August 2, 1900. Nebraska State Museum and Archives, Lincoln (UPRR Co. MS3761, SG2, Series 1, Box 128, Folder 336).

[23] *The Sheridan (Wyoming) Post*, December 17, 1903. For a comparison of privately owned homes to company homes, see *Coal Age* 8(August 1915):328-329.

[24] Frank P. Walsh, *Final Report of the Commission on Industrial Relations* (Washington, D.C.: Barnard and Miller Print, 1915), 96-97.

[25] Edward Eyre Hunt, F. G. Tryon, and Joseph H. Willits, eds., *What the Coal Commission Found* (Baltimore: The Williams and Wilkins Co., 1925), 140. The Commission was appointed by President Harding in the fall of 1922.

[26] Ibid., 143.

[27] Ibid., 146-147.

[28] Ibid., 147.

[29] John R. Lawson file, Denver Public Library, Denver, Colorado (Special Collections, Scrap Book, September 26, 1912), 17.

[30] J. W. Bischoff, "Labor Problems at Coal Mines," *Coal Age* 8 (December 1915): 1058-1059.

[31] Another article describing needed improvements is in the August 28, 1915, issue of *Coal Age*. A more favorable argument in favor of company housing is contained in the July 29, 1915, issue of *Coal Age*. However, in summing up the article the editor comments, "Rents are too low in mining towns and houses not as fine as they should be. But until the miner is ready to pay more or legislation makes the operator face the problems, rents and houses will both be much like they have been," 138.

[32] *Census of Wyoming, 1905* (Cheyenne: SA Bristol Co. Prince Brand Bookbinders, 1905), 5; *Census of Wyoming, 1915* (Cheyenne: Wyoming Labor Journal Printing Company, 1915).

[33] Ibid.

[34] Elizabeth Crouch, interview with David Kathka, Green River, Wyoming, 1975 (Ms. on file, Archaeological Services of Western Wyoming College, Rock Springs), 68-69.

[35] David Kathka, "The Italian Experience in Wyoming," in *Peopling the High Plains, Wyoming's European Heritage* (Cheyenne: Wyoming State Archives and Historical Department), 73.

[36] A. Dudley Gardner and David E. Johnson, *Cultural Resource Inventory and Mitigation of Thirty-Seven Mine Reclamation Sites in Sweetwater County, Wyoming.* Cultural Resource Management Report No. 29 (Rock Springs: Archaeological Services of Western Wyoming College, 1986), Appendix H.

[37] L. A. Cardoso, "Nativism in Wyoming, 1868 to 1930," *Annals of Wyoming* 58 (Spring 1986): 26.

[38] Coded and Deciphered Telegrams D. O. Clark to H. G. Burt, December 10 and 11, 1900. Nebraska State Museum and Archives, Lincoln (UPRR Co. MS3761, SG2, Series 1, Box 128, Folder 337).

[39] Telegram from H. G. Burt to D. O. Clark, December 11, 1900. Nebraska State Museum and Archives, Lincoln (UPRR Co. MS3761, SG2, Series 1, Box 128, Folder 337).

[40] D. O. Clark to H. G. Burt, December 13, 1900. Nebraska State Museum and Archives, Lincoln (UPRR Co. MS3761, SG2, Series 1, Box 128, Folder 337), 1-2.

[41] Telegrams from D. O. Clark to H. G. Burt, January 5, 7, and 8, 1901. Nebraska State Museum and Archives, Lincoln (UPRR Co. MS3761, SG2, Series 1, Box 128, Folder 338); Letter from D. O. Clark to H. G. Burt, January 7, 1901. Nebraska State Museum and Archives, Lincoln (UPRR Co. MS3761, SG2, Series 1, Box 128, Folder 338), 1-2.

[42] *The Omaha Daily Bee*, December 8, 1899.

[43] George L. Black to D. O. Clark, March 24, 1899. Nebraska State Museum and Archives, Lincoln (UPRR Co. MS3761, SG2, Series 1, Box 127, Folder 330), 1-2.

[44] Telegrams from George Black to D. O. Clark, July 14 and 18, 1900. Nebraska State Museum and Archives, Lincoln (UPRR Co. MS3761, SG2, Series 1, Box 128, Folder 336).

[45] *Union Pacific Coal Mines*, 163-164.

[46] *Twelfth Census of the United States*, 1900 (Washington, D.C.: U.S. Government Printing Office, 1901).

[47] *Census of Wyoming, 1905*, 5-7; *Historical Statistics of the United States, Colonial Times to 1957* (Washington D.C.: U.S. Government Printing Office, 1961), 11.

[48] *Union Pacific Coal Mines*, 163. Union Pacific separates black Americans from whites; the total of black and white native-born Americans is 438.

[49] *The Coal Age* 5 (April 1914): 686-687.

[50] *The Coal Age* 8 (September 1915): 383.

[51] D. O. Clark to H. G. Burt, April 26, 1899. Nebraska State Museum and Archives, Lincoln (UPRR Co. MS3761, SG2, Series 1, Box 127, Folder 330), 3.

[52] D. O. Clark to H. G. Burt, August 10, 1900. Nebraska State Museum and Archives, Lincoln (UPRR Co. MS3761, SG2, Series 1, Box 128, Folder 336), 4.

[53] Herman Justi, *Organization and Public Opinion* (Chicago: Illinois Coal Operators Association, 1903), 18-19.

[54] The Citizens Alliance of Cheyenne, Wyoming, Constitution. Nebraska State Museum and Archives, Lincoln (UPRR Co. MS3761, SG2, Series 1, Box 135, Folder 378), 3-4.

[55] D. O. Clark to H. G. Burt, September 25, 1903, Nebraska State Museum and Archives, Lincoln (UPRR Co. MS3761, SG2, Series 1, Box 136, Folder 379). Also H. George to H. G. Burt, October 3, 1903.

⁵⁶ Clipping. Nebraska State Museum and Archives, Lincoln (UPRR Co. MS3761, SG2, Series 1, Box 136, Folder 379).

⁵⁷ D. O. Clark to H. G. Burt, September 25, 1903.

⁵⁸ Erma A. Fletcher, *The History of the Labor Movement in Wyoming, 1870-1940* (Master's thesis, Department of Economics and Sociology, University of Wyoming, 1945), 26-27.

⁵⁹ Ibid., 29.

⁶⁰ Ibid.; *Rock Springs Miner*, May 25, 1907.

⁶¹ *The Sheridan Post,* July 26, 1907; *The Kemmerer Camera*, May 25, 1907; David A. Wolff, Cumberland, Wyoming, A Middle Generation Union Pacific Coal Camp, (Unpublished graduate seminar paper, History Department, University of Wyoming, 1988); Yuji Ichioka, "Asian Immigrant Coal Miners and the United Mine Workers of America: Race and Class at Rock Springs, Wyoming, 1907," *Amerasia*, 6 (1979): 1-23. Ichioka presents interesting observations and discussions regarding the 1907 strike. In 1908 in Sweetwater and Uinta counties, Japanese miners totaled 377 or 19.3 percent of the work force in the coal mines of these two counties. Of this strike Ichioka states, "In short, the interests of the Asian miners, the local unions, and the coal operators all happened to have converged in the unique labor situation that prevailed in southern Wyoming in 1907. For pragmatic reasons rooted in the situation, the local unions admitted Asian miners. . . . In any event, what happened in southern Wyoming was a notable exception in the history of organized labor's racial exclusion of Asian labor."

⁶² *Sheridan Post*, July 26, 1907.

⁶³ *Rock Springs Miner*, August 11, 1907.

⁶⁴ *Sheridan Post*, August 25, 1908.

⁶⁵ Ibid.

⁶⁶ *Sheridan Post*, September 29, 1908.

⁶⁷ *Session Laws Tenth State Legislature*, 21.

⁶⁸ Robert A. Divine, T. H. Breen, George M. Fredrickson, and R. Hal Williams, *America Past and Present*, vol. 2 (Glenview, Illinois: Scott Foresman and Company, 1987), 665.

⁶⁹ Larson, *Wyoming*, 378.

⁷⁰ Ibid.

⁷¹ Ibid.

⁷² Ibid., 379.

⁷³ D. O. Clark to H. G. Burt, November 20, 1899. Nebraska State Museum and Archives, Lincoln (UPRR Co. MS3761, SG2, Series 1, Box 127, Folder 333), 5-6.

⁷⁴ D. O. Clark to H. G. Burt, June 10, 1900. Nebraska State Museum and Archives, Lincoln (UPRR Co. MS3761, SG2, Series 1, Box 128, Folder 335), 3-4.

⁷⁵ Ibid., 4.

⁷⁶ *Rock Springs Miner*, November 10, 1906.

⁷⁷ *Rock Springs Miner*, January 19, 1907.

[78] *Sheridan Post,* June 21, 1907.

[79] *Sheridan Post,* June 25, 1907.

[80] *Sheridan Post,* June 21, 1907, and July 19, 1907.

[81] *Rock Springs Miner,* July 23, 1907.

[82] *Sheridan Post,* October 1, 1907.

[83] Ibid.

[84] *Sheridan Post,* February 1, 1910.

[85] *Sheridan Post,* February 18, 1910.

[86] *Sheridan Post,* February 9, 1909.

[87] Thomas A. L. Nicholas, The Gebo Mine and Miners (Ms. on file, Hot Springs County Museum, Thermopolis, Wyoming, copyrighted 1969).

[88] Larson, *Wyoming,* 380.

[89] Walter R. Jones, "Coal Mine Explosions at Almy, Their Influence on Wyoming's First Coal Mining Safety Laws," *Annals of Wyoming* 56 (Spring 1984): 55-63.

[90] James W. Calvert, *The Gibraltar Socialism and Labor in Butte, Montana, 1895-1920* (Helena: Montana Historical Society Press, 1988), 10.

[91] *Rock Springs Rocket,* June 25, 1908.

[92] *Rock Springs Rocket,* March 26, 1908.

[93] *Session Laws Tenth State Legislature.*

[94] *Rock Springs Rocket,* April 15, 1910.

[95] *Rock Springs Rocket,* November 18, 1910.

[96] *Rock Springs Rocket,* January 27, 1911; February 3, 1911.

[97] *Rock Springs Rocket,* April 5, 1912; August 9, 1912; November 5, 1912.

[98] *Rock Springs Rocket,* November 7, 1913.

[99] *Union Pacific Coal Mines,* 158-178.

[100] Ibid.

[101] *Mineral Resources of the United States, Calendar Year 1912, Part II, Non-Metals* (Washington, D.C.: U.S. Government Printing Office, 1913), 224-225.

[102] *Union Pacific Coal Mines,* 154.

[103] *State Coal Mine Inspector's Report 1920.*

5
The Economic Pendulum, 1917 - 1945

Coal mining after World War I entered a period of change. Wyoming coal was no longer in as great a demand as it had been during World War I, and in the years between 1920 and 1930, coal miners and their families had to face the ups and downs of an unstable coal market. Only World War II would end almost two decades of economic depression. To overcome the financial burdens of underemployment, women and men were forced to stretch their limited incomes. Life was not easy in coal camps where the miner worked maybe one or two days a week. At times, men would go months without work. Added to the uncertainties were changes in mining techniques that lessened the number of miners needed to dig coal. Gone were the days of the Coal Age when laborers were the principal means of extracting coal and loading carts. Machines were replacing miners, and layoffs were all too common. The years between the wars were not ones of prosperity. To miners and their families fell the job of adjusting. Immigrant families were faced with an economic crisis, something they had come to America to try and avoid. Miners' wives were then, as they had often been, forced to help lessen the difficulties. This they did admirably as families once again weathered the vagaries of the coal industry because of their ingenuity.

Stretching the Dollar

One miner's wife described how she and her neighbors helped make ends meet in the years between the wars.

> Us ladies, we were pretty adept. We made our own clothes, and people would use up everything that they had. I know when the mines would be off for two or three months, we'd live out of the garden. We'd just do everything we could to save money.[1]

Coal mining, at times, could be seasonal. When orders for coal were down, miners were laid off. Mining was always slower in the summer when there was little demand for heating fuel. With little or no money coming in, miners and their families had to stretch limited resources over lean periods. To the wives, especially, fell the task of minimizing cash expenditures.

The varied environment of Wyoming meant different strategies were used to meet shortfalls. Sheridan and Cambria had water and an adequate growing season. There, gardens could be grown, and wives and children tended the patches. The immigrants, using skills learned in the old country, pickled and canned their vegetables for use in the winter, but in the high mountain deserts of southwestern Wyoming, short growing seasons and lack of water hampered cultivating gardens. Yet some miners were undaunted: their gardens were small and at times water was rationed, but they succeeded in turning small spots of the desert green. These gardens in the desert were a source of pride and awe.

Getting even enough water for cooking and drinking was a problem in southern Wyoming. Often the only method of getting the water into the home or onto a garden was to haul it by bucket from a tank car or a centrally located water spigot. Water spigots served from four to six homes, depending on the coal company. This method of providing water was common throughout coal camps in Wyoming. One woman, who lived in a mining camp on the Colorado-Utah border, aptly described the problems the miners' families faced in arid areas. "They brought the water in on the railroad from Columbine Springs. It was probably the hardest water that ever existed outside of Deaf Smith County, Texas. All of us who grew up over there have marvelous teeth." The people in the camp made jokes about the water but also bragged "about how many times you used the water before you finally threw it out on what little green thing you could save outside. There wasn't enough water to grow things. You had to be careful with bathing and washing dishes. It was hard."[2] To grow vegetables or flowers successfully in any garden, no matter how small, required a tremendous effort. In southern Wyoming, like other areas of the West, water was not only scarce, it was also alkaline.

At Quealy, south of Rock Springs, Antone Pivik recalled his father had their "house worked out where he had the dishwashing sink water handled very carefully. The water would go out to the tree. We had one tree, and that's how it got its water." At Dines, another miner stated, "Well you come out here in the dry country like this one was, its different. . . . No kind of trees, no grass. They never did get no grass. The miners [planted] two or three trees out there, but we never had enough trees to say good morning." Water was not wasted. Antone Pivik also related, "My dad had taken an old washing machine bowl and put it on the floor so my mom could throw all the water in there. Then he plumbed it down so it [the water] went into the creek. He had horseradish growing along there. Boy, that was powerful stuff."³ The creek where the horseradish grew only ran part of the time in dry years, but the horseradish could tolerate alkaline water.

Weeding and watering gardens, making sausage and sauerkraut, bottling beer, and making wine were jobs for the miners' families. At Cambria, one garden fed a family for nine months. Caroline Flaim, who grew up in Cambria, described the importance of the family garden.

> My dad had a huge garden in Cambria. My mother and dad were out on strike for nine months, and they never went to the bank to get a dollar or got any groceries from anybody. In the meantime, my dad kept his rent paid on the house. Dad had his garden, and my mother canned. We had everything—squash, pumpkin, watermelon, lettuce—everything you wanted, almost. And there was all kinds of berries: wild strawberries, blackberries, chokecherries. I just love chokecherry jam. We had a big cellar. I never wanted for nothing. My mother made her own bread. And like I say, my mother would cook pork chops. When she got done cooking pork chops, the ones left she would grind up and use the bone to make soup. When my dad was working in the mine, he would leave in the morning and tell my mother, 'Send that kid out there to pull up those weeds.' As he was coming home, he had to go by the garden and he would be looking on his way and would say, 'Not very many weeds pulled today.'⁴

Most families did not have such large gardens, but they did a variety of things to stretch the dollar.

Miners were adept at making ends meet. Immigrants who had worked on farms in their homelands brought their agriculture know-how to the West, but changes had to be made to match their new environment. At Reliance, north of Rock Springs, one immigrant family from Yugoslavia milked cows. Of course they weren't able to grow their own hay, but as the son Henry Kovach recalled, "This was my mother's job. . . . They were farmers in the old country, and she had to have chickens and she had to have hogs and she had to have cows. She couldn't be without them." To this Yugoslavian immigrant family fell the job of milking the cows. They "had a cow barn and corrals and as many as 12 cows." The milk was delivered to neighbors before the children went to school.⁵ All of this was necessary to help make ends meet. The father worked in the mines, but the family contributed to the economic well-being in other ways.

People of different nationalities in a coal camp worked together to process meats or make traditional foods. Henry Kovach pointed out, "Of course in those days, you know the old-timers, they came from the old country and they grouped together. They worked together and did things together. Like, for instance, killing a hog. There would be a group of them come and help butcher the hog, and they would share." Then later on, "a different guy would have one, and they'd all get together and butcher his hog."[6] The meat was often made into sausages with the women joining together to prepare the spices and skins.

The making and bottling of beer and wine were other skills miners brought to the Rocky Mountain coal camps. Although they were far from any grape orchards, the miners would pool their resources and have railroad cars of grapes shipped to such coal towns as Cumberland, Superior, and Rock Springs. According to one account, the miners from southern Europe would "get carloads of grapes . . . three or four carloads at a time." Austrian, Slovenian, or Italian immigrants would get together with others from their homeland and make wine. Ernest Giorgis, whose family lived at South Cumberland, was the son of Italian immigrants. He remembered, "Everybody made wine. My mom and dad had a cement tank made in the basement that held three ton. Then we had a wooden barrel down there that held three ton, too, besides the other barrels" for storage. "My dad mostly made wine out of Zinfandel grapes, a red wine." The pressing of the grapes was a family effort. Giorgis related, "My mother always bought new boots and kept them just for the wine. We would put them on and tramp on the grapes in the barrel—about one lug at a time." Although far away from any grape vineyards, some people of the Wyoming coal camps made enough wine to serve their own needs as well as provide additional income through sales to saloons and, sometimes, to neighbors.

Drinking homemade wine could also be a social event. Hugh Crouch, a black miner at Dines, related, "When we wasn't making it, we had Italian people that always at Christmas would have us to come over and get us a Christmas drink and give us a gallon or two of wine. I had one neighbor where I had to drink wine with every evening when we came home from work. Come on over before we should take a bath. Get the coal dust out of our throats."[7] Most people made wine and beer for their own consumption; but if there was extra available, it was a good source of revenue.

Making beer differed from making wine. Polish miners and their wives commonly made beer. Brewed in a manner similar to that of the breweries in Poland, the beer was bottled and capped for use at a later time. The beer was placed behind the "coal stove to keep it warm so it would ferment." One Polish immigrant's daughter, Mary Wolney, recalled, "to start the process you put yeast and hops into the crock, and then it had to start fermenting behind the stove. You had to keep it covered, and then we'd test it out. You know, get a little bit in a cup and drink it. I don't really know how long it took before they bottled it."[8] Making alcoholic beverages and raising and preserving your own food was one way of saving money.

Prohibition

During the years of Prohibition, making your own wine or beer at home became a somewhat more colorful means of making ends meet. The majority of the miners who immigrated to Wyoming in the early part of the twentieth century came from eastern and southern Europe. In their homelands, the skills of making beer, wine, or whiskey were learned at an early age, and beer and wine were common fare at mealtime. Many miners in Wyoming who lived through Prohibition have stories revolving around bootlegging. Prior to 1919 it was legal to sell homemade wine and beer, but the passage of the Eighteenth Amendment in that year made it illegal to "manufacture, sell, or transport intoxicating liquors in the United States." To immigrants who grew up making wine and beer, the law made little sense. Selling and making alcoholic beverages continued to be part of their lives. Of course, it was illegal.

Since making liquor was no longer legal, miners had to find ways to continue making "home brew" without getting caught. Mine shafts proved ideal for hiding stills. Some people, however, made few attempts to hide the fact they were making wine or whiskey during Prohibition. One miner noted, "I don't think they had as much problem with whiskey then as they do now. A lot of times when they was running whiskey like that and you would go around the house, they would just bring some out in a water bucket with a dipper in it. Just set it down there, 'Help yourself; drink all you want.'" To some, however, "revenuers," as the law enforcement officers were called, put a stop to making home brew at least temporarily.

Rock Springs area miners Eugene Paoli, Antone Pivik, Frank Dernovich, and Mike Duzik recalled the Prohibition years in southwest Wyoming.

We had our own smokehouse. Then, of course, the biggest event in the fall was the butchering. We made wine and whiskey, and the grapes came here from California in railroad cars. I don't know how many, but substantial numbers. [E]verybody made wine. . . . I stomped many grapes. Dad would get those fishing boots and wash them off. Lot of [the vats for mashing grapes] had them squeezers: I had fishing boots. Boy, I used to get so damn tired. You would get in that tub and tramp with your feet. By the time you got through with two ton of grapes, that's a lot of stomping. When they made wine, they would ferment it right off the first batch. The second batch they would add a little sugar and would ferment it again and make second wine. But then they would take all the rest of that stuff that was left and add more sugar. Then they would distill that and make graupa [brandy].[9]

The revenuers attempts at enforcing the law were often thwarted by people who saw no harm in continuing something they had done since childhood. In Rock Springs,

You could smell it. When you went down to No. 4 [mine], you could really smell it where they throwed out the old mash after all the whiskey was out of it. They would try and bury it in the garden, but you couldn't miss it. And every house you went into around here, they always had a pitcher of wine.

My dad never did make moonshine for the family, but he made it a lot for people that owned bars, and I know to this day that I can make moonshine. I used to be with him. He must have loved to make it because he didn't make nothing out of it. They gave him a couple gallons, and he was satisfied.

My mother-in-law used to get onions, you know that red peel on the onions, and she would boil that and put a few drops of that in the whiskey. Or brown sugar; put it on the stove and carmel it, to give the color. And to test the thing, we used to have a little whiskey glass. You would catch it, put it in, and light a match to see how she burned. When she quit burning, why you had to shut it off—no more fermenting. We used to put it through the vat again until . . . it was straight alcohol!

But I can still smell that smell going down to No. 4, always the same time of year. That garden I've got down there where my father-in-law lived, if I dig down deep enough . . . [I can] still find the mash. Yeah, the seeds still come up. That's where we used to hide it all during the night. We would empty it and let it cool off in the basement, then take it out there and dig a hole. You could smell it for blocks.

During prohibition in the bars, you used to could go down there and get half a pint or a pint of moonshine anytime. My ex-father-in-law, Barney, he remembers driving it to Kemmerer. Kemmerer whiskey, that was the best. Used to load it in the back of that car and they'd take runs to Kemmerer because that was really the big bootlegging place. I remember [Barney] telling me how scared he was; he was kind of young, I guess. When I was living in Craig, we used to play baseball. One night we went to a dance, and I happened to be in the cafe when Dusty Roades came in. He lived up in Mount Harris, Colorado. I asked him to give me a ride home. So I asked him, 'Where were you, Dusty?' He said, 'Up in Kemmerer.' I said, 'What the hell were you doing up there?' He said, 'I got a load of moonshine.' I said, 'Where's it at?' Then he started telling me he had a big tank under the car. He used to fill it up and bring it clean to Mount Harris from Kemmerer.[10]

Mount Harris was a coal camp in northwestern Colorado located east of Steamboat Springs. The coal town of Kemmerer had the reputation of being one of the largest distilleries in the state. Of course, other coal towns also manufactured their own home brew.

Most nationalities had preferences for what they drank. Continuing age-old traditions, Japanese immigrants made saki. Edith Sunada, whose father worked at Superior, related

> You know, that's the funniest thing. My mother used to make . . . saki. She had those earthenware jars, and she'd take the rice and sugar, and I don't know what else, and then she'd put a cover on it. Every third or fourth day they'd take a dipper and stir it around. It ferments, you know, like it does for pickles. The longer you leave it [the stronger it gets]. [Y]ou put a lot of sugar in it. [My mother] she said she couldn't figure out why the [liquor] kept going down. She thought my dad surely wouldn't be drinking it until it was done. She knew somebody was drinking it because she'd tie a string around it and put the big dipper on it. The dipper was always put on in a different way. So she told my dad about it. . . . My dad watched just to see what was happening. It was me. See, when it was fermenting, it was real sweet stuff. It tasted real good. I'd go out and play; then I'd go into the bedroom where she'd have it, and I'd lift the lid, take a great dipper of it, and drink it. To this day I don't like liquor at all; but in those days, I thought that was the best tasting stuff.[11]

The repeal of the Prohibition Amendment in 1933 brought a sense of relief to most miners. They could make liquor in their own homes without fear of breaking the law.

Boarders and Laundry

Another way the family could help make ends meet was to take in boarders or do laundry. The onerous tasks of washing clothes and cooking fell to the wives and children. Neither of these tasks was simple. Coal dust permeated the miners' clothes. In talking about her husband's clothes, Bernice Ketcham, who lived at Monarch, complained, "the clothes he'd bring home would be just saturated with black coal dust. You'd soak them out in an old tub outside. We had no bathroom. In the summertime, especially, you'd put a big tub out in the sun and tell the kids to stay out of it. Then you'd have to go out there and dig them out, scrub them one by one, and put them out before you would go to bed." But this was just the first step. A person had to wash the "clothes by hand on the board, put them in the boiler, especially the whites, and let them boil on the stove. In the summer [heating] with coal, you can imagine how hot your house would get."[12] There were always single miners more than willing to pay a good price for laundry services.

Men outnumbered women in the coal mining towns. In Rock Springs, for example, in 1890 the ratio of males to females was about 2 to 1. The ratio would improve, but men would outnumber women in Rock Springs even into the 1960s.[13] Mine owners provided barracks for single miners to live in, but boarding houses with hot meals and laundry services proved to be more attractive. Two types of boarding houses were evident in coal camps. The first was a simple venture which provided food, clean clothes, and a bed in a spare room. This was a family enterprise and was another means for a miner's family to earn extra income. The second type of boarding house was similar to a small hotel. The operator might be a widow who had lost her husband in a mining accident. Running a boarding house was regarded as an acceptable enterprise for a woman in the early part of the twentieth century. Rooms, food, and clean linen were all part of the fare. The main attraction of a boarding house, however, was home cooked meals; so even if owned by men, it was essential to have women managers. Coal companies owned some of the larger boarding houses and employed women managers. Sizes of the boarding houses and the services provided varied, but they all attempted to offer food and clean beds for the coal miners.

Families who took boarders into their homes provided a much needed service. They often helped young miners adjust to strange surroundings. They also helped immigrants adjust to a new culture. The practice of taking in boarders was regionwide. In the Utah coal fields, "South Slavs," who came from present-day Yugoslavia, often took in Slovenian boarders. This helped "supplement the family's cash income." Women bore the responsibility "for cooking and laundering for as many as six more adults." The added guests crowded the already small homes, and "the crowding effects of taking in boarders often forced the children to sleep in the same room as the parents." As one social historian pointed out, "With coal stoves and without washing machines," taking in boarders "meant a tremendous increase in her labors and the Slavic women were not necessarily unhappy when the practice gradually ceased."[14]

Crowding was an integral part of the home turned boarding house. Catherine Miller, who worked in her Aunt Ella's boarding house at Reliance, gave an excellent description of a family-run boarding house. The boarder received room, board, and clean clothes. The boarding house had four rooms. In all there were four men in the house, and two men slept behind the house in a "shanty." In addition to those staying at the house and in the shanty, two other men took their meals at Ella's. The sleeping arrangements were tight for the family.

[T]hey had a kind of a roll-away for me to sleep in, and Jackie [Ella's young son] slept with me. [It was] a double roll-away. Cassie slept with her mother and dad, and Ruth used to sleep out in the front room on the couch.

I [would] go out at four o'clock in the morning and light the fires and put the water on to heat to wash before breakfast. Then about three o'clock [in the afternoon] I'd go out and put the wash water [in] the boilers . . . and clear the wash house out. Then [the miners] would go out there and bathe when they come home from work.[15]

There were no bathing facilities at the mine, so it was left to the boarding housekeeper to provide the men with a place to wash. As a young woman, it was up to Catherine Miller to take care of the menial jobs. According to her, in the 1920s "everybody had boarders."[16] At least coal miner's families that needed extra money took in boarders, since they helped to make ends meet.

One woman, whose husband worked in the Reliance mines, described how hard it was to make ends meet.

[H]e went back in the mine in December of '23. He worked there one or two days a week. The mines was so poor we weren't even making our rent, $12 a month rent and $2.50 for a load of coal, so we thought we'd make a change. We went to Kemmerer where my dad was, and Joe went to work in a wagon mine there with Bill Stokes.[17]

Moving to another coal camp in search of steady work was commonplace.

Feelings of Community

The shared experiences associated with coal mining and life in a company town led to strong feelings of community in most camps. There is a general consensus among coal miners that coal camps were a friendly place in which to live. Sol Williams, a black miner reflecting on his life at Superior, felt people were easy to get along with. Sol commented, "I think it was like most coal camps. Everyone tried to get along," Sol speculated, "because they worked underground together." They made their own entertainment, "and most of the people like the Italians, well most of them foreigners, they'd make their own wine and whiskey. . . . You'd go to their house and drink . . . and sit there and talk and play cards."[18] Hack Carter, another black miner who worked at Dines north of Rock Springs,

The Elk Mountain Finn Band in 1920. Miners maintained their ethnic heritage through the formation of groups such as the Finn Band and the establishment of clubs. (Courtesy of the Wyoming State Archives, Museums and Historical Department)

said of the people who lived in the coal camp, "They were friendly; they'd help one another."[19] Many miners concurred with this assessment.[20] Since everyone lived in company houses, there was a feeling that "everyone was in the same boat." Hugh Crouch related, "I know for over twenty years there were four of us in our party that fished and hunted. [There] was a Finlander, two Italians, and me myself. . . . Them same people now is the same friends I've had for the last forty years."[21] Prejudices might have existed, but there was a sense of community in most coal towns.

Churches helped bring about a sense of community. Since the company owned all the property within a camp, miners felt a sense of pride and accomplishment when they could secure land and erect a church or a place of worship. Churches in the coal camps were as varied as the immigrants who lived in the towns. Greek Orthodox, Lutheran, Episcopal, Roman Catholic, Methodist, and Mormon congregations were common. To begin with, most church services were held in homes. Where the coal companies had community halls or other suitable buildings, church services were held in company-owned buildings until something better could be found. In those camps where there were but a few structures, a variety of buildings served as meeting places, including basements. The Finnish Lutheran Church in Hanna held services in various homes until 1904 "when the old Carbon Finnish church was moved" to town. The Slavic Catholics in Rock Springs worshipped for thirteen years in a variety of structures until a church was completed in 1925.[22] The churches served as another means of pulling the town together.

Another means of developing a sense of community was through maintaining ethnic associations. Especially common among the Finnish immigrants were Finn Halls and Finnish baths. The Finnish baths were saunas, a carryover from bath houses in Finland. Finn Halls provided places to meet and discuss politics and concerns. Before the halls were constructed, the meetings were held in homes. Once the hall was constructed, various meetings were held there and community functions planned. Community functions sponsored by the Finnish residents had the positive effect of fostering good will and teaching children about life in the home country. The Finnish were not alone in constructing meeting halls. Slovenians constructed halls called Slovinski Doms. These meeting places served not only as community centers but housed various churches. The primary function of the Slovinski Dom was to provide a place where Slovenians could continue the culture of the old land while adapting to the coal camps. Towns such as Rock Springs developed large Slovinski Doms that continue serving the community even today.

Most miners and their families were fun-loving people. The majority of the mining towns had baseball teams and bands. At times, the competition between coal towns was heated, and more than one miner was hired

The Gebo Women's Band circa 1920. Bands were a source of entertainment and pride for the mining camps. (Courtesy of the Hot Springs County Museum)

because of his ability to play baseball. The bands were noted for their skills, and concerts and dances served as entertainment for many mining communities. Since diverse ethnic groups made up coal towns, the baseball teams and bands provided a means of drawing the community together. In addition to the shared living and working conditions, the various forms of entertainment helped weld the town together. Sports and music were an international language everyone could understand. Because a sense of community developed, there was a sense of sadness when mines were abandoned and towns dismantled. With the abandonment of a town came the end of a community in which the miners and their families had worked, lived, and played together.

The mining communities never lacked a focus. As the coal mines went, so went the towns. Layoffs affected everyone. Even if a person avoided a layoff, he wondered if he might be next to be fired. Slowdowns were nearly as bad as layoffs because a miner might work only one day a week. These

The 1922 Hanna baseball team. (Courtesy of Bud Tebedo, New Studio, Rock Springs)

slowdowns were the result of few orders for coal. The only good thing about slowdowns was that the company would let you stay in your home and charge goods at the company stores. Of course, this kept you in debt; but in the Depression years, having a house in which to live was a major concern.

Since the mine was the focus of the company town, when layoffs or slowdowns occurred, everyone felt the "pinch." Hard times went a long way towards creating camaraderie. It also heightened the need to be frugal and work together to make ends meet. Frank Dernovich, who began working in the mines during the late 1930s, recalled, "In the summertime it was terrible." Beginning in about March, the slowdown began. In the winter you might work each day, but in the spring "You would work two or three days a week, and then it would go down to one. As a result there wasn't much of a paycheck."[23]

Increased Mechanization

In addition to slowdowns and layoffs, miners began to witness increased mechanization underground during the 1920s and 1930s. More machines meant fewer miners were needed. All aspects of coal mining became more sophisticated. Even setting explosives was done scientifically. But wages were slow in reflecting the new skills needed in mining. Worse yet was the fact that miners were losing jobs to new equipment.

By the 1920s, most undercutting of the coal was done by machinery. As soon as you finished undercutting the coal, the process of setting charges began. Setting blasting charges and setting props to support the mine roof was "dead work," meaning you did not get paid for your efforts. Also, setting black powder charges and blasting the coal contained an element of danger. Frank Dernovich described the process as follows:

> Well, you would clean up the place; and then, of course, you were cutting all the time you were loading. Just as soon as you got the place cut, you drilled it. Then you went ahead and tamped [the powder]. . . . You used to have to go up there and shoot them shots. They wanted you to shoot shots one at a time on the account of it would make lump coal. You would walk up there in that smoke, and half the time the face was on fire.[24]

With the smoke still hanging in the air, you prepared your second charge.

During the Depression years, shooting the charges was a sophisticated process. Lump coal was easier to handle than powdered or small chunks of coal. The process of obtaining lump coal could be partially controlled by

Electric cutting machines introduced in the 1920s greatly increased productivity. The undercutting of the coal on the working face had previously been done by hand, requiring many man-hours.

how the miner set his blasting charges; therefore, care was taken in placing the explosives. The powder was contained in something similar to a dynamite stick. These were tamped into the holes drilled in the face of the coal. Powder dummies were placed behind the sticks of powder to force the blast inward and downward, and the powder sticks were ignited by electric charges. To get the lump coal desired, you had to blast one hole at a time. After setting the electrical charge, the first shot was blown off the face. Then the worker returned and set another charge. When the miner returned, "the smoke and that heat from the powder" would make the face "just light up . . . like it was on fire."[25] Miners were paid only for the coal weighed at the surface and received no pay for setting the charges.

Mechanization caused changes underground. Mechanization began early in Wyoming, but during World War I and through the Depression years, the use of machines underground accelerated. Along with machinery came workers who specialized in operating the equipment. In addition, mechanics were needed to repair the machines. These specialized miners were paid first by the day and later by the hour. Unlike company men of the past, these men were miners whose wage scale was negotiated by the union. This was an important change. No longer were key personnel company men who owed their allegiance only to the coal company, they were part of the general mining crews. These miners, who had learned the skills of operating underground machinery, were indispensable to a successful underground operation. Machines, while displacing some workers, made trained miners more valuable. Although wages rose slowly because of the Depression, even during slowdowns there was a need to retain these skilled men whenever possible.

One of the most important pieces of machinery underground was the "cutter," or cutting machine, to undercut the coal. The use of the cutting machine greatly increased productivity as men were no longer required to lay on their side and undercut the coal with a pick. Henry Kovach, whose job was to repair underground equipment, provided an excellent description of underground machinery.

[W]hen I was [at Reliance, north of Rock Springs,] they finally got cutters. What it was, was like a big chain saw. [Miners] would go into the face with it and cut along the bottom between the rock and into the coal. They wanted to miss the rock because that would dull the bits. They wanted to cut into the coal but as close to the rock as they could to keep smooth bottoms so they could keep advancing. They would cut the bottom, and they would drill holes in a certain pattern. They had electric drills, big electric drills in my time, to do that with. Some of them had materials to hold them with, booms and so forth, but most of them were hand held. The auger was usually about six feet long. They would start the hole with a short auger and extend the length as they went. They would drill holes in a certain pattern and load them with explosives and blast. Then they had what they called a duckbill that was mounted to a ratchet that actually fed a pan with a big snout on it . . . a big duckbill. There was kind of a snout that would get under the coal. It was hooked to a shaker. It would go in and shake back the coal. They would tie the base of the ratchet to a cutting machine that had a rope on it and a drum, like a winch, to pull this mechanism across the face. It was hooked to what they called a pan that would allow this duckbill to swivel. The anchor point would let it move in a radius the width of the face in a kind of half-circle. So they had to shovel the corners a bit, into the duckbill. There wasn't as much shoveling as there was in the olden days. In the olden days what they'd do is drill and blast and [they did not] even have a cutting machine. They'd have to pick underneath it and blast and hand load it.[26]

With machinery, the process of moving the coal from the face to the surface was simplified. From the underground workings to the railroad cars, the process became mechanized. From the duckbill the coal was conveyed away from the face through a system of shakers on a panline. Henry Kovach described the process of moving the coal from the face to the surface.

> The system of [moving] the coal [involved getting it] into the shakers on this panline. It would shake down to what they called a loading head. A loading head was arranged to where they had cars under that pan. As the pan would shake, [the coal] would drop into steelies, as we called them. They were wooden cars in the olden days. That's the reason they got the name steelies; they were steel cars. They would dump the coal into steel cars that were on rails. They had a locomotive [that] would pick them up from the working areas and take them out to the mainline. They actually had

Electric drills augered holes in the working face for the placement of explosive charges to break the coal into chunks.

Electric loading machines and haulers made the loading of coal underground and the hauling to the surface much more efficient.

switching areas in there where they'd put the loads and the empties so that when they brought a loaded trip out, they could pick up [an] empty trip and come back in with it. That's how they did it. They would pull the loads out and push the empties in so that the locomotive would be on the right end all the time. They had an electric locomotive that pulled the cars out from the working areas out to the slope. [There] they had a hoist that would lower and pull out the trips. That's how they got the coal to the outside. Then from the outside they had the high line, and they had a motor line outside too . . . at our mine anyway . . . all of them weren't the same. They'd drop their coal down into the tipple, and the tipple would process the coal and load it into big railroad cars and ship it out.[27]

During the early decades of the twentieth century, there was a mixing of mining processes. Alongside machines, men would continue the age-old process of hand digging and loading coal. In the hauling of coal, mules were used alongside electric locomotives. In time the mules were phased out, but even during the 1930s they were commonplace. The mule was a sturdy animal and the bane and pleasure of most miners. Mining folklore has it that when explosions occurred underground, mine foremen would ask, "Were there any mules killed?" Trained mules were in great demand. One miner who went to work in the southern Illinois coal fields before moving to Dines in 1936 related that when he was younger he drove mules in Illinois mines. In the early 1930s,

> I used to drive mules.... They got more sense than a horse. I had one [mule] could count them [coal] cars better than you could count. [I]f you put on one [car too many], he wasn't going to move. You could stay there and beat him all you wanted; all he gonna do is kick until you unbuckle that car. Then you go, 'geddup,' and he'd go on about his business. And when quitting time came, they [would] blink the lights. When them lights blink, them mules know you ain't got a cargo; they goin' to the barn. They make a beeline.[28]

The mules were often stabled underground and never brought out of the mine unless there was a work stoppage or a mine shutdown for repairs. The hardy mule would continue to be a fixture in smaller mines for years to come; however, the larger mines began replacing the mules with "electric motors," or locomotives, early in the twentieth century. By the late 1930s, most large mines had replaced their mules with mechanical hauling equipment.

With the arrival of mine machinery came new dangers. Miners would lose hands or fingers in machines, and sometimes, unfortunately, their lives. William Harris, who worked in the Kemmerer mines, described the mixing of horses and machines and the dangers associated with mine equipment.

> Well, down in the mine in the entries, they used to have horses. These horses would pull these homemade cars in to the diggers. The [drivers] would drop a car off in one room, and the next one would go on to the next room and they'd drop another one off, until they got all the empties scattered out. And then when they would turn around and come back, [the diggers would] generally have them loads sitting there. [The drivers would] pick up all these loads, and they'd pull them out to the main slope with the horses they had. There would be four or five cars to pull with one horse. And these horses, they used to have a big leather shield over their head, right on top of their ears, because they used to hit the crossbars. They'd pull these loads out to the slope, and then they'd hook on to [the cars] with the main hoist and pull them outside and drop them down to the tipple.

Where they had these rooms inside, they used to have what they called magennies [for hauling coal] and these had an endless rope [or cable]. [The rope] used to go up to the case of the room to a shiv, and it come back down and run around this magennie—they called it. Well, they'd hang a car on that rope, and they'd say, 'Jig it down.' When they'd say, 'jig it down,' they'd kick that car loose. When that car come down, the loaded car would pull the empty car up the other room, see. And that's how they got them cars up into the rooms. A lot of times I seen them try it, these ropes would get stuck. These guys would get ahold of the ropes and pull on them to get the car started. And I seen a Jap one time, he got ahold of that rope with both hands and give that rope a jerk, but he never turned loose of it fast enough. It pulled both his hands into the pulleys, and it cut all his fingers off, both hands.[29]

In the mines surrounding Kemmerer, the transition from mules to electric locomotives took place in the 1920s. The locomotives, known as motors to the miners, usually weighed about five tons. Most motors ran on a trolley line. An electric cable was placed in the roof of the mine and as the motor traveled, the lines would flash, sending sparks above the locomotive. As more and more electrical equipment was used underground, a good source of electricity in the mine became essential. The trolley line served as one means of getting electricity into each room.[30]

To power the equipment, electric generating plants were constructed. Power plants were built at the mining camp of Frontier to power the mines near Kemmerer. Another plant was constructed at Rock Springs, and later a small plant was built at Superior. At Acme, a generator was built to power the mines near Sheridan. The construction of power plants had a beneficial side effect. While many rural communities lacked electricity prior to the Depression, coal camps usually had electric lights and services. As early as 1892 the first electric motor appeared in the Rock Springs mines. "Charlie Smith," as the locomotive was called, was the first electric mine locomotive built in the United States.[31] With coal as a source of energy, it was natural that electric generating plants would be constructed near coal mines. Coal was available to fire the first electric boilers, and in places like Rock Springs, pipelines were constructed to haul in water for steam. The steam powered electric generators provided power for mines and towns alike. The powerful locomotives used underground required a good power source, and coal mine operators who could not afford to build their own generating plants purchased electricity from the larger coal companies. The electric generating plant became a part of coal mining in the early twentieth century.

The electric locomotives increased the amount of coal that could be hauled out of the mine in a given time; they also increased the dangers.

William Harris told how his brother was killed while "hauling" coal cars in a mine near Kemmerer.

> [H]e was running one of them locomotives, and he was going in with a bunch of empties.... [W]hat I think happened [was] after he got inside, right next to the workings, there was a place where you come off of the lower tracks to a kind of a little hill to get onto the high tracks. I think when he was out there he got a little heave, and it shoved up the bottom, or something, because when he went up that little hill, the top of his hand [was pinned]. [A]ll the bones in his hand [were crushed]. You could see all his bones where it took the hide and meat off. ... When he got that hand caught, he jumped. And when he jumped, it drove his head right down against the corner of that locomotive. He was dead. Well, he was hanging over the side of the locomotive, and it was going into the entry and my other brother, he was in there. Happened to be standing on the off side from where he was [and saw] the cars was coming. When he happened to see my brother laying on that motor, he run and jumped in that locomotive and shut it off. Picked him up off there. Well, he was dead. Pert near cut his head off.[32]

Deaths underground were all too common but, for the most part, took place in the form of isolated accidents.

Even though coal mining was becoming more mechanized, working underground followed patterns established in the nineteenth century. In a study prepared for the Colorado Fuel and Iron Company, an attempt was made to describe the miners' "working place." Written in 1924, the study described the rooms in an almost literary style.

> There is bustle here. ... A driver, bringing empty cars to diggers or taking loaded ones away, hurls a strange mixture of profanity and cabalistic words at his mule. 'Timber men' are sawing logs into props and crossbars, notching them and fitting them together to brace roofs as miners advance. 'Trackmen' are either repairing or laying new tracks. The rooms, corresponding to city lots, are the working places to which the miners are assigned, usually in pairs. In order to keep the roof of a mine from caving in, 'pillars' of coal are left as the men advance. Hence the name given to this method of coal mining is 'the room and pillar method.' The pillars are 'pulled' after all the other coal has been mined.[33]

Even with electric lights, the dust and darkness underground took getting used to. Often the miner's first days underground were filled with a mixture of awe and fright. One young miner recalled that when he used to hear a pop, he would start to run. His father, for whom he was working, would say, "I'll tell you when to run."[34] One writer wrote, "Work places change daily as the mine is extended further along its underground course," and went on to add,

[M]ining is essentially a dirty, unpleasant, and extremely hazardous occupation. The miner works underground, with the darkness relieved only by the lamp in his cap, and often in a cramped physical position. He does not know when a section of the roof may cave in and crush him, or leave him crippled and dependent for life; or when explosive gas may be accidentally ignited, and burn him and his fellow-workers to death, or cause the mine to cave in to such an extent that it will be impossible for a rescue party to get near him and his friends. If you wish to hear gruesome and blood chilling stories, listen to veteran coal miners who have gone through mine explosions, either as victims or as members of rescue crews. In addition, miners work more or less apart from one another, a few hundred scattered over a wide area.[35]

Water spraying machine used by the Union Pacific at Rock Springs to help keep down coal dust in the mines. Coal dust was a major health and safety problem in the mines. (Courtesy of Bud Tebedo, New Studio, Rock Springs)

Men adjusted to "the isolation, the darkness underground, [and] the constant presence of danger" in order to make a living.[36] In spite of the sacrifices, coal miners too often were unable to make ends meet. Miners attempted to address the safety hazards on their own and through their unions. Union leaders negotiated for safer working conditions as well as lobbying legislators to enforce existing mine safety laws. Coal companies also attempted to train their men better. Safety classes and safety teams were slow in coming, but eventually they were developed. The safety teams were established to perform mine rescues in case of disasters. Each mine had its own team. To sharpen their skills, the men competed with other teams across the state. Safety teams took their jobs seriously, and the events were hotly contested. An awareness of safety procedures helped prepare the miners for the working conditions underground. With the coal companies taking an active role in mine safety, positive steps were taken to control underground disasters. Unfortunately, during the 1920s, two major mine explosions once again rocked Wyoming.

The Explosions of 1923 and 1924

On August 14, 1923, Kemmerer Coal Company's Frontier No. 1 exploded, killing ninety-nine men. In September 1924 Kemmerer Coal Company's Sublet No. 5 exploded, killing thirty-nine men. The Frontier No. 1 explosion was the second worst mining disaster in Wyoming history. William Harris recalled, "I was sitting over here in the house where we used to live, and I happened to look up on the hill over there. I seen this big cloud of black smoke come out of the fan. And I ran in and I told Dad, 'there's a big cloud of smoke just come out of the fan on the hill.' He said it blowed up. Boy, she had too. Killed ninety-nine men."[37] The cloud of smoke coming out of the fan house was a telltale sign of an explosion. Most of those killed were born overseas. The state coal mine inspector report for 1923 shows that of those killed, 37 were Italian, 17 Japanese, 14 American, 12 Austrian, 11 Finnish, 5 Mexican, 2 Slovenian, and 1 Canadian. Ninety-eight children lost their father in the explosion.[38]

When Frontier No. 1 exploded, rescue teams arrived quickly. Union Pacific Coal Company's Safety First Department lent assistance as did the Bureau of Mines rescue car. Their efforts were to no avail. The explosion of gases and coal dust covered too wide an area, and nothing could be done. The local UMWA sent relief funds to the families immediately. The national headquarters of the UMWA sent $10,000 for the relief of the bereaved families. The UMWA local at Kemmerer also helped meet the pressing problem of burying the dead. To the union members fell the task of digging the graves.[39] The miners were buried in the Catholic and the city cemeteries. A mass burial was given to the Japanese victims in the city cemetery, with all seventeen victims being buried in one grave.[40] The papers reported that there was "scarcely a home in Frontier . . . that wasn't bereft of a loved one. At one place, there were seven cabins in a row where the husband had left never to return."[41]

The *Rock Springs Rocket* called the miners "Martyrs to Industrialism." An editorial claimed, "All Wyoming bows its head today in silent grief, in mourning for ninety and nine of its stalwarts, who lie before us in cold death, martyrs, if you please, to modern industrialism." The editor, Lester G. Baker, went on to write, "On the faces of the living may be seen the lines of sorrow; none possessing human sympathy but that grieves on this solemn day, when the last sad rites are performed for our brothers and on all sides we observe the heart-broken mothers, wives, and children over whom a cloud of sorrow has descended, cutting deeper, with more lasting pain than that brought by the great gulf of flame that destroyed their loved ones." The coal miner, Baker claimed, was a major force "in our industrialism, who takes his life in his hand, even as the soldier, as he enters the caverns of danger that we may live in comfort. . . ."[42] To bring home his point, the editor published a second short piece defending the coal miner's right to strike, "Hard toil underground, with a tendency to early exhaustion and serious disease, and continued risk of sudden death in dreadful forms, is not conducive to any special breadth of view tolerance of thought and speech or a 'light touch' in negotiation. Since the peril of death is ever present," concluded the editor, "the requirements of life itself . . . must be considered."[43]

On the heels of the 1923 disaster came the explosion of Sublet No. 5 in 1924. The editor of the *Rocket* was livid again. Baker responded by writing, "Thirty-nine more lives have been added to the toll of the hazard of coal mining in Western Wyoming."[44] As a result of the gas explosion, 11 Austrians, 7 Americans, 6 Japanese, 6 Italians, 3 Germans, 3 Slovinians, 1 Bohemian, 1 Montenegrian, and 1 Englishman lost their lives. Forty-five children lost their father.[45] The newspapers once again pointed to the "attitude of poignant grief" felt throughout Kemmerer. The Rock Springs editor wrote, "Their loved ones were gone and now remained but to shed a final tear and render the last loving tribute and then to face the world without the fellowship and companionship to which they have been accustomed."[46] The newspapers of the period reflected an attitude felt by most of their readers. Miners and their wives knew too well that when a mine whistle blew it could be signaling a death or disaster in the mine involving a friend, neighbor, relative, or spouse. The mine whistle was a dreaded sound. The shared losses and dangers served as another means of uniting the people of the coal camps.

Possibly as a result of the 1923 and 1924 explosions near Kemmerer, the Wyoming legislature passed twelve different pieces of legislation in 1925 to improve underground working conditions. In addition to new safety laws, a bill establishing a "Coal Mine Catastrophe Insurance" plan was enacted. The insurance was designed to help the state cover claims filed by miners' dependents. Premiums were to be paid by "employers operating coal mines" at the rate of "one-fourth of one percent of his Wyoming payroll for the preceding month." The catastrophic insurance bill was designed to help the state pay workmen's compensation claims growing out of major mine disasters or "a series of accidents or occurrences" that resulted in death or injury.[47] Included in the safety laws enacted was another somewhat anti-foreign piece of coal mining legislation passed in 1925. This law required "Shot Inspectors in Mines" to "be citizens of the United States and be able to speak and understand the English language." Shot inspectors' jobs were to ensure conditions were safe underground prior to setting off explosives. There was a positive side to the law. Wherever possible, shots would only be fired once a day, and then by the shot inspector. In mines where more blasts were required, permission to fire the powder had to come from the shot inspector. This had the effect of reducing dust and the possibility of igniting gas within a mine.[48] In addition to the legislation requiring shot inspectors, bills establishing minimum standards for working conditions underground were passed. Mines were required to be cleaned and sprinkled, barrier pillars had to be left in place, ventilation had to be improved, and new safety lamps that measured the amount of explosive gases in the mines had to be used in all mines. The various legislation enacted in 1925, combined with previous coal mine safety laws, had the effect of minimizing deaths due to underground explosions. Never again would the state experience the devastation witnessed by the mine explosions in the first quarter of the twentieth century. The Vail mine, northeast of Afton, was the only coal mine to have an explosion that resulted in the loss of life after this time. In 1938 five men lost their lives in an underground explosion at Vail.[49] Although the legislation did not end the dangers associated with underground mining, it went a long way towards the prevention of mine explosions.

Work Stoppages

Mine accidents were not the only problems plaguing miners in the 1920s. Following World War I, the coal industry entered a slump that affected the coal industry for almost 20 years. This slump came on the heels of a decade of growth. During World War I, the coal industry prospered. "In World War I, bituminous coal furnished 69.5 percent of the total mechanical energy of the country, a mark never reached since." Nationwide "the aggregate net income for the soft coal industry was set at $149 million."[50] While feeling they did not have adequate wages, the miners shared in the prosperity in the form of steady employment. During the war the unions had promised not to strike for better wages; however, as the end of World War I approached, they grew impatient. John L. Lewis, President of the UMWA, issued the order for unions to walk out of the mines nationwide on November 1, 1919. This walkout, or work stoppage as it was called, came ten days before the Armistice was signed in Europe. Since the war was not officially over, Woodrow Wilson stepped in to end the strike. On December 3, eighty-four national union officials were arrested, as were striking miners. Four days later John L. Lewis called off the work stoppage saying, "I will not fight my government, the greatest government on earth." It was not a wasted effort. The miners received a fourteen percent increase in wages. Later, a more lasting settlement increased the wage of contract miners by thirty-four percent.[51]

In Wyoming, people viewed the strike of 1919 as a serious threat. The commander of a federal military post, Fort D. A. Russell in Cheyenne, issued an order warning "all persons engaged in unlawful combinations, assemblages, or conspiracies, tending to obstruct or hinder the execution of the laws . . . will be [prosecuted] in accordance to the laws and usages of war."[52] In essence, the military would intervene if it was necessary to keep the coal mines open. In Wyoming police arrested workers. John Wolney, whose father worked at the Kooi mine north of Sheridan, recalled

[M]y dad was Financial Secretary in Kooi [for the union] and that was in 1918, 1919. They had a real deal. At one time they told him you can't strike. They said, 'You guys just keep working' because it was during the war time. These other boys went . . . on strike. They loaded them up in a cattle car and took them up to . . . the VA hospital [just north of Sheridan] and put them in jail.[53]

John Wolney's father was among the miners jailed. Happily for the miners, the strike ended with a wage increase.

Only for a brief period following World War I would the coal market remain strong. In 1920 Wyoming coal production was at record levels, but the strong market did not last. During the period when the market was strong, miners felt that they were not sharing in the prosperity. The miners, remembering that the coal companies had profited handsomely from a wartime economy, felt that they should have an increase in wages to offset the nonstrike policy they had followed through most of World War I. The expected increases had not come even in the post-war coal boom. Unfortunately, an economic downturn was in the offing. Statewide from 1920 to 1922, coal production fell by 3.4 million tons.[54] Diminished orders for coal created hardships for miners and mine owners alike. The owners, faced with a weak coal market, wanted the miners to take wage cuts or at least not to ask for wage increases. The two differing points of view came to a head in 1922.

One point of view appeared in a newspaper article entitled "Don't Blame the Miner." The reporter stated, "When the statement is made that a miner receives as high as $7.50 a day for his labor, if that's all the outsider has, he is likely to think the miner has no cause for complaint." Some might think, the article contended, "Why at that rate the miner can earn almost $200 a month. The miner . . . according to the highest estimate, does not work much more than half time and instead of earning $45 a week receives only $22.50." This amount is "not sufficient to keep their families in comfort."[55] Where wages were adequate, there was not enough work. The second point of view, held by mine managers, was that there were simply not enough orders for coal. Cutbacks were needed to maintain their companies. Decreasing wages was one way to solve the problem. The two sides could not agree on a fair wage. On April 1, 1922, John L. Lewis, President of UMWA, called for a work stoppage in America's coal mines.[56]

The shutdown of Wyoming mines was complete. By July 24, little had changed. In an attempt to end the coal strike, Wyoming's Governor Carey called together the coal operators and union representatives for a meeting in the state capitol. "The Governor called the meeting following [a] request . . . by President [Warren G.] Harding to encourage the immediate resumption of coal production, urging the necessity for police protection and guaranteeing the support and cooperation of the Federal Government and its troops."[57] As a result of the meeting, P. J. Quealy, president of the Wyoming Coal Operators Association, offered to give the miners the same wage scale in effect prior to the strike. Union representatives were not ready to accept the old wage. The Wyoming UMWA would not negotiate without word from the national organization. The governor, with both union and mine operators present, was "perplexed." Frustrated, the governor's conference ended without settling the three-month-old strike.[58]

"The welcome news" that the strike was over reached Wyoming in August 1922. The UMWA was praised by the *Rock Springs Rocket*, which claimed, "Throughout the entire five months the strike has lasted, there has been no hint of disorder or disturbance of any nature." The miners went back to work at "old wages and old conditions." While not taking a decrease in pay, the union did not gain any wage concessions, and its contract was extended until 1923.[59] What the strike did prove was that the union would stick together not only locally, but nationally. The statement "Wyoming coal is UMWA coal" was more than a slogan in 1922.

The effects of the strike were reflected in a drop in coal production. In 1922 coal production dropped by 1 million tons. With the labor issues resolved, coal production once again rose to 7,554,066 tons in 1923. Unfortunately, due to a weak coal market, production declined steadily until 1926 when it leveled out at 6,495,815 tons.[60] The decrease in production led to layoffs. Between 1923 and 1927, 1872 coal miners lost their jobs.[61] The layoffs came as a result of a decrease in coal orders and an increase in mechanization. In 1900, three percent of the nation's coal was mined by machinery; by 1926, 70 percent of America's coal was mined by machines.[62] Possibly in response to the weak market for Wyoming coal, when a strike was called for the coal fields in the eastern United States in 1927, Wyoming miners voted to remain on the job. Nor were they alone, miners in both Montana and Washington also remained at work.[63] The West was experiencing a recession, and miners could ill afford to man the picket line in 1927. Moreover, increased mechanization was decreasing the number of miners needed to extract the same amount of coal. Uncertain of the future, Wyoming miners cared most about maintaining their "present wage."[64]

Strip Mining Makes an Entrance

While mechanization was increasing underground, another change in coal mining was taking place in northeast Wyoming. At the Peerless Mine east of Gillette, the United States Geological Survey, whose job it was to survey federal lands and report on the presence of available natural resources, reported that as early as 1924 the overburden was being stripped to expose the coal in the Roland coal beds. The coal was only 25 feet below the surface and about 90 feet thick.[65] Strip mining, or the process of stripping off the overburden, was feasible in the Powder River Basin of northeast Wyoming. The process had its basis in the old quarrying techniques of mining. Quarrying was simple. A person located a coal seam, dug a hole into the seam, and removed the coal. As the hole became deeper, the miner had a choice of either tunneling or abandoning the hole and looking for another seam. The miner might also expand his hole, exposing more of the seam. In most areas of Wyoming in the 1920s there was too much cover or rock over the coal to make strip mining profitable using existing mining procedures, and the most efficient way to reach the coal was through a tunnel. In places like the Powder River Basin, however, this was not the case. The cover was soft, and the coal seams were thick.

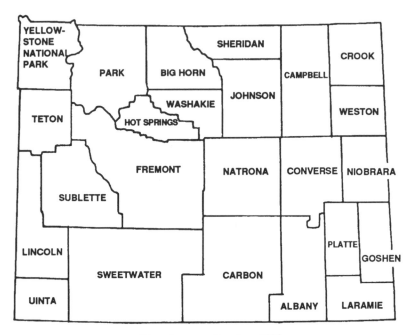

Wyoming counties since 1923

A horse-drawn scraper, called a fresno, was adequate to peel back the overburden. With the development of steam shovels, motorized graders, and, later, bulldozers, removing the surface cover over the coal was a simple process. As equipment improved, strip mining coal like that found in the Roland coal beds generated profits unthought of in underground mining. While most strippable coal is not as high in BTUs as deeper coal, it is easier to mine; and fewer men are needed to extract the coal. The Peerless Mine was but a harbinger of things to come.

The advantages of strip mining were numerous. Through strip mining, the mine operator eliminated the need for expensive ventilation systems, drainage pumps, and hauling coal long distances to the surface. It was considered to be a safer means of extracting coal, and the strip mine also reduced the need for large numbers of workers.[66] Following the the old line of reasoning that machines were easier to manage than men, the strip mine offered both efficiency and a means of reducing the number of laborers needed.

The first large strip mine was opened by the Wyodak Coal and Manufacturing Company near Gillette. In 1925 the state coal mine inspector reported that 15 men extracted 33,579 tons of coal from the newly opened mine.[67] It was, moreover, the only strip mine listed in the 1925 report. The men working there averaged 2239 tons of coal per person for the year. Statewide the average amount mined per man was 1030 tons. The average production for each man in a strip mine far exceeded the amount mined by their underground counterparts. It should be pointed out, however, that 38 percent of the coal mined underground in Wyoming in 1925 was still mined by undercutting the coal with a pick.[68] By 1935, Wyodak Coal was still the only strip mine reported operating in the state. Its productivity was impressive. In that year Wyodak extracted 120,502 tons of coal with 30 men: Wyodak had more than tripled its production while only doubling its work force. Each man was mining 4017 tons a year. To keep abreast of these changes in the coal industry, Wyoming underground mines increased their mechanization. Only nine percent continued to extract coal by manually undercutting the coal in 1935. On the average, miners extracted 1263 tons of coal per year.[69] While increasing underground mechanization by 29 percent between 1925 to 1935, Wyoming coal operators were only able to raise production per man by 233 tons. During the same ten years, the Wyodak strip mine increased production per man by 1778 tons. Strip mining was the wave of the future. It was hoped that the efficiency enjoyed by strip mining might offset the economic reverses the coal industry experienced in the 1920s.

A Declining Industry

The coal industry during the 1920s was beginning to feel the effects of competition from other forms of fossil fuels.[70] The increased use of natural gas and oil cut into markets once held exclusively by coal. To compete with the cheaper fuels, the coal industry viewed strip mining as a means of cutting costs. In the 1920s and into the 1930s, strip mining in Wyoming was in its infancy. Production of strip mined coal during this period never came close to that of coal taken from mines through shafts and portals. Therefore, strip mining did not provide the cheap fuel necessary to compete with the petroleum industry. As long as the railroads used coal for steaming their engines, there would be a market for Wyoming coal. But with oil becoming more popular for home heating and the emergence of natural gas as a heating and cooking fuel, coal began losing its domestic market. On the high seas, ships once fueled by coal were relying on diesel and oil. Railroad mines, that is mines owned by railroad companies, still had markets and would weather the changes for a time; however, companies dependent on other markets began to feel the competition and were forced out of the marketplace. As a result of competition from other fuel sources and a nationwide depression, Wyoming coal miners lost their jobs. Continuing the trend of the 1920s, overall Wyoming coal production declined even further in the early 1930s. As a point of comparison, more coal was mined in Wyoming in 1909 than in 1930. Beginning in 1930, coal production plummeted. By 1933, only 4,004,602 tons were mined. This was 2 million tons less than in 1930. Not since 1900 had Wyoming coal production been so low.[71] The reason for Wyoming's rapid decline in coal production grew out of the Depression. When Black Thursday hit Wall Street on October 24, 1929, the Wyoming coal industry had already experienced almost a decade of recession in the coal industry. When the nationwide depression struck, Wyoming's chief coal consumer, the railroads, was hard hit. With fewer passenger trains running and less freight to haul, the railroads consumed less fuel. The coal mines quickly felt the pinch. Layoffs were inevitable. In 1929, 5081 men were employed in Wyoming coal mines. By 1934 this number decreased to 3778 men.[72] By comparison, in 1920, 7986 men had worked in Wyoming coal mines. As a result of the recession in the 1920s and the increase in mechanization, the number of miners working steadily decreased. With the onset of the Great Depression, the number of layoffs increased and production dropped to a low point in 1933.

Miners were often affected by economic forces outside their control. Changes in technology, which replaced men with machinery, were something they could not stop. Miners were also susceptible to the ups and downs of the national and international economies. Little could be done to prevent the layoffs that followed downturns in the economy. The shift from coal to petroleum in America's industries cost jobs. Outside forces changed the coal industry. Between 1922 and 1934, 5414 Wyoming miners lost their jobs. The total of 9192 men working in the coal industry in 1922 was at an all time high.[73] Never again would there be that many men working in Wyoming coal mines.

Even through the recession in the 1920s and the Depression of the 1930s, many miners and their families decided to remain in Wyoming. In places such as Sheridan, Kemmerer, and Rock Springs, miners were permitted to weather the economic downturns in company housing. If the coal company felt it would reopen its closed mines, or if the company was operating at reduced capacity, it allowed the miners to charge goods at the company store. It was not a prosperous period, but those that had jobs felt lucky.

Mine Closures

Mines closed throughout the state. Some closed and reopened several times during the two decades between 1920 and 1940. The changes in markets led to closures, but so did the depletion of coal. In some coal camps the miners extracted all the available coal. In other camps, the coal companies could no longer get contracts for the coal they mined. A lot of the major coal producers closed mines during the recession years of the 1920s and the Depression years of the 1930s. During these decades, however, there were still other mines in the state to which the miner could move.

After producing over 14 million tons of coal, in 1930 the coal camps at Cumberland closed because it was becoming difficult to mine the coal in the existing mines.[74] There was still coal available, but since the actual mining was still done by hand, a major overhaul would have been needed to work the coal seams to the north. Joe Bozovich, who worked at Cumberland from age 15 until it closed, said that the coal was a good grade but that it was essentially mined by hand and black powder. When Union Pacific was about to close the mine, they slowly reduced their working force. Joe Bozovich pointed out:

> My dad and I [at Cumberland Mine], we were in easy money. . . . U.P. figured that they was going to close that mine in not too long, and there was some fellow that was working there that owed U.P. a lot of money in the store. He couldn't afford to go anywhere, so he just charged everything. They seen he had a big debt, so they put him to work with us. And with us working like that, it wasn't long before he was out of debt. Usually whenever you owe [the company] money, at the bottom of your statement all they do is put a couple of lines. They call them rails. When he saw his first statement where there was no rails, there was actually money, he cried he was so happy. He said 'This is the first time I've ever seen cash for a long time.' It was easy coal, see. He was fairly old, you know, and did the best he could, but I was young and I was willing to work. So that helped him out a lot—all of us did.[75]

Miners often helped one another. Their similar plight and understanding of what the other was experiencing drew the miners together. When Cumberland closed, because he was young and a hard worker, Joe Bozovich was transferred to Union Pacific's mines at Superior. Other miners from Cumberland that the company decided to retain were sent to Reliance, Rock Springs, or one of Union Pacific's other mines.

In 1928 the coal mines at Cambria closed. Even though they were operated by different companies at different ends of the state, there were similarities in the two coal camps of Cambria and Cumberland. Both were laid out as planned communities. It was said of Cambria that "the company built and maintained an exceptionally neat and well-ordered mining camp . . . no saloons or professional gambling operations were allowed on any part of its land tract."[76] Cumberland was laid out with well ordered streets much like a midwestern town grid. It was also held that liquor could not be served inside the town limits, but neither Cambria or Cumberland were dry communities. To the south of Cumberland the privately owned village of South Cumberland emerged with saloons and a Golden Rule Store, the forerunner of J. C. Penney's Golden Rule store. There was little Union Pacific could do to stop miners from shopping or drinking in establishments not owned by the company. Inside the company-owned communities, it was also impossible to stop the use of liquor. Since the road into Cambria from Newcastle was maintained by the county, "there was no legal way to prevent [a dealer from] taking orders for liquor from the road." The company had to relax its rules somewhat. "Thus, there became daily 'beer wagon' trips from Newcastle to Cambria with rather stiff competition between dealers."[77] When both Cumberland and Cambria closed, there was a sense of loss. "Hundreds of persons were present for the closing celebration held on June 21, 1930," at Cumberland. "[M]any men and women [came] from distant points to do honor to the camp where they had formerly lived and worked."[78] At Cambria the families left slowly until the mine was completely closed. "When each family left, a farewell party was given in the departing family's honor. A good time was had at these parties as they tried to forget that they would be leaving the next day."[79] The cycle of opening and closing coal camps displaced workers and families alike. In spite of this, many miners and their family members retain happy memories and a particular bond to the coal camp where they lived.[80]

Mine closures during the Depression were somewhat harder to take because there were fewer mines operating. In describing the Depression, Hugh Crouch recalled,

It wasn't good, but when you set down and talked to a lot of the other people in the other parts of the country, I guess it wasn't so bad here after all. . . . But there was several years there when we just drifted along. I don't know how we did it. When you eat everything in the house today and don't know what you're going to eat tomorrow, why you just driftin' along.

I done a lot of huntin' and fishin'. . . . I always had a few chickens and rabbits. In the late thirties there I got ahold of a pig or two. We hunted and fished mostly the year round. I guess they had a [hunting] season, but we ignored it. . . . When it comes to survival, you're not going to worry too much if it's season or not.[81]

The problems in making ends meet during the Depression were due in a large part to the very nature of coal mining. Coal mining had always been seasonal. With the Depression, the seasonal layoffs were lengthened. For example, in 1933 the mines in Wyoming operated an average of only 145 days for the year. By 1935 the number of days Wyoming mines operated had increased to only 184 days per year. On the average, Wyoming mines operated about eight months during the year of 1935.[82]

Federal Programs

Several federal programs were initiated during the Depression to assist the unemployed and underemployed. Since coal mining was the principal source of employment in Sweetwater County, it provides a good example of the efforts made by the federal government to improve the plight of the miners in coal towns. Among the more prominent New Deal Programs in Sweetwater County were the Works Progress Administration (WPA) and the Civilian Conservation Corps (CCC). These programs helped unemployed miners and also provided a means of improving school facilities at several of the coal mining camps. In actual contributions to coal mining communities, the WPA provided the most direct assistance. In 1935 alone, the WPA provided $40,340 in federal funds for Sweetwater County. Projects initiated in 1935 included "work on the school grounds at Winton and street improvements in Superior." Interestingly, Winton and Superior were completely owned by a private company, Union Pacific Coal. At the coal town of Superior, a swimming pool and "other athletic facilities were constructed."[83]

Various other federal programs, including the Civil Works Administration (CWA) and the Federal Emergency Relief Administration (FERA), provided Sweetwater County with direct federal funds. From 1933 to 1935 they expended $400,000 in Sweetwater County. In 1933 they employed 900 men, providing relief to those who had lost their jobs in the mines. Their accomplishments were impressive. The athletic stadium at East Junior High in Rock Springs was built by these men. At Superior, water controls were constructed along Horsethief Draw. At Dines, Winton, and Reliance, playgrounds were enlarged and playground equipment installed. At Reliance and Superior, the school facilities were improved.[84] These programs were beneficial to the unemployed miners and improved the coal camps where they lived. Again, with the exception of Rock Springs, all the improvements were made in company-run towns. Only Dines did not belong to Union Pacific Coal. But these improvements, while benefiting coal companies, also helped make the lives of the miners better.

In 1935, 1638 people received relief in Sweetwater County. To help these individuals, "relief work" was provided. The idea was to try and find jobs for those that could work and were not already enrolled in other government programs. One such program was the Community Sewing Center. This program, begun in December 1934, provided work for women with children and unemployed single women. They produced clothing, quilts, and other items which were "issued to the needy." Statewide, the *Rocket* reported, "of the number employed, ninety-two per cent [are] widows, with from two to nineteen dependent children, six per cent are women whose husbands are disabled and the remaining two per cent are single women most of whom had dependents." In Sweetwater County during 1935, 85 women were employed in three Community Sewing Centers, two in Rock Springs and one in Green River.[85] Although it is not known how many of these women lost husbands in mining accidents, it is safe to assume that at least some of the widows lost their husbands in the coal mines.

During the Depression, mining accidents were, unfortunately, all too frequent an occurrence. Sweetwater County never had a major mining disaster; however in the period from 1909 to 1948, the county often accounted for the majority of mine fatalities recorded yearly by the state coal mine inspector. Rarely did the county fatalities fall below 40 percent of the total. In the decade that spans 1930 to 1940, Sweetwater County, while leading the state in production, had less than 30 percent of the shipping mines; yet it accounted for almost 50 percent of the fatalities. These deaths resulted from accidents while hauling coal, from roof falls, and from a variety of other reasons, but not from a major disaster similar to the explosions at Almy or Hanna or Kemmerer. The yearly mining fatalities for Sweetwater County were tragically high considering they were ongoing and not the result of a single mining accident. Sweetwater County's total fatalities from mine accidents still exceeds that of any other county in Wyoming.[86]

Strip Mining Takes Hold

In 1939 there were only four strip mines. Statewide there were 140 mines reporting coal production. The majority were small operations. For the entire state, 5,411,018 tons of coal were produced. The bulk of this production came from commercial mines, that is, mines owned by Union Pacific and the other large coal companies. The Wyodak Coal and Manufacturing Company near Gillette was still the largest strip mine in the state. With 29 employees, it removed 107,923 tons of coal in 1939. Each man at the Wyodak mine was extracting 3721 tons per year compared to the 1007 tons per man mined in Union Pacific's No. 4 underground mine in Rock Springs. The profits to be made by strip mining were becoming apparent. In 1939, Campbell, Sheridan, Carbon, and Converse counties each had one strip mine. With the exception of the Wyodak mine, they were small operations.[87]

Nationwide, strip mining was increasing. In 1937, 32 million tons of bituminous coal was mined by stripping operations. By 1941, approximately 97,300,000 tons of soft coal was extracted from strip pits. "Finding competition within their own industry from the oncoming strippers, many deep-shaft operators . . . included stripping in their enterprises."[88] As Duane Smith noted, "Strip mining went into production faster and used less complicated mining processes. Illinois miners were overwhelmingly convinced; from 1920 to 1945, strip mined coal jumped from less than 1 percent to 22 percent, while the rest of the industry stagnated."[89] With a relatively thin overburden and thick seams of soft coal underground, Wyoming was perfectly suited for strip mining.

Early strip mining ventures were often small-scale operations. Homer Alley, who began working in a strip mine towards the end of the Depression in 1939, described camp life at a small-scale operation north of Sheridan.

> In the winter of 1939-40, I went to work at the old Riverside Coal Mine, a strip mine, for Leslie Sharp, who was at that time running the only strip mine operation in this end of the state. Real fine man to work for. He and his wife lived on the property. We had absolutely no labor agreements whatsoever. We would go to work in the fall. Mr. Sharp would divide up the cash every Saturday night. We'd clean off a little spot on the ground, and we'd lay the cash out and count it out. At that time there was four of us working. In say September or October, we, the workers, would take most of that money. But then in November, December, January, February, and March, Mr. Sharp made his money, and we all got paid pretty good. I sometimes made as high as $12 or $14 in a week. That $12 and $14 went a long ways because my second year Mr. Sharp went to Sheridan, and I moved into his abode, so to speak, and took care of the money and seen that the mine was open and ready to go. There was no lights, no electricity, no toilet facilities, no water bills, there was nothing. We had a Coleman lantern, and two gallons of gasoline a week would take care of that. We hauled our drinking water and water to use— personal water—from Dayton in a wooden barrel on a two-wheeled trailer. We had all kinds of water running through the property in an irrigation ditch, which we used for bathing. There was absolutely no expense other than food.[90]

Strip mining began slowly in Wyoming, but it would gain momentum.

World War II

In 1940 Wyoming coal mines extracted 5,850,702 tons of coal. Five years later this production total had jumped to 9,836,798 tons.[91] To accomplish this jump in production, it required hiring more men, but fewer were needed than in earlier times because of mechanization. In 1940, 4321 men worked in Wyoming coal mines; by 1945, 4814 men were employed. Their production, however, jumped from 1354 tons per employee in 1940 to 2,043 tons in 1945. Almost 6.5 million tons of coal mined in 1945 came from Union Pacific mines, primarily underground operations centered in Sweetwater County.[92] The outbreak of hostilities with Japan in December 1941 was the principal reason production increased. With America dependent on steam locomotives to haul men and materials over the transcontinental railway, there was a need for more coal. Located along the principal rail route connecting the industrial East to San Francisco, the mines along the Union Pacific railroad became more important.

Increased efficiency resulted from using new equipment underground. Ninety-two percent of all coal mined was mechanically loaded, and 99.4 percent of the coal was undercut by machines. By increasing mechanization, the amount of coal an individual could mine also rose. The jump in production witnessed in 1945 was the result of more and newer mining equipment. While strip mines played a role in rising production, it was not a major factor in World War II. At the peak of wartime production in 1945, only eight percent of Wyoming's coal came from strip mines. However, in some northeastern counties, strip mining was playing a more important role. Campbell County, for example, extracted all of its coal from strip mines. While the future lay with strip mining, during World War II the underground miner and his machines did most of the work.[93]

Unfortunately, World War II brought with it new racial tensions. The bombing of Pearl Harbor caught America by surprise. Fears grew out of the surprise attack. One fear held by the Union Pacific Railroad was that Japanese working along the mainline through southern Wyoming might sabotage the railroad. At the time, Union Pacific had a number of Japanese working along the railroad and in the coal mines in and around Rock Springs. Possibly due to the diverse ethnic make-up of Rock Springs, the prejudice that resulted from the Japanese bombing of Pearl Harbor did not manifest itself in the extremes seen in other parts of the country. Immediately after Pearl Harbor, on December 7, 1941, the Japanese, Italians, and German "aliens" in Rock Springs and surrounding areas were ordered to register at the county seat in Green River. The *Rock Springs Daily Rocket* chronicled this registration, concentrating on the Japanese population in

Sweetwater County. Among the first to register were the Japanese miners. Only four days after Pearl Harbor, the paper reported, "Officers had said the registration had been orderly and that no disturbances had occurred. All Japanese are being urged to stay at home and avoid public places as much as possible for the present time." Six days after Pearl Harbor, Union Pacific Railroad ordered timekeepers in Rock Springs to "freeze all paychecks of Japanese nationals." Japanese, Italian, and German residents were soon required to obtain certificates of identification.[94]

It was estimated that there were "500 Alien Enemies" living in Rock Springs in 1942. All were required to have photographs and identification with them at all times.[95] Fearful of what might happen to their rail line, on February 13, "all Japanese nationals employed by the Union Pacific Railroad in the area were dismissed. . . ." Since the Japanese all lived in housing owned by the railroad, termination of their jobs also meant the loss of their homes. The newspaper in Rock Springs stated

> Japanese nationals . . . were given notice to have their belongings and families aboard special cars spotted at sections preparatory to being transported to either Salt Lake City or Cheyenne. They were given three days in which to comply, it was reported.
>
> The sheriff's office reported that no official orders had been received here for removal or evacuation, but it was understood that the railroad took the step as a precautionary measure.
>
> It is not known how many Japanese will be affected by the railroad's action, but it was stated officially that Japanese nationals not employed by the railroad would not be affected.[96]

In essence, the Japanese working in the mines were not affected but those working for the railroad lost their jobs.

According to George Okano, an American of Japanese descent, this action by the Union Pacific Railroad directly affected his family.

> My brother was one of them. I was lucky, I was at school then. But heck, you come home, and they laid off all the citizens, noncitizens, whatever, up and down this line. . . . [Y]ou were just off the property. You couldn't even be close to the railroad. Then the railroad comes right through the city [Rock Springs], and there was people living right along side the railroad tracks in the city. It didn't make much sense.[97]

Indeed, Japanese did continue to live in Rock Springs and the surrounding coal camps. The Japanese even continued making powder dummies for the mines. After World War II, their numbers dwindled. In 1940, 130 Japanese lived in Sweetwater County; by 1950, only 63 remained.[98]

During World War II, America's railroads were pressed into service to transport war materials. Since the railroads were one of Rock Springs' major coal markets, production climbed dramatically. In 1940, Sweetwater County mines produced 3,859,426 tons. By 1945, production had risen to 6,251,662 tons.[99] To achieve these high production levels, miners were recruited from outside Wyoming. Interestingly, due to the manpower shortage, Japanese miners were allowed to continue working underground and even on the Chicago Burlington and Quincy rail line in northeastern Wyoming. One Japanese miner, who began working at Reliance in 1937, spent the entire war digging coal for Union Pacific. He was not alone.[100] To retain workers already working underground, the federal government acted to prevent them from changing jobs. Coal mining was considered to be a critical war industry, and the majority of miners were frozen in their jobs.[101] With few immigrants coming into the coal fields from overseas, miners were recruited from other states to fill the vacancies created by the expanding coal industry. To achieve high production levels, additional manpower was needed. A drain in manpower brought about by the war coupled with a need for more miners created new problems. The influx of new workers needed to mine large quantities of coal gave rise to severe housing shortages. Nonetheless, following as it did on the heels of the Depression, the new era of prosperity was welcomed.

One of the major areas of the country from which coal miners were recruited was Oklahoma and Arkansas. Commonly called "Okies" and "Arkies," they were given menial jobs in and around the mines and were also given the worst homes, namely, boxcars. To alleviate the housing shortage in Sweetwater County brought on by the accelerated growth of the coal industry, boxcars were placed along railroad sidings at Superior, near Winton, at Rock Springs, and at other points near the mines as a stopgap measure. Carpenters working for Union Pacific Coal Company remodeled the railcars to serve as homes.[102] Numerous families moving from elsewhere in Wyoming to Rock Springs were also forced to live in boxcars. One miner who moved into a boxcar in Rock Springs said, "They had three big rooms . . . [and were] just like a house."[103] Others did not think they were so nice. They complained of cramped quarters and the dust, heat, and wind. Some people modified the boxcar, cutting holes and tightening cracks where needed.

According to several accounts, the men recruited from Oklahoma and Arkansas had little knowledge of coal mining. Apparently they were promised easy jobs and told:

Oh, you don't have to do nothing; everything is mechanized up there. Maybe once in a while you pick up an old rusty shovel. And they let them charge [at the company stores]. They had them so far in the hole, they couldn't go back [home] if they wanted. . . . They would go charge a gun, take it to the bar, and sell it for booze and cigarettes or something like that. They would go buy a carton of cigarettes and then sell it for half price just to get the money. Or ham. Heck, you could buy anything in the bars. Many times I had a guy come up to me and say, 'I'll take you down to the store and let you buy $20 worth of anything you want, groceries or anything, just give me $10 cash.' They kept them in the hole with a charge account.[104]

Since the newcomers were unfamiliar with the mines and especially with the way the company stores operated, they were at a disadvantage.

The shortage of miners during World War II brought women into the mines of Sweetwater County. Traditionally women were not allowed to work underground in the mines. "Women in the mines were believed to be bad luck. . . ."[105] One old-timer recalled, "They always said that if a woman worked down in the mine, they were going to walk out—that it's bad luck"[106] Even during the war, they usually worked outside the mine. Prior to World War II, most of the women employed by the mines worked as clerks or in other office positions; however, during the war this changed. Amy Pivik, who lived and worked in Rock Springs during the war, stated

What I remember then mostly was that most of the fellows were gone, and the women were working picking the boney at the mines and working the filling stations. I don't remember the wages being that good.[107]

Picking boney was a dirty job.

Men and women worked side by side in the tipples. At Reliance, Japanese women worked beside women of other nationalities. The dust covered everyone and everything. Most tipples, while enclosed, were cold in the winter. In the summer the black dust coupled with the heat made working conditions almost unbearable. The coal company allowed women and teenagers to work inside the dirty, ill lighted tipple, but rarely would they allow them to work underground. Wyoming women and Japanese Americans were making a contribution to the war effort by helping process coal. Agnes Tabuchi, who lived in Reliance, related, "one of my good friends worked at the tipple. . . . They were so short of men that they hired women too. But they wouldn't let them in the mine."[108] The jobs were not easy. The dirt in the tipples was often worse than in the mines.

Female boney picker at Hanna during World War II. The increased demand for coal production during the war, along with the shortage of men, created new job opportunities for women in the coal industry.

There were no laws dictating that coal should be sprinkled or ventilation provided in the tipple. Eugene Paoli, who worked alongside women in the tipples during World War II, stated, "Picking boney, there was 6 foot of cloud. You couldn't even see the person standing right by you."[109]

The prosperity brought on by World War II was felt throughout the state. At Monarch and other northern Wyoming mines, however, the need to bring in miners from outside areas was not as pressing as it was in southern Wyoming. Miners were "deferred by the Draft Board," and locked into their jobs.[110] The mines, which had been working only part-time through most of the Depression, began working seven days a week. In addition, some of the equipment was updated and production rose through mine improvements. World War II brought prosperity mainly because there were jobs available. "The wages weren't that good. The wages were frozen. . . ."[111] But to the miners, the most important thing was steady work. Their plight had been improved because they were no longer subject to periodic layoffs and part-time unemployment. As one miner stated:

I think that, on the whole, you used to work one to three days a week, and then you went to five to seven days a week. You had more money than you had ever had.[112]

Prosperity had returned briefly to the coal camps. Steady employment was something that Wyoming coal fields had not witnessed consistently for two decades.

Notes

[1]   Bernice Ketchum, interview with author, Sheridan, Wyoming, July 1987 (Ms. on file, Archaeological Services of Western Wyoming College, Rock Springs), 8.

[2]   Marie Havens Kaczmarek, interview with author, Vernal, Utah, December 1983, in *Oral Historical Accounts of Northwestern Colorado*, ed. by A. Dudley Gardner and Verla R. Flores (Rock Springs: Western Wyoming College Contributions to History, 1986), 1-2.

[3]   Frank Dernovich, Mike Duzik, Eugene Paoli, Norma Paoli, Antone Pivik, and Amy Pivik, interview with author, Rock Springs, Wyoming, 1984 (Ms. on file, Archaeological Services of Western Wyoming College, Rock Springs); Dines information from Hugh Crouch, interview with David Kathka, Green River, Wyoming, 1975 (Ms. on file, Archaeological Services of Western Wyoming College, Rock Springs), 75.

[4]   Caroline Flaim, interview with Jodie Gardner, Rock Springs, Wyoming, May 1988 (Ms. on file Archaeological Services of Western Wyoming College, Rock Springs), 29-30.

[5]   Henry Kovach, interview with Todd Horn, Rock Springs, Wyoming, March 1987 (Ms. on file, Archaeological Services of Western Wyoming College, Rock Springs), 19-20.

[6]   Ibid., 33.

[7]   Ernest Giorgis, interview with Linda Newman, Fort Bridger, Wyoming, November 1985, in *Archaeological Investigations at South Cumberland*, A. Dudley Gardner and David Johnson (Rock Springs: Archaeological Services of Western Wyoming College, 1986), Appendix A, 2-3. Description of Christmas and neighbors, Hugh Crouch interview, 77.

[8]   Mary Wolney, interview with author, Dayton, Wyoming, July 1987 (Ms. on file, Archaeological Services of Western Wyoming College, Rock Springs), 28-29.

[9]   Frank Dernovich, et al. interview, 30. The story about whiskey in the bucket is from the Hugh Crouch interview, 77.

[10]   Ibid., 30-34.

[11] Edith Sunada, interview with author, Green River, Wyoming, 1986. (Ms. on file, Archaeological Services of Western Wyoming College, Rock Springs), 40-41.

[12] Bernice Ketchum interview, 14.

[13] *Eleventh Census of the United States 1890* (Washington, D.C.: U.S. Government Printing Office, 1892); *Eighteenth Census of the United States 1960* (Washington, D.C.: U.S. Government Printing Office, 1963).

[14] Joseph Stipanovich, *The South Slavs in Utah: A Social History* (Saratoga, California: R. and E. Research Associates, 1975), 79-80.

[15] Catherine and Joseph Miller, interview with Shirley Black, Rock Springs, Wyoming, February 1987 (Ms. on file, Archaeological Services of Western Wyoming College, Rock Springs), 20-21.

[16] Ibid.

[17] Ibid., 14.

[18] Sol Williams, interview with Margie Krza, Superior, Wyoming, April 1982 (Ms. on file, Archaeological Services of Western Wyoming College, Rock Springs), 8.

[19] Hack Carter, interview with author, Rock Springs, Wyoming, Fall 1984 (Ms. on file, Archaeological Services of Western Wyoming College, Rock Springs), 3.

[20] Guido Silla and John Wolney, interview with author, Sheridan, Wyoming, July 1987 (Ms. on file, Archaeological Services of Western Wyoming College, Rock Springs), 7.

[21] Hugh Crouch interview, 64.

[22] *History of the Union Pacific Coal Mines 1868 to 1940* (Omaha: The Colonial Press, 1940), 242, 238.

[23] Frank Dernovich, et al. interview, 8.

[24] Ibid., 9.

[25] Ibid., 10.

[26] Henry Kovach interview, 46-47.

[27] Ibid., 48-49.

[28] Hack Carter interview, 29-30. See also William Harris, interview with author, Frontier Wyoming, fall 1983 (Ms. on file, Archaeological Services of Western Wyoming College, Rock Springs), 11, for the importance of mules to Wyoming coal mining.

[29] William Harris interview, 30-31.

[30] Ibid., 31-32.

[31] *Union Pacific Coal Mines*, 167, 172.

[32] William Harris interview, 41.

[33] Ben M. Selekman and Mary Van Kleeck, *Employees Representation in Coal Mines, A Study of the Industrial Representation Plan of The Colorado Fuel and Iron Company* (New York: Russel Sage Foundation, 1924), 43-44.

[34] Joe Bozovich, interview with author, Rock Springs, Wyoming, 1987. (Ms. on file, Archaeological Services of Western Wyoming College, Rock Springs).

[35] Selekman and Van Kleeck, *Employees Representation in Coal Mines*, 53-54.

[36] Ibid., 54.

[37] William Harris interview, 7.

[38] *State Coal Mine Inspector's Report 1923*, 27-30. (All state coal mine inspector's reports are on file, Wyoming State Archives, Cheyenne.)

[39] *The Rock Springs Rocket*, August 17, 1924.

[40] Lorenzo Groutage, *Wyoming Mine Run* (Kemmerer: Independently Published, 1981), 20.

[41] *The Rock Springs Rocket*, August 17, 1923.

[42] Ibid.

[43] *The Rock Springs Rocket*, August 31, 1923. The article is supposedly taken from the *Alexander Gazette*, Alexander, Virginia, which reported on the Frontier disaster.

[44] *The Rock Springs Rocket*, September 26, 1924.

[45] *State Coal Mine Inspector's Report 1924*, 22.

[46] *The Rock Springs Rocket*, September 26, 1924.

[47] *Session Laws of the State of Wyoming Passed by the Eighteenth State Legislature, 1924* (Sheridan, Wyoming: The Mills Company, 1925), 242-245.

[48] Ibid., 54.

[49] *State Coal Mine Inspector's Report 1945 and 1970*.

[50] McAlister Coleman, *Men and Coal* (New York: Farrar and Rinehart, 1943), 90.

[51] Ibid., 98-98. See also *The Rock Springs Rocket*, December 12, 1919.

[52] *The Rock Springs Rocket*, November 7, 1919. The *Rocket* published the proclamation in order of points the commander deemed important. This quote, while accurate, reverses the original order. The proclamation reads "(1) the power of the Government of the United States of America having been invoked by the Governor of Wyoming to assist in the preservation of law and order in the state, the undersigned assumes military control of the State of Wyoming. . . . (3). . . . All persons will be protected in their lawful, peaceful pursuits 'Military control will be exercised in accordance to the laws and usages of war.' . . . Warning (5) All persons engaged in unlawful combinations, assemblages or conspiracies, tending to obstruct or hinder the execution of the laws; All persons committing acts of violence or inciting others to commit such acts; All persons interfering in any of the rights and privileges, immunities, or protection guaranteed by the Constitution and the laws, to individual organizations, or corporations will be summarily dealt with."

[53] John Wolney and Guido Silla interview, 16.

[54] *State Coal Mine Inspector's Report 1921-1922*. There are conflicting totals for statewide production. The state coal mine inspector reports for 1920 through 1923 give the following totals for coal production: 1920, 9,580,274.15 tons; 1921, 7,276,496.92; 1922, 6,128,366.64; and 1923, 7,554,066.21. These totals seem fairly reliable but conflict slightly with the *Wyoming Coal Mine Wage and Employment Survey, 1982* (Cheyenne: Wyoming Department of Labor Statistics). This conflict is slight and possibly due is to rounding of figures when totals for each county were tabulated.

[55] *The Rock Springs Rocket*, April 7, 1922.

[56] Ibid.

[57] *The Rock Springs Rocket*, July 28, 1922.

[58] *The Rock Springs Rocket*, August 18, 1922.

59 *The Rock Springs Rocket,* August 25, 1922.
60 *State Coal Mine Inspector's Report* 1923-1927.
61 *State Coal Mine Inspector's Report* 1923, 29; 1927, 48.
62 *The Rock Springs Rocket,* March 25, 1927.
63 *The Rock Springs Rocket,* March 11, 1927.
64 *The Rock Springs Rocket,* February 25, 1927.
65 C. E. Dobbin and V. H. Barnett, *The Gillette Coal Field, Northeastern Wyoming,* U.S.G.S. Bulletin 796-A (Washington, D.C.: Government Printing Office, 1927), 63.
66 Coleman, *Men and Coal,* 6.
67 *State Coal Mine Inspector's Report 1925,* 12. The state inspector lists the "average number of men employed" each year.
68 Ibid., 12, 42.
69 *State Coal Mine Inspector's Report 1935,* 16, 61.
70 Duane Smith, *Mining America, The Industry and the Environment 1800-1980.* (Lawrence: University of Kansas, 1987), 109. Dr. Smith wrote, "Coal mining, which was hurting because of inroads that natural gas and oil made into the fuel market, also took it on the environmental chin."
71 *State Coal Mine Inspector's Report* 1900 to 1933.
72 *Wage and Employment Survey,* 6.
73 Ibid., 6.
74 *Union Pacific Coal Mines,* Appendix.
75 Joe Bozovich interview, 32-33.
76 *Newcastle (Wyoming) Newsletter Journal,* March 29, 1984.
77 N. E. Wells, *A Brief Biographical Sketch of Some of My Experiences as a Country Doctor* (Newcastle, Wyoming: privately published, 1953), 20. Copies of the publication are contained in the Cambria and Newcastle file, Wyoming State Archives, Museums, and Historical Department, Cheyenne.
78 *Union Pacific Coal Mines,* 135.
79 Jodie Voiles Gardner, A Childhood in Cambria, 1918-1928, (Ms. on file, Archaeological Services of Western Wyoming College, Rock Springs, 1988), 6. The Caroline Flaim interview contains good information on camp life in Cambria.
80 This is reflected statewide and articulated in the interviews of Mary Wolney, Joe Bozovich, Caroline Flaim, Antone Pivik, and others.
81 Hugh Crouch interview, 63-64.
82 *State Coal Mine Inspector's Report* 1933, 59; 1935, 61. The calculation of eight months was arrived at by dividing 184 days by 22. The work month, not counting weekends, was estimated at 22 days per month.
83 *The Rock Springs Rocket,* August 10, 1935; August 28, 1935.
84 *The Rock Springs Rocket,* March 28, 1935.
85 *The Rock Springs Rocket,* January 16, 1935.
86 *State Coal Mine Inspector's Report* 1886-1970.
87 *State Coal Mine Inspector's Report 1939.*
88 Coleman, *Men and Coal,* 6.
89 Smith, *Mining America,* 110.
90 Homer Alley, interview with author, Dayton, Wyoming, July 1987 (Ms. on file, Archaeological Services of Western Wyoming College, Rock Springs), 4-5.

⁹¹ *State Coal Mine Inspector's Report* 1940-1945.

⁹² *Wage and Employment Survey*, 6; *State Coal Mine Inspector's Report* 1945, 71.

⁹³ *State Coal Mine Inspector's Report* 1945, 14-16 and 78.

⁹⁴ *The Rock Springs Daily Rocket*, December 10, 1941; December 11, 1941; December 13, 1941.

⁹⁵ *The Rock Springs Daily Rocket*, February 26, 1942.

⁹⁶ *The Rock Springs Daily Rocket*, February 13, 1942.

⁹⁷ George Okano, interview with author, Rock Springs, Wyoming (Ms. on file, Archaeological Services of Western Wyoming College, Rock Springs), 58.

⁹⁸ *Sixteenth Census of the United States, 1940* (Washington, D.C.: U.S. Government Printing Office, 1942); *Seventeenth Census of the United States, 1950*, (Washington, D.C.: U.S. Government Printing Office, 1952).

⁹⁹ *State Coal Mine Inspector's Report* 1940-1945.

¹⁰⁰ Yoshio and Agnes Tabuchi, interview with author, Reliance, Wyoming, spring 1986 (Ms. on file, Archaeological Services of Western Wyoming College, Rock Springs), 5.

¹⁰¹ Alice Antilla, interview with author, Kemmerer, Wyoming, fall 1983 (Ms. on file, Archaeological Services of Western Wyoming College, Rock Springs) 25; Joe Bozovich interview, 1985.

¹⁰² Joe Bozovich interview.

¹⁰³ Hack Carter interview, 20.

¹⁰⁴ Frank Dernovich, et al. interview, 38.

¹⁰⁵ Duane Smith, *Colorado Mining, A Photographic History* (Albuquerque: University of New Mexico Press, 1977), 43.

¹⁰⁶ Frank Dernovich, et al. interview, 37.

¹⁰⁷ Ibid., 36.

¹⁰⁸ Yoshio and Agnes Tabuchi interview, 12.

¹⁰⁹ Frank Dernovich, et al. interview, 43.

¹¹⁰ John Wolney and Guido Silla interview, 40. See pages 33, 36, and 37 for further descriptions of World War II and coal mines near Sheridan.

¹¹¹ Frank Dernovich, et al. interview, 36.

¹¹² Ibid., 39.

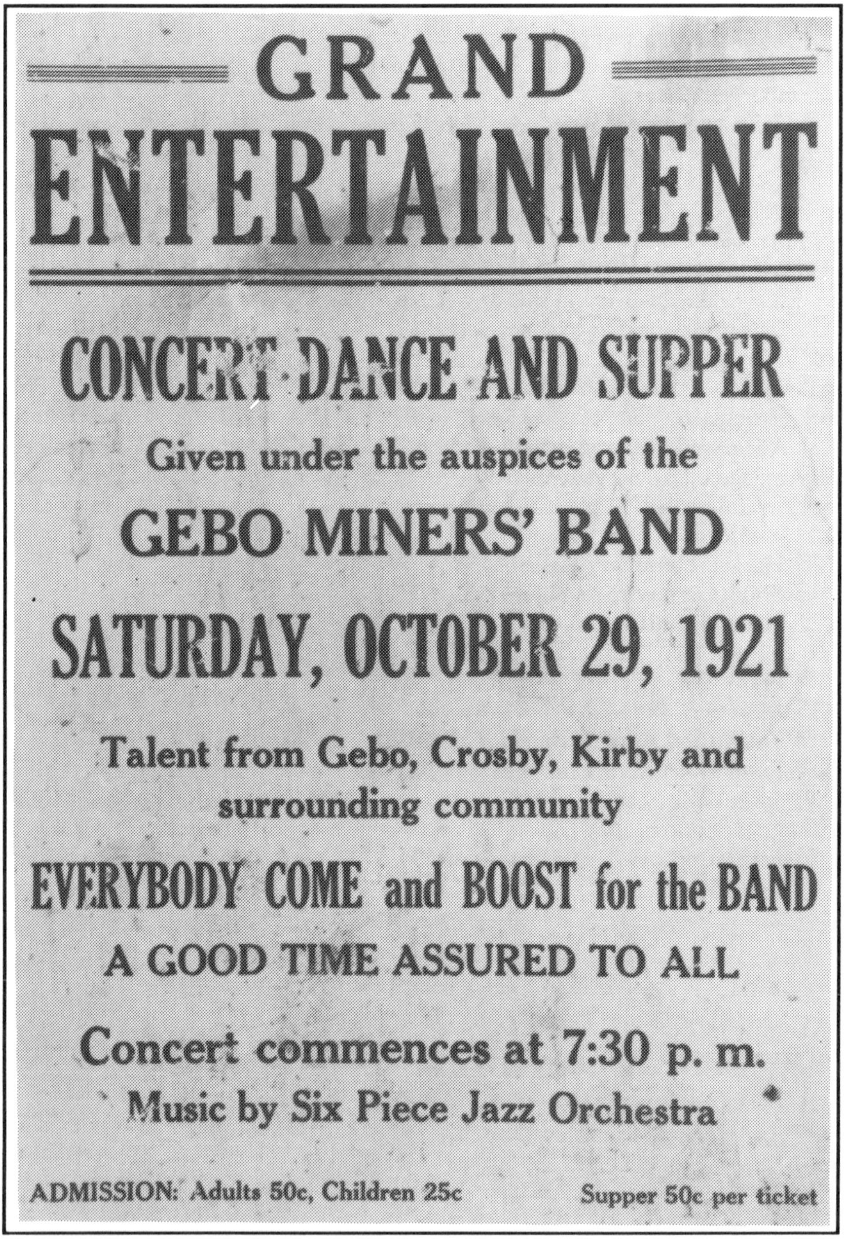

GRAND

ENTERTAINMENT

CONCERT DANCE AND SUPPER

Given under the auspices of the

GEBO MINERS' BAND

SATURDAY, OCTOBER 29, 1921

Talent from Gebo, Crosby, Kirby and
surrounding community

EVERYBODY COME and BOOST for the BAND

A GOOD TIME ASSURED TO ALL

Concert commences at 7:30 p. m.

Music by Six Piece Jazz Orchestra

ADMISSION: Adults 50c, Children 25c

Supper 50c per ticket

(Courtesy Hot Springs County Museum)

6

Booms and Busts,
1945 to the Present

At the end of World War II, there was little to indicate what lay ahead for the Wyoming coal industry. Throughout America in general, prosperity followed the war and continued into the 1950s. The country was entering the atomic age. Wealth and technological advances seemed in store for the nation as a whole. Some people felt the use of an archaic fuel such as coal would naturally drift into the past as did the windmill and wood-powered steam engines at the beginning of the Industrial Revolution. Coal had powered the Industrial Revolution, but with the dawn of the atomic age, it seemed coal would no longer be needed. Gas and diesel engines would replace steam engines. Jet engines and sleek racing machines were the wave of the future. Bulky, coal-powered locomotives were seen as a thing of the past. While America's economy forged ahead, the Wyoming coal industry stagnated.

Wyoming war veterans returning home to coal camps found few jobs awaiting them. During World War II, coal production had reached an all-time high, peaking at 9.8 million tons in 1945. One year later production had dropped by 2.2 million tons. With the onset of a recession in the industry, men lost their jobs. It would take almost two decades for the coal industry to revive. The prosperity experienced during World War II had been too short-lived. For the Wyoming veterans returning home from the war, the recession meant they would have to find jobs outside the mines. To some it meant moving away from Wyoming.

The strip mines offered one form of employment for returning veterans. Big Horn Coal, owned by Peter Kiewit and Sons and located north of Sheridan, was one of these mines. After taking over part of the old Riverside mine, the Big Horn Coal Company began strip mining in Sheridan County on a large scale. Changes in mining equipment were revolutionizing strip mining. Turnapulls, a rubber wheeled scraper that traveled up to 12 or 14 miles an hour, were speeding the process. Homer Alley, who returned from the Pacific Theatre after World War II, recalled that Cats (bulldozers), scrapers, and turnapulls were the most important

Shovel and hauler used in the Big Horn Coal Company strip mine in the 1950s. The efficiency with which this type of large equipment could mine coal led to the eventual closing of underground coal mines. (Courtesy of Homer Alley, Sheridan)

stripping machines. At Big Horn Coal, the overburden varied from 50 to 60 feet when the mine first started. Modern stripping equipment was used to remove the overburden and expose several seams of coal. "At Big Horn ... first came small veins of 5 and 6 feet. These were low [in] BTUs. Then they got down to a 17-foot vein and a small parting, and then into a 24-foot vein, which was the best."[1] The coal from these various seams was blended together. By mixing the top coal with the lower coal, a consistent BTU was obtained. Only a parting (a separation between the seams) interrupted the process of removing 47 feet of coal. Strip mining was a profitable way to mine.

The strip mine at Big Horn would eventually prove too efficient for the underground coal mines to compete against. The result was that underground mines in Sheridan County were slowly put out of business. John Wolney, the son of a Polish immigrant, provided an excellent description of how the mines at Monarch met their end.

In the mine they had 9 or 10 feet of coal. Then above that was a parting. [The boss] said they figured it out they had 5 more feet of coal up [above the parting]. So he said, 'Why not get that coal up there.' So what they were doing was shooting that parting down. Then they were shooting that top, and they were timbering [with] 16-foot poles. They just about lost a bunch of machinery in there at that time. First thing you know they were getting this rotten coal, and they [c]ouldn't get [a market]. The orders went to Kiewit, and that was the end of it in '53. I'll tell you, that was really something.[2]

The company's effort to remove the top coal prior to the closure of the Monarch mine in 1953 created an unstable roof, especially when pulling props. John Wolney told how the props were pulled.

We were in there with a shuttle car, and they wanted to cave this one place up there. The boss said, 'Well, John, [we'll put] a big cable on them cars and we'll start from there.' We had about four of them . . . big old shuttle cars, and we pulled them posts out. Then we unhooked, and he said, 'Let's get out of here 'cause the rest of them are coming.' Boy, I'll tell you, it's still spooky now. A lot of times at night I'd wake the little woman up and she'd say, 'What's the matter?' I would say, 'Oh, nothing. Just old times, that's all.' There was some close ones, I'll tell you. I had some close ones.[3]

Pulling props was one of the more dangerous jobs underground. Many men lost their lives in Wyoming mines pulling props.

The practice of pulling props and caving mine roofs was supposed to be a beneficial process. Mine roofs exerted a great deal of pressure over mined out areas. This pressure would eventually increase to the point where mine props would buckle and the roof collapse. These collapses were unpredictable and, therefore, dangerous. To alleviate the danger, the props were pulled and a controlled cave-in created. This served a dual purpose. The roof no longer had the stress above the mined out areas, and the mine became more stable to work in as the rubble had a tendency to support the rest of the mine. The debris from the roof fall actually became a mine support. With the benefit of preventing unwanted roof collapses and at the same time supporting the mine workings, prop pulling was viewed as worth the risk.

When a mine roof collapsed, when coal was moved, or when blasting took place, the mine filled with dust. In the 1940s and 1950s miners became acutely aware of the danger of coal dust although it had been known since early in the nineteenth century that coal dust caused lung disease. By the 1950s, respirators were used to filter some of the dust, but this was never completely successful in keeping the dust out of a person's lungs. In describing the problems of dust in the Sheridan field, one miner related:

Even in early years my dad . . . used to cough up phlegm or coal dust. It was worse then than it is now. Finally they were trying to get these respirators. . . . But you had dust in there continually. The cutting machine was supposed to use water, but half of [the miners] didn't want water 'cause it was harder to shovel wet coal dust instead of dry. You know what I mean. The cutting machine had a 9 foot bar; and when it would cut, [there would be a] fine dust. They'd shovel that and [the boss would] say, 'Put water on it.' Well, they'd put water on it while the boss was there, but then they'd shut it off. [There would be a lot of] dust in there. There was dust on the coal when you were loading it out too.[4]

Underground mining machines created new sources of dust, but even on the surface in the strip mines, heavy equipment created clouds of dust. On the surface, coal dust mixed with blowing dust could be as suffocating as the conditions underground. The difference was that in the strip mines, the wind would blow the dust away from the machines and across the countryside.

When the Monarch mines closed in 1953, the last large underground mine in Sheridan County became part of a strip mining venture. Two small underground mines owned by the Storm King Coal Company continued mining, but their production for 1953 totaled only 10,464 tons. On May 1, 1953, the Monarch mine was sealed. The Sheridan-Wyoming Coal Company, which owned Monarch, entered into a joint venture with Big Horn Coal. This joint venture stipulated that Big Horn Coal would do the mining while Sheridan-Wyoming Coal would sell the coal.[5] Unfortunately, the strip mine required far fewer men than did the underground operations at Monarch. Consequently, men lost their jobs, and the mining camp was closed. Only a few fortunate workers were able to gain employment at the strip mine. As a result of mine closures, layoffs became all too common in the 1950s.

While layoffs were taking place statewide, owners began taking a different view on how to manage mines. Mine managers became more sensitive to the problems facing the coal miner. One reason for this change of heart was that the mines had to be more efficient to compete with other sources of energy. Threatened with competition from the oil and gas industry, underground mines had to increase productivity. Statewide in 1953, 5.2 million tons of coal were extracted; only 1.6 million tons came from strip mines.[6] In 1953, underground mining held a tenuous lead over strip mining. To keep production levels high underground, equipment as well as management practices were improved. In the *Union Pacific Coal Company Code of Standards* (a manual for managing mines), the coal company told their supervisors:

> Courtesy is an unfailing source of power. Many men object to being told to do a thing in a rough, commanding tone of voice. Such are frequently the very best men, and they will respond cheerfully to a more considerate

approach. Men can no longer be induced to give loyal service through fear, and discharging a man for trivial causes is unfair; it savors of cowardice. Men are not given capital punishment for petty offenses; admonishment and advice will go further in the majority of cases. It is only the persistent and flagrant offender who should be dismissed, and he should be taken out for his own good and that of the men who work with him.[7]

Unfortunately, the Wyoming coal industry was on the verge of experiencing the worst collapse in its history. New management policies did not prevent the loss of jobs, yet the new policy was refreshing when compared to labor policies practiced at the turn of the century.

A Major Recession in the Coal Industry

In 1952 Wyoming mines produced about one-third of the coal mined in the Rocky Mountain region. This production amounted to 6.1 million tons, a considerable drop from the levels reached during World War II. Sweetwater and Carbon counties led the list of producers. Machines removed 96 percent of all coal taken from the mines. The mechanization of underground mines was almost complete. Underground mines accounted for three-fourths of Wyoming's total coal production; but strip mines were gaining on the deep mines.[8] The days when underground mines out produced strip mines were numbered. The death knell to underground mining, however, did not come in the form of a steam shovel stripping coal from the earth, it came in the form of a diesel engine.

Since World War I, petroleum products had been making inroads into markets once held solely by coal. The gasoline industry had greatly increased its domestic markets through the growth of the automobile industry. By volume, coal was simply too low in BTUs and too bulky to compete in the automobile industry. Natural gas was quickly becoming the fuel of choice for home heating and cooking. The railroads, with their large steam engines, seemingly stood as the last major market for coal. When railroad locomotives switched to diesel after World War II, the last major market for coal vanished. The coal industry in the West, and especially in the Intermountain West, witnessed a major recession.

Union Pacific and other railroads in America had experimented with diesel locomotives for years and found that diesels were more efficient than their coal-fired counterparts. The first diesel passenger trains arrived on Union Pacific's mainline in the mid-1930s. Dieselization of the UP system was well advanced in the 1940s when many steam engines were displaced by diesels. Old steam engines were sent to the Wyoming division, which became the last refuge for steam locomotives in the Union Pacific system. The principal market for Wyoming's coal from underground mines was to fuel these steam engines. In the 1950s the transition to diesel power was completed. Within seven years, between 1950 and 1957, all but two of the underground mines in Sweetwater County ceased operation. In the years between 1950 and 1955, coal production statewide dropped 4.7 million tons, and only 587 men were employed in all of Wyoming's mines.

Even though the change from steam locomotives to diesel engines was fairly rapid, there was a transition period. Union Pacific and the Burlington Railroad needed time to purchase engines and to make changes in machine shops and other facilities. Until the changes could be made, the railroads continued running steam locomotives. To keep the men in Wyoming mines working, in the midst of a threatened strike, Union Pacific promised, "If there is a work stoppage in the nation's coal mines, you keep on mining coal here and whatever the national settlement is we'll go along with it." This promise came in an address to 2000 people in Rock Springs. Given by P. J. Lynch, vice president of operations of the Union Pacific Railroad, the speech points out how important coal still was in 1953. Lynch went on to promise, "We are not giving up coal and the day when we do is too far away for us to consider tonight. . . . Only the future can answer the outlook for coal burning on the railroad." Lynch added, "We are operating in coal burning territory today less diesels than we were four years ago." Appealing to the coal miners "to stay on the job," Lynch went on to assure miners that if there was a steady supply of coal, there would be a "conversion of oil burners back to coal."[9] Lynch proved to be a false prophet. By the end of 1954, all but three Union Pacific coal mines were closed in Sweetwater County. In 1954, one year after Lynch gave his speech, Union Pacific laid off 760 miners in Sweetwater County.[10] They lost their jobs for good; there would be no new coal mines opened in Sweetwater County. The layoffs were the result of the Union Pacific Railroad converting to diesel power.

The year 1954 was devastating for the coal industry in Wyoming. In January, Union Pacific promised not to "shut down its Wyoming coal mine operations entirely," but officials for the railroad went on to say its coal mines in Wyoming would be "considerably smaller operations from now on." They were true to their last promise. With 190 diesel engines on order, Union Pacific was ending an era.[11] Over the Christmas holidays of 1953, Union Pacific began closing both the Reliance and Hanna mines. In February 1954 Union Pacific completed the closure of the Hanna mines by laying off 180 miners.[12] The closure of the Hanna mines was the last in a series of layoffs that began as early as December 1953.

In January of 1954 the federal government pledged surplus food to the miners in the Rock Springs area. "The plea for surplus food was wired to the Wyoming [Congressional] delegation by local 8038 of the United Mine Workers at Stansbury . . . after approximately 500 miners were laid off." The union claimed that the hardships experienced by the miners were "due to slow working times in the mines, followed by work reductions." Many of the miners' families were in "dire circumstances," and federal aid was promised in the form of surplus food.[13] Some of the miners in need of aid had worked for Union Pacific for decades. One coal miner, who worked in Sweetwater County, recalled, "When the mines closed, you couldn't buy a job."[14] The economic downturn was felt statewide. In 1945, 4814 men had worked in Wyoming mines; by 1955, only 979 men were working, and the decline was just beginning.[15]

In 1954 statewide production decreased 46 percent from the previous year. In that year, Wyoming's strip mines out produced the underground mines for the first time. The turnaround came about due to the closure of underground mines statewide. Of 2,833,352 tons of coal mined, 1,438,957 tons came from strip mines. Requiring fewer men to operate, the strip mines could not offset the loss of underground jobs. Wyoming's mining labor force was cut 45 percent. By 1955, only 979 miners remained in the coal industry. Not since the state began keeping records in 1888 had there been so few men mining coal. There were few jobs open to displaced miners. Among all states, Wyoming was in last place "in number of firms . . . and number of employees employed" in manufacturing.[16] Without employment opportunities, the miners had to move elsewhere. By the end of 1956 there were only 24 mines operating in Wyoming, whereas in 1945 there had been 70.

In February 1957 the Stansbury mines north of Rock Springs were closed. Of the closure, company president I. N. Bayless said, "It's an action we take with regret." Bayless went on to add that the "present conditions in the coal industry force us to take these steps."[17] There was still coal underground, but there was just no market. One hundred and ninety miners lost their jobs. Only Union Pacific's coal mines at Superior were still operating; but then in October, 150 miners were laid off. In all, 340 miners lost their jobs in Sweetwater County in 1957. Without elaborating on the reasons for the layoffs, Union Pacific simply held "the company doesn't need the coal."[18] By 1958 Wyoming coal production reached its lowest level—only 1,631,234 tons were mined.[19]

The year 1962 brought with it the closure of Union Pacific's last mine at Superior. The *Rock Springs Daily Rocket* reported, "Superior's colorful era, during which coal mining was king for more than a half-century, ended this weekend with the closing of the last big mine, the D. O. Clark."[20] Only one Union Pacific mine remained opened. Four months later the last Union Pacific Coal Company mine in Wyoming closed. Fittingly, the last coal mine Union Pacific closed was in Rock Springs. On August 28, 1962, Rock Springs No. 8 mine ceased operations.[21] In the fall of 1868 Union Pacific had first begun to depend on Rock Springs coal. The closing of No. 8 marked the end of Union Pacific's almost century-long dependence on Wyoming coal.

In 1954 coal produced from strip mines exceeded the amount produced from underground mines. In part this was the result of more efficient mining techniques which employed large heavy equipment. This dragline bucket, employed at Hanna, could move many tons of overburden and coal quickly and more cheaply than conventional techniques. (Courtesy of the American Heritage Center, Photo Archives, University of Wyoming)

Sweetwater County's black gold had fired locomotives for almost 90 years.[22] The end came like its beginnings, with a note in a newspaper. Union Pacific, however, did not give up its mineral reserves. It still owned vast tracts of land gained through the original land grant. Under this land lay coal. Union Pacific could afford to close mines, the earth would hold its untapped wealth. One day in the not too distant future coal mining would again be profitable. The coal miners, whose needs were more immediate, could not wait. The coal camp at Superior was dismantled and only nearby South Superior with privately owned homes remained.

One miner described the sadness he felt as he watched the dismantling of the town of Superior. Sol Williams, who lived and worked in the mines, remembered

[People] gradually, slowly would move out and down in[to] South Superior. There's very few peoples livin' in these houses today out here that was livin' here then. Peoples just, what can I say, givin' their houses away out here in South Superior. Course, up in the camp, the U.P. started to sell 'em. You could buy 'em, but you had to move 'em. Some houses up in camp went as far as Logan, Utah. Well, quite a few is in Rock Springs; some's in Green River and different places like that. You could buy a house up in the camp at the time and move it to Rock Springs for about $600. And a lot of peoples was takin' them and movin' them down there and then fixin' them up. 'Cause peoples just frettin' and just goin'. Course Rock Springs at that time was just as bad. Once they closed down, there was nothin' no more there. Reliance was still goin', but it was just Reliance and that's all. Stansbury had closed down; it was phased out. They was takin' all the houses out of Stansbury. Green River was just as bad. They'd taken the round house and the railroad shop out of Green River and put it in Ogden, Utah. So there you are. Sweetwater County was nothin'.[23]

Sol was describing the passing of a way of life. The company town, with all its ills, had instilled a sense of belonging and a common focus. There was sadness in seeing homes of co-workers dismantled. The common bond of town and mine was gone. Company towns would continue to be part of western mining, but not in the same way as in the late nineteenth century and the early twentieth century.

When people move to a new area, they try to define it in terms they can understand. They bring with them successful adaptation patterns used in their homeland. Some define settlement as staying in one place forever. Wyoming, however, did not lend itself to definitions generated in the Old World or the eastern United States. Instead, life had to be defined in terms of winter deserts and high elevations. There was a short supply of water and a lot of wind. Cold was more common than humidity, and newcomers had to learn new lessons if they were going to stay. Staying in Wyoming was not easy. People in company towns did not own the property on which they lived. When the mines closed, the miners had to move. In some cases the miners did not want to move, but there were no choices. Rented houses were sold out from underneath the renter. In more a congenial climate, such as Iowa, the miner might have moved to a small farm and weathered the downturn. Or the miner might have found employment in another industry. This was not the case in Wyoming where ranching dominated the economy. There were few farms, and ranching required a lot of land but not many workers. At Kemmerer, Gebo, and Sheridan there were no major industries to employ out-of-work coal miners. Wyoming in the 1950s and 1960s was the least industrialized state in the Union. The coal miners and their families without jobs had to leave Wyoming.

When mines closed, men and women sought work. Near Rock Springs there was one option. Some men who lost their jobs in the coal mines found work in the newly opened trona mines west of Green River and could continue to live in Rock Springs. This was not the case for those living in Winton, Dines, Superior, and Stansbury. When the mines closed at these towns, the company houses were moved. In the coal camps surrounding Kemmerer, the mines closed over a period of time. Most structures were dismantled or moved into Kemmerer and other towns. Glencoe, Oakley, Sublet, and Susie became places of the past. Near Sheridan the towns of Acme, Monarch, and Carneyville were also abandoned and dismantled. The environment around Sheridan is less harsh than the southwestern desert, and a number of miners turned to ranching and dryland farming while working at the coal mines. Those miners with jobs or farms or ranches stayed near Sheridan. The others had to move.

While some miners who moved to Wyoming originally did not intend to stay, others came seeking new opportunities. Immigrants from around the world who worked in Wyoming coal mines found a place to begin anew and raise families. When the mines closed and the towns were dismantled in the 1950s and early 1960s, the hope of several generations staying in one place was lost. Immigrants from places such as Yugoslavia had been raised in families where generation after generation had lived in the same village,[24] and some hoped that in America new generations could be raised with similar deep-running roots. While the complete dismantling of entire towns ended such hopes, these were adaptable people. If staying in Wyoming meant moving to a new town nearby or changing jobs, some were willing to make the change. Others, finally dissatisfied with the economic situation in Wyoming, chose to leave. Even those deciding to stay saw their children move away because of the lack of job opportunities. In the 1950s there was an exodus of Wyoming youth who could not find jobs after they finished school. T. A. Larson, in discussing Wyoming as the energy state, noted that for many years Wyoming's "exports had included its youth."[25] Moving elsewhere, for the younger generation, was more of a necessity than an option.

Coal camps were literally dismantled in the 1950s. To avoid paying taxes on vacant buildings, coal companies sold the structures for a minimal amount. Since there is a scarcity of wood in the region, buying a structure from Dines, Gebo, or elsewhere was an attractive means of obtaining a home. Paul Krza, an editor for the *Casper Star Tribune,* interviewed one of the men who moved these homes. Of his interview with Avelino Gutierrez, Krza wrote:

> Over the years, Gutierrez had moved hundreds of houses, many from now-defunct mining camps when area coal mines closed in the 1950s. With their newly attached wheels, the formerly stationary homes left the dying towns of Superior and Stansbury to find new resting spots in Rock Springs, Pinedale, and even neighboring states.
>
> The homes were sold then for 'a couple hundred dollars, and some were even cheaper than that,' Gutierrez said. For another $250 to $400, he would move the dwellings to Rock Springs. About every three days, there was one house in transit.
>
> The houses went everywhere. Some went over South Pass to Hudson and Lander. Others were moved to Utah, Idaho, and Colorado. And at least nine went north to Pinedale and Big Piney, a trip that lasted seven or eight days.[26]

In Sweetwater County between 1950 and 1965, the coal camps of Superior, Dines, Gunn, Quealy, Winton, Lionkol, East Plane, and Reliance were dismantled. Elsewhere in the state, houses at Monarch, Gebo, Glencoe, and Susie met similar fates. Some buildings were torn down, instead of moved, and the wood and other materials used in nearby towns. Currently, all that remains of these once-thriving coal camps are concrete walls and foundations.

While coal miners in Wyoming were struggling to find jobs, much of America prospered. Other Rocky Mountain states and the Plains states did not share in the nationwide wealth, but the nation as a whole was prospering to an extent not dreamed of during the Depression. "The GNP [Gross National Product] grew to $440 billion by 1960, more than double the 1940 level." This growth in the GNP was felt by most Americans. "By the mid-1950s, the average American family had twice as much real income to spend as its counterpart had possessed in the boom years of the 1920s." More important, one historian contends, "The American people, in one generation, had moved from poverty and depression to the highest standard of living the world had ever known."[27] The Wyoming coal miners who lost their jobs in the 1950s and early 1960s did not share in the wealth. The lost jobs were gone forever. Technological changes ensured underground mining would never again play the role it had played prior to 1953. As the rest of the nation enjoyed the fruits of prosperity, Wyoming miners sought employment.

New Issues Raised

But the situation was not to remain static; coal mining would again pick up. Slowly, from its lowest point in 1958, the production from Wyoming mines increased. In 1965 there were only 327 people mining Wyoming coal; but as the decade of the '60s neared its end, the number of men employed began to rise, as did the output from Wyoming mines. Not even the most optimistic miner in the Coal Age could have foreseen what was to come.

As Wyoming's coal production began to climb slowly from the doldrums, new issues began to face the coal industry. The issues arose out of the impact strip mining was having on the landscape. In 1965, 327 miners extracted 3,257,314 tons of coal. Wyoming miners were extracting 9,961 tons of coal apiece.[28] Productivity was rising as the result of strip mining. Awesome and powerful pieces of equipment removed tons of coal each hour. In their wake, the machines left behind rubble and man-made canyons. The coal industry was focused on the thick seams buried under the northeast prairies. Complaints began to surface regarding a need to reclaim the land left open by the removal of coal. As the mines expanded, the voices against strip mining grew louder.

In the mid-1960s, Wyoming's coal industry expanded in response to a nationwide demand for more electricity. Power plants built to produce this electricity increasingly selected coal as fuel. Using coal to fire the boilers, companies began constructing power plants near known coal reserves. The cheapest means of obtaining coal was to strip mine. Strip mines and power plants were a profitable combination. In their wake, however, the strip mines left scars across the landscape. Wyoming wanted and needed jobs, but the question of whether they wanted their lands permanently marked by mining was asked more often. Wyomingites had seen coal companies come and go too often and abandon their problems when they left. This time, with the scars so deep and wide across the prairies, some people asked if there was not a better way to mine. Two issues came to the forefront. The first was the issue of jobs in a depressed industry; the second was the preservation of open spaces for future generations. Some felt you could not have both. The issues were open to heated debate. The need for coal to fire power plants brought the debate to a head.

The principal markets for Wyoming coal in the 1960s were electric generating plants. Some were even constructed in Wyoming. The first of a new generation of large, coal-fired generating plants in Wyoming was constructed near Glenrock in 1958. By 1959, the strip mine for the Pacific Power and Light Dave Johnston power plant produced 465,492 tons of coal.[29] The coal from the strip mine was fed directly into the power plant. This modern power plant required large quantities of coal, and the nearby Dave Johnston strip mine became the state's leading coal producer. Converse County, with both the power plant and mine located inside its borders, became Wyoming's new leader in coal production.

Coal-fired electric generating plants were designed as high capacity generating facilities. In Wyoming, the process involved stripping the coal and transporting it by truck or conveyors to a silo. The silo took the place of the historic tipple. In the silo the coal was crushed and then conveyed into the boilers along conveyor belts. By the time it reached the furnace, the coal had been pulverized to a fine dust. The dust was shot into the furnace where it literally exploded. Like the underground explosion of coal dust, the controlled explosion generated intense heat. In the boilers, water was converted to steam under high pressure. The pressurized steam spun the turbines that generated the electricity. Wyoming coal, though lower in BTUs than its eastern counterparts, was low in sulfur. When the black cloud of smoke escaped from the stacks at the power plant, it was cleaner and less harmful to the environment. Still, by 1963 clean air had become a political issue.

In the 1960s, environmentalists and mining interests locked horns. To the mining companies, environmentalists were obstructionists bent on destroying the mining industry. To the environmentalists, strip mines left ugly scars depriving future generations of usable land. Mine owners who callously hollowed the land with no thought of the future were modern pirates pillaging and plundering the land. To the mine owner, the environmentalist was a misguided do-gooder with no concept of economic realities. Battle lines formed early in the 1960s. As historian Duane Smith accurately observed, "The storm that had been coming for years, the great environmental awakening, was now at hand."[30]

Public awareness of industrial pollution and the damage strip mining could impose on the land if not controlled led to a popular outcry against anything that might harm the planet Earth. Through a variety of books and magazines, people were made aware of past, present, and future environmental problems. In works such as *My Land is Dying*, Harry M. Caudill wrote and gave clarity to the problems associated with strip mining.

In the 1960s the environmental effects of strip mining were becoming an issue as the demand for coal was once again on the rise. With increasingly larger, more modern equipment, large tracts of land could be devastated in a short period of time. (Courtesy of the American Heritage Center, Photo Archives, University of Wyoming)

Writing about strip mines in the hills of Kentucky, Caudill said, "Here, the scene was altogether different: jumbled mounds of loose earth, slabs of bluish slate, half-buried trunks of dead trees, pools of stagnant acid-yellowed water, and raw cliffs of sandstone newly scoured; a litter of mechanical relics already rusting, from the bulldozers, trucks, and power shovels, whose work completed, had left this desolation."[31] The Appalachian Mountains, which formed the hills of Kentucky, became associated with an environmental nightmare. Americans were warned it might happen anywhere. Caudill warned

> of the coming devastation of the rest of the continent—the creation of an 'American Carthage, plowed and salted'—as millions of acres in the Mid- and Far West (especially Ohio, New Mexico, Arizona, Colorado, Montana, and Wyoming) fall before the blades of giant earth-destroying machines.[32]

Caudill was not alone in pointing out environmental issues. Activists throughout the nation decried pollution. Their voices did not go unheard. During the presidential terms of John F. Kennedy and Lyndon B. Johnson, the federal government became actively involved in environmental issues. As Duane Smith noted, "Even a brief survey of the enacted legislation gives a clear indication of its sweep and its impact on mining. The 1963 Clean Air Act awarded the federal government the enforcement power over air pollution."[33] This law was followed by the Water Quality Act of 1965; the Air Quality Act of 1967; and then during Richard Nixon's administration, the National Environment Policy Act (NEPA) of 1969, which was the most sweeping legislation to date. Signed into law in 1970, NEPA created the Environmental Protection Agency (EPA).[34] The purpose of the EPA was to protect America's land, water, air, and environmental quality. Coal companies cursed the act. Coal miners and construction workers sported bumper stickers in Wyoming and Colorado stating, "If you're hungry and out of work, eat an environmentalist." Strangely enough, the EPA and the environmental laws of the 1960s and early 1970s would create a boom for Wyoming's coal industry. Ironically, strip mining would be the principal means of extracting the fossil fuel.

The environmental legislation of the 1960s led to an awareness of problems facing America. "One nationwide problem which could no longer go unnoticed by lawmakers and other citizens was dirty, unhealthy air." It was not until 1967 that the importance of using low-sulfur coal was emphasized as one means of reducing air pollution. "The passage of the Clean Air Act of 1970, which mandated that coal-fired generating plants must assist in the effort to improve air quality, became the catalyst for action." Following this 1970 act, power plants were required to emit less ash, sulfur oxide, and nitrogen oxide. There were two options open to power plant operators: They could either build "scrubbers" to remove the ash, sulfur, and nitrogen, or they could burn coal low in sulfur. Scrubbers were expensive, "often representing 20 to 25 percent of the total cost" of producing electricity. Low-sulfur coal meant western coal. The sub-bituminous and lignite coal found in the West had always had difficulty competing with coal mined in the East. "[I]t produces approximately one-third fewer BTUs of heat than eastern coal, but it also produces much less sulfur oxide. Users were quick to realize that they could satisfy the Environmental Protection Agency and still pay the stockholders a respectable dividend by switching to western coal."[35] Almost overnight Wyoming coal gained an advantage over coal mined in the East. The environmentalists gave Wyoming's coal industry an economic shot in the arm.

Coal from Wyoming's Powder River Basin proved to be the principal source of low-sulfur fuel. While not the only source of coal shipped to power plants in the East, northeast Wyoming had the richest deposit of easily strippable coal. The year following the passage of the Air Quality Act of 1967, "78,000 acres of Campbell County coal lands were leased."[36] America, dependent on electricity for most of its amenities and necessities, needed a cheap source of clean-burning fuel. With coal-powered generating plants being the principal source of electricity, a nationwide market emerged. The Powder River Basin, with its vast underground coal deposits, provided the clean fuel America needed. As historian Robert Righter noted

> The largest unbroken concentration of coal in the United States is the remarkable Wyodak bed, centered in Campbell County, Wyoming. This bed penetrates the surface continuously along a line extending 120 miles at thicknesses ranging from 25 feet to 150 feet. To a depth of 200 feet, it contains an estimated 15 billion tons of strip mineable coal.... To a depth of 2000 feet, it contains perhaps 100 billion tons of coal.[37]

Also, coal from the Powder River Basin could be easily hauled over the Burlington Railroad to markets throughout the East.

Harry M. Caudill, in *My Land is Dying*, prophesied in 1971 the future demand for western coal. He claimed, "As the demand for coal goes up, the proportion obtained by stripping also rises." Caudill continued, "New power stations near sources of coal supplies may bring the strip mining boom to states like North Dakota, Montana, and Wyoming."[38] In retrospect, Caudill was farsighted. In 1970 Wyoming produced only 7,380,930 tons of coal. Although a decided increase over 1960 production, the industry still had not regained the stature enjoyed during World War II. Moreover, only 621 men were employed in coal mining. More men had been employed in 1957 than in 1970.[39] Yet there were those who could see what was coming. Arnold Miller, president of the UMW in 1973 warned, "The moral is simple, beware of industrialists bearing gifts. Fifty years ago they promised to develop Appalachia, and they left it in wreckage. Now they promise to develop the Northern Plains. They will leave in in ruins."[40] Wyoming was on the verge of its biggest mining boom in history.

The final push that returned the Wyoming coal industry to its dominating position in the state's economy came in the form of what has been called the Energy Crisis. In 1973 the nation was hard hit by an oil embargo imposed by the Organization of Petroleum Exporting Countries (OPEC) cartel. America had become too dependent on petroleum. Almost every American became "aware of our petroleum habit and its effect not only on

New technologies and the increasing population of the United States created a greater demand for electrical power. Coal-fired power plants provide one source of electricity. Power plants, such as Jim Bridger near Rock Springs, were constructed near mineable coal deposits to reduce the overall cost of electrical production.

our pocketbook, but on our national pride." Throughout the nation, people began to search for an energy source that would not make the United States dependent on foreign fuel sources. National pride mandated that America free itself from the whims of OPEC. Coal, in abundance throughout America, was one of the first energy sources the nation looked to to meet its needs. "We also began to realize, from the White House on down, that it had probably not been the wisest of policies to have phased out the use of coal, which was, after all, a still very abundant source of energy." Coal was seen as the "energy source to combat our oil dependency. As the nation began to focus anew on its reserves of coal, its vision turned westward."[41]

In the northern plains of the American West, particularly in the states of Wyoming, Montana, and North Dakota, "there could be found billions of tons of sub-bituminous coal."[42] When the environmental issue of clean air was followed by the need for cheaper energy sources, Wyoming coal became especially attractive. The power plants expanded or constructed near Glenrock, Kemmerer (1963), and later Rock Springs (1970) were forerunners of things to come. In 1970 unit trains were delivering low-sulfur coal from strip mines near Rock Springs, Hanna, and Sheridan to power plants in Iowa, Illinois, and Wisconsin. By the time the oil embargo hit America, Wyoming coal was being delivered to seventeen states.[43]

However, the state's production in 1973 was modest. Although coal output exceeded 14 million tons in 1973, it paled in comparison to the 102 million tons mined in 1981.[44] Wyoming was about to become, again, an energy frontier.

The Energy Frontier

People in the West had experienced booms throughout their history. The last coal boom had come during World War II when people were hurriedly moved to Sweetwater County. At that time, one of the most common forms of housing available for newcomers was boxcars. Temporary quarters for entire families, the boxcar was not a pleasant residence; but westerners tolerated it as part of prosperity. Temporary quarters and substandard living conditions were just part of the price one paid during booms. "Although the people of the West have had plenty of experience with boom towns, it is not at all surprising that when the booms of the 1960s and 1970s hit, Westerners were caught off guard."[45] When the boom exploded in the 1970s, Wyoming was ill prepared. The prosperity it had long desired came in a flood. And as in all floods, there was damage brought about by the rapidity with which it struck. For decades there had been tales of exploiting Wyoming's coal, natural gas, oil shale, and petroleum reserves. The promises of growth had come too often without results. Therefore, the promise of a new boom was met with "guarded skepticism, if not downright indifference." As Robert Righter noted, "After all, no shepherd boy can cry 'wolf' forever without losing some of his credibility. Nor could the region anticipate that the worth of uranium ore or the increased value of trona, oil, and gas would draw many corporations to this land of little rain."[46]

What Wyoming experienced in the 1970s "was nothing less than an invasion of a new frontier." Whole new communities were created and old ones doubled in size. The new frontier, as Righter described it, was properly called the energy frontier.

> But it was a corporate frontier. Apart from a brief period in the 1950s, when anyone with a geiger counter and a four-wheel drive truck could make a uranium strike, the individual has played a subservient role in this frontier. Coal mining had always been a corporate frontier. It takes capital—vast amounts of it—to play a part in the energy frontier.

Wyoming's coal industry had always been dominated by large companies. As in the days of the underground mines, individuals were needed to mine the coal; but the companies controlled where and when the effort took place. The federal government and Union Pacific were still the largest landowners in Wyoming, and they dictated where the new pioneers would live. They were not going to sell their land to a small family, not when there were bigger profits to be made in leasing the land to corporations. The individual could not compete in such a high stakes game. Yet "individuals were needed to explore for resources, to construct massive facilities, to provide transportation and services, and finally, to staff permanently the mines and plants."[47] With the federal government owning 48.1 percent of the land, there became a shortage of land on which to live, an unlikely situation for the least populated state in America.[48] Coal miners in the nineteenth century had sought to earn a better living through their own efforts. In coming to the coal fields of Wyoming, the coal miner of the last century had found the land owned by the coal company. The individual energy pioneers of the twentieth century had similar dreams of finding new opportunities, but the hoped for wealth would be funneled down to the miner by an energy corporation. Often the pioneer would lease a spot to park his or her trailer from an energy company. In some areas, privately owned trailer courts were available; but these spaces were quickly filled, and mobile home owners had to turn to their employers for a place to live. Some things had not changed since Union Pacific began building its company towns in the nineteenth century.

To the energy pioneers of the 1970s fell the tasks of building new power plants and opening new mines. The influx of people was rapid. "Services were taxed to the breaking point. Sewer and water systems proved inadequate, schools were overcrowded, and law enforcement agencies were understaffed and ill equipped to do their jobs. Social services were often nonexistent, and medical facilities were woefully inadequate. Craig, Colorado, and Rock Springs, Gillette, and Evanston, Wyoming, are a few of the towns that felt such impacts."[49] Almost simultaneously with the surge of employment in southwestern Wyoming's strip mines came an increase in trona markets. Added to this was a statewide oil boom.[50] "First Gillette and later Rock Springs resembled the 'Hell on Wheels' boom towns of the 1860s with their flimsy, temporary housing . . . and high incidence of vice and crime."[51] With the boom at their doorsteps, some Wyoming residents began remembering the problems of the past.

Corporations were going to prosper from the energy boom, but what about the state of Wyoming? Something had to be done. Even though most saw the coal resources of Wyoming as limitless, farsighted individuals knew that coal could be mined only once. It is a nonrenewable resource. Every ton of coal stripped from the ground by the present generation meant less coal available for future generations. People had seen coal companies come and go before. Possibly remembering the past booms that took coal from the ground and left empty caverns that collapsed, causing homes and streets to subside into the abandoned mines, the state legislature began to take notice.

Two questions were on the minds of many individuals in the 1970s: what to do when there was no more coal, and what to do when the boom ended. The long years of recession in the coal industry that followed World War II had taught the people of Wyoming a lesson. That lesson was once coal companies decided mining was no longer profitable, they left Wyoming. Often they left ugly scars on the land and unemployment. There was, moreover, an added problem. When the mines were working, funding schools and community services was shared by the corporations and by individuals through tax revenues. When the mines closed, the burden of operating schools and continuing social services fell to the

During the boom of the 1970s, one of the problems encountered was providing housing for a rapidly expanding population. Mobile homes were one answer to the housing shortage. (Courtesy of Val Brinkerhoff, Rock Springs)

government. With coal companies gone, there was not enough revenue to pay unemployment benefits and continue health services unless taxes were raised. Unemployed workers were unlikely targets for tax increases. The complex lesson learned from earlier booms was that after a coal mine closed, stresses and strains on the local economy were not easily addressed. More than one community had been left with hospitals or schools filled with patients or students with too little money left to operate the facilities. Problems arose when a city put in a new water system to accommodate growth only to find that before the system was paid for, a mine closed and entire portions of the town became vacant. One need only look at present-day Hanna, where trailer courts and homes lie empty, to witness the waste that results from a boom gone bust.

People in Wyoming knew how desperate a state could become when there were too few sources of revenue. Having a small population and a large land area, Wyoming could hope for little tax revenue to provide needed services. Consequently, the state decided to tax its underground wealth. A tax on its mineral resources might soften the blow of future economic downturns.

Severance Taxes

The idea of taxing coal was not a new concept. Several members of the state's Constitutional Convention in 1889 suggested a coal tax at a rate of one and a half cents a ton. Proponents argued a tax of this nature should become part of the State Constitution. The president of the convention, M. C. Brown, "warned that coal was subject to depletion and therefore ought to be taxed before the deposits were exhausted." Spokesmen from the coal industry opposed the tax and convinced the members of the convention to reject the tax. However, the constitution "did include provision for a production tax on minerals." But it would be years before the state legislature would tax coal.[52]

Predictably, coal companies would oppose coal taxes. During the downturn of the 1950s, representatives from the mineral exploration firms resisted any form of natural resource tax. In 1957 "representatives of mineral exploration concerns said today that a proposed natural resource tax act would 'place the hand of paralysis' on future development in Wyoming." Some companies issued veiled threats that they would not open new mines in Wyoming. A representative from Ohio Oil said a resource tax "would stop development of four or five additional wells in this state annually." In the 1950s, businesses and energy concerns alike opposed any legislation that suggested such a tax.[53] Using the old argument that taxes would hamper development, the coal industry closed mines in the 1950s, even though the state legislature followed this line of reasoning and failed to pass any meaningful tax on coal. Despite the argument that additional taxes would hurt the coal industry, mines were opened and closed not because of taxes, but because of economic realities elsewhere. When there were no markets, mines closed. Economics more than taxes dictated the energy industry.

Moves to tax Wyoming's natural resources were afoot throughout the 1950s and 1960s. But it would not be until 1969 that a severance tax would become part of Wyoming law. "The concept of a mineral severance tax is based on the fact that when a nonrenewable natural resource is removed from the earth, the value of that resource to the state is irretrievably lost. Therefore, the people of the state are justified in recapturing a portion of this lost value through an excise tax on the severance of the natural resource which is removed and sold for private profit." Eventually Wyomingites would view taxes on mineral development as a means of revenue and a way of offsetting, "the social and environmental costs imposed on the state due to mineral extraction."[54] Passing a tax on resources extracted from Wyoming was not easy. Powerful forces within the state, such as the mining and railroad lobby, were opposed to taxes on minerals. Yet, there is also a philosophy in the state that political scientists call a "libertarian thread . . . [that] makes the people suspicious of big government, big labor, and big business."[55] This skepticism might have contributed to the passing of a severance tax over the objections of the energy industry. By 1969, however, additional revenue was much needed, and Wyoming minerals seemed a good source.

In the late 1960s public pressure for a severance tax finally grew to a point that passage of such a bill became a reality. In 1967 a proposal for a severance tax on oil and gas was easily turned back in the state legislature. When the bill returned to the legislature in 1969, "pressure for a severance tax was so great that one percent had to be conceded." According to T. A. Larson in his *History of Wyoming*, the reason the tax passed in that year was because the "State government had to have more revenue and the alternatives, higher sales tax or an income tax, were even more dangerous politically."[56] The need for more revenue overrode some of Wyoming's more traditional ideas of not taxing private enterprise. When the oil crisis of the 1970s increased demand for Wyoming oil and coal, severance taxes would also increase.

When the coal rush of the 1970s struck, legislators decided the time to levy additional taxes on Wyoming energy resources had come. No longer could mining companies hope to remove Wyoming coal without paying for it. The 1973 State Legislature "raised the fossil fuels severance tax from 1 percent to 3 percent." In 1974, Wyoming amended its constitution to provide an excise tax on coal and created a permanent Wyoming mineral trust fund. The amendment to the State Constitution was approved in a general election held November 5, 1974, and "proclaimed in effect on December 12, 1974." The amendment stated, "The Legislature shall provide by law for an excise tax on the privilege of severing or extracting minerals, of one and one-half percent on the value of the gross product extracted. The minerals subject to such excise tax shall be coal, petroleum, natural gas, oil shale, and such other minerals as may be designated by the Legislature." The state's voters held that extracting minerals from Wyoming was a privilege. "In 1975 another 1 percent tax was added. Also in 1975, a special tax of .4 percent was added on coal." In the minds of some people, Wyoming was still not receiving the benefit of its natural resources. In 1976, "reports indicated that midwestern states which were using Wyoming coal took more revenue from the coal than Wyoming did." However, the severance taxes did generate revenue. In 1976 alone, over $40 million were provided to the state coffers, most of it coming from oil.[57] Perceiving that past taxes had not gone far enough in generating much needed revenue, the legislators moved once again to pass new taxes on coal.

Impacts on State and Local Government

Severance taxes would be levied against the coal industry at a steadily increasing rate throughout the 1970s. "Originally all minerals had a 1% severance tax rate. Over the years that rate grew to 10.5% for coal; 6% for oil and gas; 5.5% for trona and uranium; and 2% for all other minerals." From 1969 to 1973 the percentage rate was stable, but by 1979 the rate had jumped to 10.5 percent on coal. This jump in taxes coupled with increased production led to a windfall in revenues for the state. In 1975 the coal industry paid $1,095,230 in taxes; nine years later it paid $120,860,054. Statewide severance taxes levied on coal, oil, gas, and other minerals jumped from $18 million in 1975 to well over $380 million in 1984. This jump in revenue led to an expansion in state, county, and local governments never before seen in the state of Wyoming.[58] The coal industry played no small role in this statewide revolution.

The Wyoming legislature enacted special severance taxes on coal and other minerals to fund the expansion. "Trona, coal, and uranium are subject to a 1.5% tax which is deposited to the Capital Facilities Revenue

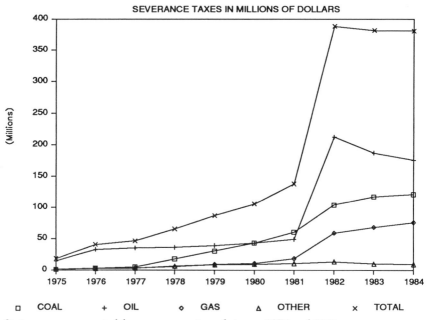

State revenue generated from severance taxes between 1975 and 1984.

Account. This revenue is distributed to community colleges (10%), and to local school districts (30%) for capital construction purposes and to the Highway Fund (60%)." Above this tax, coal has five additional severance taxes. "Revenue from a 1% tax is deposited to the State Highway Fund for construction and maintenance of the state highway system. Revenue from a 1.5% tax is earmarked for such Wyoming water development projects as the legislature deems feasible." Add to this a 2.5 percent tax to be deposited in the permanent Wyoming Mineral Trust Fund, a 2 percent Coal Impact tax, and a 2 percent tax that provides revenues to the General Fund, and coal production in 1978 was taxed at a rate of 10.5 percent.[59] The proceeds from the Permanent Mineral Trust Fund are placed in a permanent trust fund which is invested or loaned to political subdivisions of the state. All income generated from this fund is deposited annually in the general fund. In the boom towns of Wyoming, revenue was especially lacking in cases where municipalities were strained by a large influx of new workers and families. Some form of relief was needed. In 1979 additional relief came in the form of a tax on coal to help local and state governments provide financing for "water, sewer, highway, road, or street projects."[60] The coal industry was paying for a lion's share of Wyoming's expansion in the late 1970s and 1980s.

The funds from severance taxes were used to generate a veritable revolution in the size and function of state government. Funds went to such state agencies as the Wyoming Department of Environmental Quality (DEQ). Established by the legislature in 1973, DEQ was given the "authority to regulate air and water quality and mined-land reclamation."[61] To assist communities impacted by the energy boom, the legislature passed a series of bills that would help communities deal with increased demands for services. They included the Joint Powers Act (1974), the Coal Tax for Impact Assistance Act (1975), and the Community Development Authority Act (1975).[62] The net impact of this legislation was the enlargement of the state government's role in local communities. In providing funds for education and new highways, the state helped improve the quality of life in rural areas, but it also brought more state control into the lives of the people. Thankful for the economic assistance provided by severance taxes, many communities did not appreciate the state's increased presence in their lives. In the years from 1975 to 1984, Wyoming's government grew at an annual rate of 17 percent per year.[63] This growth was the result of an expanding energy industry.

In the 1980s, severance taxes would be the single largest source of state revenue. "In 1984, severance taxes on coal production were $121 million." The oil industry paid $175 million and the natural gas industry paid $75 million. "Of the $381 million severance taxes levied, 97 percent were attributable to coal, oil, and natural gas production." For the year 1984, roughly 57 percent of the revenue from severance taxes on coal came from Campbell County, while Sweetwater County generated 17 percent as the second highest coal producer in the state. By 1986, severance tax revenues were at $387,000,000, or 49 percent of the total tax revenues.[64] The state of Wyoming owes much to its energy industries.

A Different Kind of Boom

While the state was acting to generate revenue from its nonrenewable resources, the federal government moved to pass laws that provided additional protection to the environment. The laws came in a variety of forms including the Mineral Policy Act of 1970, the Threatened and Endangered Species Act of 1973, the Federal Land Policy and Management Act, and the National Park System Mining Regulation Act of 1976. All of these new laws directly affected and regulated mining activity.[65] As a result of the new laws, reclamation became an important part of mining. Preserving America's landscape was something no longer taken for granted.

Coal companies stripping away prairies and deserts would no longer be able to dump their waste wantonly across Wyoming. With the establishment of the Abandoned Mine Reclamation Fund in 1977, Congress levied a tax on coal that would be used to reclaim mining waste left by centuries of thoughtless mining practices throughout America.[66] It was a much needed reclamation. As West Virginia's Congressman Ken Hechler said,

> I have seen what havoc and obliteration are left in the wake of strip mining. It has ripped the guts out of our mountains, polluted our streams with acid and silt, uprooted our trees and forests, devastated the land, seriously disturbed or destroyed wild life habitat, left miles of ugly high walls ... and left a trail of utter despair for many honest and hard working people.[67]

America wanted no more Appalachias. Federal environmental laws passed by Washington in the 1970s were designed to try and prevent the wide open plains, mountains, and deserts of the West from becoming a wasteland. These laws would make the boom of the 1970s different from those that had come before.

Washington, in creating a whole new series of environmental laws, brought about a different type of boom; moreover, it brought a different type of individual into the western mining towns. The new laws, coupled with laws passed in the 1960s, required an Environmental Impact Statement (EIS) be prepared to document the effects that mining would have on the environment. To satisfy the requirements of the federal regulating agencies, sociologists, psychologists, and economists were called upon to determine the impact energy exploration would have on small communities. To determine the impact mining would have on the environment, archaeologists, soil scientists, wildlife biologists, water quality specialists, botanists, historians, and a host of other specially trained individuals were needed. Coupled with the need to hire environmentalists was a need to hire geologists, petroleum engineers, structural engineers, and technicians. Descending on Wyoming towns were women and men armed with newly won college degrees. Along with their lesser educated counterparts, they encountered the problems of inadequate housing, poor social services, and inadequate sewer systems. Many an archaeologist or soil scientist came to town to find they had to live in the back of their car until housing became available. Like their construction worker counterparts, the scientists of the 1970s found boom town living anything but convenient.

Ideally the environmentalists would come first, followed by construction workers and miners. But during the frenzied years following the energy crisis, things did not work ideally. There was a feeling that power plants, mines, and oil wells had to be put into operation as quickly as possible. The coal industry was on the verge of unparalleled expansion. Within ten years, coal production skyrocketed. In 1973, 14,840,857 tons of coal were mined. In 1979, 71,445,178 tons of Wyoming coal came from the earth.[68] The need for Wyoming coal had reached an all-time high, and the strip mines had made it possible to meet the demand. With the push to achieve unparalleled production, miners, merchants, environmentalists, and construction workers descended on towns overnight.

In addition to opening mines, rail spurs, loading facilities, repair shops, and offices needed to be constructed. Enticed by jobs paying from $8 to $18 an hour, women and men alike came to Gillette, Hanna, and Rock Springs. Changing jobs and moving west was a good investment in the future. America needed energy; opportunity for a better life lay in the West. The best part about the new boom was that in your car or truck, within days you could be where jobs were seemingly unlimited. Quickly the newcomers learned what the '49ers in the California Gold Rush had learned: while wages were high, so were prices. The promise of easy money accompanied by a high cost of living were part of any new frontier.

The reality of what the boom actually meant began slowly to sink in. At Gillette, located amidst the Powder River coal fields, the reality of the boom became apparent early in the 1970s. "According to the U.S. Department of Housing and Urban Development, a growth rate of 10 percent per year for a small community begins to strain local service capabilities, [a growth rate] above 15 percent begins to break down the service delivery system." In the 1970s, Wyoming communities exceeded this 15 percent growth rate.[69] The strain on towns, such as Gillette, taxed all segments of society. Red light districts and drug and alcohol abuse were common in many boom towns. People problems, as they were called, resulted in "alcohol abuse, child abuse and neglect, depression, loneliness," and a host of other maladies.[70] The boom invigorated Wyoming's economy but left numerous individuals scrambling for places to live and searching for solutions to problems created by the boom.

The trailer house provided the quickest solution to housing shortages. Being portable, they were easily set up and provided a modest amount of comfort. Washing machines, dryers, refrigerators, radios, and televisions were common. All one had to do was park the house trailer and hook up water, sewer, and electricity. Sizes varied, but a 60 x 14 foot trailer house contained two bedrooms, a bath, a kitchen, and a living room. On the surface, the mobile home seemed a model of efficiency and comfort. The new pioneers were, after all, soft twentieth-century folk with a need for

creature comforts. But looks were deceiving. Because they were aluminum and thin walled, wind whipped through the cracks in the trailers.
Insulation was often inadequate. The cold, biting wind went directly from
the surface to the inside of the trailer. During the winter it was not
uncommon for furnaces to run all night. Sometimes the wind would blow
out pilot lights, and the owners of the trailer would awake to find water
and sewer lines frozen. Even when things were going well, frozen
plumbing was commonplace. Wind battering the trailers and rippling the
aluminum, coupled with the cold, made trailers less than comfortable.

As researchers began taking stock of what the boom actually meant, one
of the things they pointed out was the poor living conditions found in
trailer towns. Social workers writing about problems in Wyoming boom
towns noted, "Trailers are rarely of adequate size; there is a perpetual fog
of dirt. In trailer parks, there is a scarcity of transportation which increases
isolation, and there are few playgrounds making it necessary for mothers
to remain home with their children."[71] In April 1974, Jane P. Sterba
reported

> Gillette, Wyoming, is a raw jumble of rutted streets and sprawling junkyards,
> red mud and dust, dirty trucks and crowded bars, faded billboards and
> sagging utility lines, and block after block of house trailers squatting in the
> dirt like a nest of giant grubs.[72]

The trailer was maligned not because of its appearance but because it was
usually ill suited for dusty, windy, and cold environments.

The coal boom in Gillette, Wyoming, followed on the heels of an oil
boom. The town grew too rapidly. The *New York Times* held that 42 percent
of Gillette's population lived in trailers in 1974. The *Times* reported,
"Massive typically unplanned mobile home parks spring up.... Even
if these parks are zoned to be off by themselves they create aluminum
ghettos." Some of the trailer parks were well planned and were attractive
places to live. However, "at worst, mobile home squatters form sprawling
colonies often lacking water and sanitation. In some cases, families are
forced to live in tents, even into the Wyoming Winter."[73] Living in tents,
camper trailers, trucks, or cars was not uncommon. It created problems of
major proportions. Without revenue, towns like Gillette could not hope to
meet the problems created by rapid growth. Revenues entering the city
treasury did not come in as fast as the people. Human services could not
keep pace with changing demands. One county nurse claimed, "I never
saw so many depressed young mothers. They just hibernate in these
trailers. They get cabin fever. They hardly ever meet the people living next
door."[74] It was not uncommon to find isolation in trailer towns. Isolation

Mobile and modular housing were also employed as quarters for many single men. Large modular units were subdivided into small one- and two-room quarters. This type of housing was operated by both private enterprise and the energy companies. (Courtesy of Val Brinkerhoff, Rock Springs)

grew out of a host of reasons sociologists call Boom Town Bifurcation.[75] Moving into a new town and a new environment, people commonly felt isolated. The trailer became the focal point. People became dissatisfied with living conditions. Some stayed only days, others only a few weeks. Some did not give the town a chance. One engineer for a coal company said, "I know some guys who brought their wives up to look for a place to live, and the wives wouldn't even get out of the car."[76] There were, however, those who stayed. In 1974 the coal boom in Gillette was just beginning.

Across the state in Rock Springs the coal boom was in full swing. Like Gillette, the trailer house was the first home for many moving to southwest Wyoming. Trailer parks were built overnight in the high desert. Dust was everywhere. Poet Barbara Smith, in the late 1970s, found Rock Springs surrounded by newly bladed trailer courts. In her poem "Sisters," she captures the essence of the situation.

The wind blew down the valley from Green River
in the afternoon
about 2:30.
She looked at the clock,
the usual time.
The dust sifted in through the sliding glass doors,
lingered a bit in the air, settled softly down to rest.
She wiped the top of the dishwasher
and thought of other women.
Back then, when the wind blew, what did they dust?
The shelf on the side that served as a cupboard?
The hand-made table?
The dirt floor?
What did they dust, those women?
She remembered pictures of pale, wisp-blonde women,
not-yet-grandmothers, homesteading, standing by the sod
with aprons blowing in the wind.
Hair twisted in a knot, arms folded tight under their breasts,
bellies big under full skirts, as usual, they stood tall.
She bent over to pick up a toy
the baby pushed back hard under her ribs
a strand of fine hair fell across her face.
She remembered a story told often when she was young.
Two pioneer women would dance together
around and around their kitchen when they visited.
They danced twice in five years;
they saw no one.
What did those women do when the men were gone in the fields
and the wind came every day at 2:30?
She sat down at the table by the sliding glass door
and watched a dust squall whirl its way into the subdivision.
She didn't know her neighbor.
She wondered, did she dance?
She drove off every day in her new car.
Some pioneer women took laudanum for headaches.
Some died in the long afternoon.
Some waited five years to dance together and dream.
Sisters, she thought, we're sisters.[77]

There were common features in the booms of the nineteenth century and
the booms of the twentieth century. There was the dust. There were the
discomforts of living in dugouts, company houses, boxcars, and trailers. In
each case the housing was substandard by the standards of the day. There
was a tie between the building of the company town of Wright on the
energy frontier of northeast Wyoming and the building of Carbon in

southern Wyoming in 1868. The tie was a long ribbon of steel that carried coal eastward or westward on the railroads, but always out of the state of Wyoming. Coal might go to electric power plants in Wyoming, but the majority of the electricity these plants generated was transported to other states. Wyoming energy went elsewhere. Only when coal was transported out of state was it profitable to mine. Large corporations owned by people living outside Wyoming sold the state's energy resources. Like Union Pacific controlled from Boston, New York, or Omaha in the 1800s, in the 1970s and 1980s Wyoming was mined by AMAX, Peter Kiewit, and NERCO, all companies with corporate headquarters outside the state. The pioneers of the Energy Frontier were, as the poem suggested, truly sisters and brothers of the coal miners of the last century.

There were differences, of course; televisions, microwaves, and 4 x 4 pickups were something a Welsh miner in Rock Springs would never have dreamed of in the 1800s. However, the principal difference between the miners of the nineteenth century and those of the late twentieth century came in how coal was mined. Strip mining had revolutionized the industry. In minutes miners could extract more coal than the historic producers had mined in months. With shovels capable of holding dump trucks, drag lines could strip off overburden with ease. Underneath the overburden, especially in the Powder River Basin, were thick seams of coal. From the mine to the railroad car the process was simplified. Once the mine facilities had been constructed, few miners were needed to operate the mine. As a result, production per person skyrocketed in the twentieth century. In 1888 Wyoming miners mined 602 tons of coal apiece; in 1974 that amount was 14,635 tons per mine employee.[78]

Labor Relations

The years of the 1970s energy boom were rarely quiet. With prosperity once again returning to the coal industry, miners wanted better wages. When negotiations between management and labor failed, men walked off the job. In January of 1975, forty-four miners were arrested near Hanna. "Carbon County attorney, Oscar Hull said the arrests came after officers repeatedly warned the picketers to disband. When they refused, officers began firing tear gas." The pickets were set up on Rosebud Coal Company land, according to the reports. Since none of the miners were Rosebud employees, according to the coal company, they had no reason to picket its mine. The picketers were handcuffed and bused to the State Penitentiary in Rawlins. Violence spread as, "Vehicles driven by three supervisors had their windows and mirrors smashed at the Rosebud mine."[79]

The strike at Hanna flared over the issue of which union would represent the Rosebud coal miners. The United Mine Workers (UMW; previously UMWA) had been replaced by the Progressive Mine Workers (PMW). Peter Kiewit and Sons Inc. owned the Rosebud mine at Hanna. It also owned the Big Horn Coal Company mine in Sheridan and the Decker Coal Company mines at Decker, Montana. In early 1975, all of its mines were picketed by the UMW. In January 1975, both the Rosebud and Decker mines had UMW picketers outside their gates. At Decker violence flared when members of the PMW, who worked in the Decker strip mine, began throwing rocks at the UMW picketers. As a result, the Decker mine closed.[80] In Wyoming, Governor Ed Herschler promised to use the State Patrol at Hanna if the situation warranted it. This promise came "on the heels of allegations by a UMW official that Highway Patrol men had 'hit, kicked, and stomped on the backs of those arrested.'"[81] On January 14 union leaders claimed, "50 heavily armed patrolmen appeared. The patrolmen aimed their guns at the picketers and told them they had 15 minutes to get out of the county." Union leaders alleged that once "the 15 minutes was up the patrolmen began firing tear gas canisters at the [picket] lines." In Hanna the strike began to take on nasty overtones. Jim Marketti of Denver, the western regional director and organizer of the UMW, warned, "If the governor and Kiewit think they can bloody the heads of coal miners, let them try. . . . But the blood will be on their hands."[82] By January 22, in spite of pickets, the workers at the Rosebud mines returned to work. This resumption of work came as a result of an agreement between UMW attorneys and Peter Kiewit lawyers.[83]

Meanwhile at Sheridan, UMW strikers remained on the picket lines. But the strike north of Sheridan was considerably more calm than that at Hanna. This was due in part to the fact that two unions were not fighting against each other. Cooler heads prevailed in Sheridan. On February 14, 1975, pickets were removed from the road to the Big Horn mine. The company, however, wishing to push the issue, chose to use supervisors to haul coal from the mine.[84] This flew in the face of union organizers, and the union decided to return to the picket line.

Those who operated big equipment in the strip mines were well trained. It took experience to operate a drag line, and the operators were well paid. Bulldozer, belly dump, and grader operators were equally well paid, but there were still labor tensions. In 1975 workers at the Big Horn Coal mine north of Sheridan walked out. Tensions mounted as the company and the UMW could not reach an agreement. For sixty-four days the strike continued. This was a different breed of miner. Like their nineteenth-century counterparts, they were tough, and determined; but they were also better educated, and they waged the strike in a sophisticated fashion.

Homer Alley, the union steward for the Sheridan local, gave his impression of the strike.

[T]his is where I learned that these people could stand up to a big company if they did it lawfully. I had gotten to know Bill Johnson real well, the local sheriff. [He was] a Republican, but still a real good man. I knew that the company was going to try to pull some real fast legal maneuvers on us, so I talked to Bill several times and said, 'Bill, now I don't want any violence with those men. I want you there when we call you immediately,' and Bill agreed to this. We had been up on a portion of the old Highway 87 with our picket line, which was still a county road and was running through the mine. I was told by the union to stay off mine property with our picket line. But when we found out through an early morning call that the company was going to start hauling coal with supervisors, I said, 'Let's get down to that gate immediately,' on company property. . . . We agreed that we would let Bill Johnson come out and arrest us. But when he did arrest us, we would go to his jail. We weren't going to defy the law, we were going to work with the law. So I talked to Bill on the telephone. He said, 'Homer, what in the world am I going to do with these 80 people. My jail's not big enough.' I said, 'Bill, just tell them what you want them to do and they'll do it.' He went down on the picket line . . . all good American citizens, all good community citizens . . . every one of these people are good people. Bill said, 'I hate to arrest people like this, but I have no alternative.' I said, tell them what you want them to do. [S]o he says to the men, 'I'm going to arrest you.' So they put an American flag on one car up front. Bill led the whole group into Sheridan. No way in the world he could put them in his jail, but we went through all the process of putting the money up to bail them out. We proved right then and there to the community that we're not going to use a pick handle and we're not going to use a picket line unless it's legal. I think we won the hearts of our community right then and there because we were community people and good law-abiding citizens. During that strike, Linda [Linn, a reporter] would come out on that picket line . . . and we're dressed in our greasy clothes and our old helmet liners, and we're all looking pretty cruddy. Well, we're just coal miners. We came to court . . . and I never will forget this . . . Linda says [jokingly], 'Well, you look like real people.' Well, we are real people. These people are pillars of the community in the labor world. Every one of these young people and the older ones are substantial people in their churches and in their rod and gun clubs and in their community affairs. Therefore, we established the fact that we could do this legally, and we won legally that time, I thought, a good contract.[85]

Strikes are always emotional events. Jobs and livelihoods are at stake. There were diverse viewpoints and different sides to the story. Homer Alley presented his particular viewpoint well, but within his story are germs of change and fact. Linda Linn, who reported the strike, reflected back over the event and stated that "indeed miners were the hard working backbone of the community."[86] Historically, coal mining communities were led by miners. Coal companies might have managed the town, but miners were the heart and soul. They cared about what happened in their towns. As the miners became better trained and better educated, their view of the world changed. They understood the energy crisis and nationwide issues. Television and radio brought the news quickly to their isolated communities. Unlike the historic coal camp where they were lucky to have one newspaper, the national news media made them aware of critical issues and different sides of those issues. The miners on strike in 1975 were better educated and more aware of the law. They strove to change things through protest and legal channels. Indeed, it was called a strike, but miners had learned from protesters in the 1960s to involve the media and attorneys in attempting to gain what they wanted. The Hanna strike represented the old way, the Sheridan strike the new. At least in Sheridan in 1975 it became apparent that more could be gained with attorneys and with community support than could be gained on the picket line alone.

The picket line was changing. Throughout Wyoming the PMW and the UMW attempted to gain members. Wyoming was no longer strictly a UMW state. In 1975 some observers forecast that the UMW's future was not bright. Gillette was seen as one of the battlegrounds that would determine the UMW's future. At Gillette, eleven mining firms owned land and were opening offices. One of these firms was AMAX Coal Company, which began shipping coal from its Belle Ayre mine in 1973. AMAX did not mind paying UMW wages, but it did not want to be forced to let UMW have jurisdiction over the new mines it opened in the West. Furthermore, AMAX "no longer wanted to pay royalties to the union's welfare and retirement fund." UMW officials in 1975 felt "the western campaign [to be] one of the toughest fights in the union's 85-year history." The UMW understood that if the future followed current trends, the West would take the lead in coal production. Part of UMW's fight centered around Gillette's Belle Ayre mine. While Hanna and Sheridan miners manned the picket lines, the Belle Ayre miners also walked out. The AMAX workers went on strike on January 12. By July 1, 1975, the strike had still not been settled. Since wages were not an issue, the ranks broke. Twenty-eight miners returned to work in the spring; twenty-six remained on the picket line. The papers reported, "Day after day the remaining 26 sit in mud spattered pickup trucks at the mine entrance gates watched by mine entrance security guards hired by AMAX. Despite the picketing the mine is again producing coal."[87] Fewer men were needed to produce coal at strip mines, and AMAX was showing how few were actually needed.

Profits were there for the making. "Strip mining in the West is highly profitable," most businessmen contended. The Belle Ayre mine, which produced 3.3 million tons of coal in 1974, was forecast to mine 30 million tons by 1979. The projected output of 19 million tons annually made the Belle Ayre mine worth "3.2 billion dollars, according to industrial figures."[88] With sales guaranteed to utilities under long-term contracts, AMAX was anxious to avoid disruptions caused by "wildcat strikes" and labor disruptions common in the eastern coal fields. To avoid these disruptions, AMAX did not want the UMW to gain strength in its Wyoming mines. More important, as the UMW so aptly pointed out, "companies are more interested in keeping profits high by avoiding the union's welfare and retirement fund, financed by royalties on each ton of coal mined." This was the crux of the matter. According to newspaper reports in 1975, "A [single] strip miner in the West produces an average of 100 tons of coal daily, compared with an average of 11 tons a day for an underground miner." Western coal mining companies argued that they should not have to pay the union benefit funds and subsidize the less productive eastern coal mines. Since the retirement fund was paid for by the ton, western mines would be paying the bulk of the UMW benefits. For this reason, companies even encouraged competing unions to organize in their mines. "Competing unions, such as the Operating Engineers and the Progressive Mine Workers, [held] some contracts that provided wages similar to those won by the UMW. However, they have no welfare retirement funds and thus meet less resistance from the operators."[89] Under the expansive coal boom of the 1970s, the UMW lost ground.

In Summary

The coal boom of the 1970s and early 1980s provided an air of excitement to an industry that had waned in the 1950s and early 1960s. The boom brought an upswing in production unparalleled in history. In 1975 the United States Geological Survey estimated that the United States contained just under 4 trillion tons of coal. It was estimated Wyoming contained 936 billion tons, or roughly one-fourth of all America's known coal reserves. Wyoming ranked first in total coal resource reserves. Of that amount, it was estimated that 31 billion tons could be strip mined.[90] Between 1973 and 1983, 681,851,449 tons of coal were mined. In all the years prior to 1973 only 461,084,934 tons of coal had been extracted from Wyoming mines. In 1983 alone, 112,187,874 tons were taken from the earth. Each miner in Wyoming in 1983 extracted 20,772 tons of coal on the average.[91] The boom of the early 1980s has slowed considerably, but

Wyoming's energy resources still loom high as a part of the state's net wealth. In 1986 the state's gross product stood at $8.5 billion. Of that amount, mining accounted for $2.16 billion. This was down from Wyoming's all-time high in 1981 of $9.755 billion, of which mining accounted for $4.204 billion.[92] As was true historically, in the 1970s and 1980s a lion's share of the state's wealth came from coal mining.

Between 1981 and 1987 Wyoming witnessed a sharp economic decline growing out of a decreased demand for its energy resources. In the coal industry this bust, or downturn, came in the form of layoffs, not necessarily in the form of decreased production. In 1981, 6231 people were employed in coal mining, this decreased to 5401 in 1983. Yet during the same time period, production increased by more than 17 million tons. Large strip mining equipment and improved haulage allowed these layoffs to take place without reducing output. Not until 1986 would coal production drop.[93] It was not the first time that the industry had witnessed a downturn, but in comparison to past recessions, the coal industry in Wyoming was still relatively strong. In fact, while oil output diminished by 3.9 million barrels between 1982 and 1983, in the same period coal production increased by 5.5 million tons.[94] This increase was more than the entire output of all Wyoming mines as recently as 1969. However, the fact remains that people lost jobs. Layoffs once again became part of coal mining.

While the coal industry witnessed a modest downturn, the oil industry in Wyoming took a nosedive. The 1980s brought with it a depressed market for Wyoming petroleum products. The per-barrel prices for crude oil plummeted. New fuel-efficient automobiles, coupled with OPEC's failure to keep prices high, resulted in decreased demand and an increased use of foreign oil to supply the nation's needs. The decreased demand affected Wyoming deeply. Because prices dropped, the assessed value of oil fell by over $5 per barrel.[95] Counties dependent on oil revenues for the tax income felt the pinch immediately. Once oil rigs drilling new wells dotted most of Wyoming. With oil prices plummeting, the oil rigs came down and jobs were lost. As a result, there was an outward migration of families whose source of income had been the oil industry. The coal industry would also witness a decline in production in 1986, but unlike the oil industry its markets were more stable and quickly rebounded.

During the 1980s public utility companies continued to use Wyoming coal for generating electricity, and some eastern utilities gave Wyoming coal companies long-term contracts for their fuel. Low-sulfur coal was still needed, and the contracts from utility companies helped stabilize the industry. The appetite for Wyoming coal, while somewhat diminished in the mid-1980s, was still strong. Eastern utilities wanted the black fossil fuel. Slowly output from mines in northern Wyoming increased, and by 1989 the demand for Wyoming coal would propel it to a point where the state held the distinction of being America's number one coal producer. The coal industry had weathered a storm and provided jobs and revenue for a state hard hit by recession and declining revenues.

The Future of Wyoming Coal

Predicting the future of the Wyoming coal industry is problematic at best and falls under the category of predicting Wyoming's weather, something old-timers warn is best left to fools and newcomers. There are too many unknowns. Yet there are some historic trends that seem to set the present stage and will more than likely affect the future.

With almost a fourth of the nation's coal reserves, it appears that the coal industry will be important as long as anyone in America mines coal. But the past shows us that the coal market might weaken and Wyoming residents would again lose jobs, as occurred in the 1950s. Not only would the loss of jobs be devastating, but because the state government is so dependent on severance taxes for operating funds, a downturn similar to the one witnessed in the 1950s would be catastrophic to the state's well-being.

But for the moment, Wyoming is flush with pride knowing that in 1989 the state was the leading producer of coal. If Wyoming's clean, low-sulfur coal is the only source of fuel that can be burned cheaply enough to ensure that clean air standards are met, the present trend will continue. However, there is an ongoing search for cleaner, cheaper fuel. What happens when coal is no longer an attractive fossil fuel? Knowing that booms and busts are common in the mining industry, preparations for downturns should be made before they occur. Busts as well as booms disrupt people's lives. Continually dismantling and building new towns or communities to accommodate the immediate market is too painful to people who choose to make Wyoming home. As some political scientists contend:

> The most recent conditions as throughout the history of Wyoming, reveal a constant struggle with the limitations created by the environment, an economic system tied to outside markets and manipulators over which Wyoming has no control, and a population of rugged individuals who through no desire of their own, have often unwittingly been at the mercy of decision-making beyond Wyoming's borders.[96]

Indeed some plans have been made for the future. The Permanent Wyoming Mineral Trust Fund stands as an example of state legislators understanding that one day the energy resources will be gone. Coal is currently a bright spot in the state's economy, but will the market for low-sulfur coal always be strong? Will new environmental laws make Wyoming coal more attractive to consumers outside the state in the future?

While future markets for Wyoming coal might be an unknown, there are certain things that are known. Wyoming needs to keep in mind it has vast deposits of coal. That is a proven fact. Buried underground, it lies in the best bank vault ever built. The deposits are there for the present and the future. If prices for the state's birthright go down, it might be best to just leave the wealth buried waiting for a better day. Writers of old always warned not to sell a birthright cheaply. Once the coal is mined, there is no way to redeposit the wealth. We are keepers of a trust, one that can ensure that future generations experience a good life in Wyoming. While the state might never be able to control the markets outside its borders, it can certainly control what it does with its resources. Wisdom is needed to ensure the future is as bright or brighter than the past. Wisely managing our coal reserves is one of the best ways of ensuring a better tomorrow.

While markets are uncertain, one mining trend that has remained constant in Wyoming is the tendency to increasingly mechanize the coal industry. Currently, strip mining has greatly reduced the number of people needed to extract coal. Changes are constantly being made that save labor and reduce the number of workers needed in mines and in the transporting of coal to market. One need only look at the railroads in Wyoming to see how quickly men are replaced by machines. In 1980 the trains that hauled coal out of the state had cabooses managed by two men inside. Today, most trains have no cabooses. A mechanical device has replaced the men and the caboose. Machines and mining have become synonymous.

Perhaps one day mining will be done completely by machines. Mechanics and technicians will repair futuristic equipment, and the sound of men cursing mules and dust-filled caverns will be forgotten. Yet even the technology used to power these machines will owe a debt to the solitary miner who labored underground. They began the process of laboring to fire furnaces that powered the iron and steel mills making the Industrial Revolution possible. They also initiated technological changes that led to mechanization underground. In essence, miners paved the way to the future. Wyoming's future probably lies in mining, but it is women and men of the past that made this future possible.

A lot of quaint sayings have evolved from coal mining. Some have become part of folklore, and it is difficult to know exactly where truth ends and fiction begins. One old saying attributed to West Virginia coal miners holds "Tough times don't last, but tough people do." Whether or not this saying came from West Virginian coal miners is hard to know, but there is a ring of truth in the statement. In the 1970s more Wyoming women began working in the mines as coal miners. They played an increasingly important role in Wyoming's mines. Initially they were scoffed at and even abused by their male counterparts, but slowly they were accepted. They lasted. This is the case throughout the history of Wyoming. Miners came to Carbon but were later forced to move to Hanna. In the 1950s when the mines closed in Rock Springs, miners took jobs in the trona mines. People were forced to move because they lost their jobs, but many decided that in moving they should not leave Wyoming. They knew something about the land and were willing to stay. In sticking with it, they were determined to last.

These hardy individuals knew that coal mining fortunes go up and down, but being miners, they knew that while people move, the coal stays buried underground until someone digs it out. The land and its resources endure. Underlying the vast openness of Wyoming is coal. Howard Stansbury noted coal in 1850; children playing in the backyards of Rock Springs today still bring coal home. Rock Springs children care little that this black nugget excited railroad investors in the 1860s and 1870s, yet they are touching something that has made Wyoming what it is today. Buried underground, the coal awaits the next boom or the next market. Wyoming's coal reserves are vast. What the downturn of the 1980s has shown is that booms come and go, but the prairies and basins endure. The wealth of Wyoming remains buried underneath the land in spite of the passing of time.

Threatening often that they would leave if coal was taxed, corporations still mine coal even though severance taxes are part of the industry in Wyoming today. Wyoming knows what those who did not leave Rock Springs and Sheridan in the 1950s and 1960s knew—one day someone is going to want the coal. The taxes serve as a way of promising future generations that once the coal is gone there will still be opportunities in Wyoming. Now that mining operators are required to reclaim their waste piles, future generations will also know what wide open spaces are. Neil Morgan observed in 1963, "Except for Alaska there is no American state on which the passage of time and man has left so small an imprint as Wyoming."[97] Some things have changed since 1963, but Wyoming remains largely untouched. The future will determine which direction mining will take, but in the 1970s Wyoming temporarily warded off becoming another Appalachia. The boom did go bust temporarily, but Wyoming remained intact, a land where the myth that the cowboy is king can continue because, indeed, the land is still spacious and uncluttered. But the truth is mining is king. In 1986 mining generated 25 percent of the state's gross product, agriculture only 2 percent.[98] And in 1989 Wyoming became the nation's leading coal producing state. For the first time in American history, a state west of the Mississippi is the leading coal producer. It is also a milestone in that the least populous state is the leading producer of one of America's most important energy resources.

Wyoming coal mining history has been dominated by large coal mining companies. From the opening of the first mine to the building of the Dave Johnston power plant, large amounts of capital were needed. But, these companies could never have opened and operated their mines without people. From the British miner in the 1860s to the women miners who came from the Midwest seeking jobs in the 1970s, it was people who lived in Wyoming that made mining ventures a success. Homer Alley, in describing the strikers in 1975 said, "They were good people."[99]

Friendly and resourceful, the Wyoming miners and their families are tied together with a heritage of making it through boom and bust. Mary Wolney, in describing her life, stated

> It was pretty difficult because you didn't have any money at all, hardly . . .
> a few cents. We hauled our own coal from my dad's homestead. In the fall
> we would go up and help dad dig and then haul the coal and fill up sheds for
> the whole winter use. Even [today], we live in Ranchester now, John and I
> dig . . . our own coal.[100]

"Tough times don't last, tough people do."

Notes

[1] Homer Alley, interview with author, Dayton, Wyoming, July 1987 (Ms. on file, Archaeological Services of Western Wyoming College, Rock Springs), 19.

[2] John Wolney, interview with author, Sheridan, Wyoming, July 1987 (Ms. on file, Archaeological Services of Western Wyoming College, Rock Springs), 41-42.

[3] Ibid.

[4] Ibid., 35.

[5] *State Coal Mine Inspector's Report 1953*, 16. (All state coal mine inspector reports are on file, Wyoming State Archives, Cheyenne.)

[6] Ibid., 7.

[7] *The Union Pacific Coal Company Code of Standards, To Govern Safety Work, Including Construction and Operation.* First issued July 15, 1925, last revision January

1, 1954. (Ms. on file, Archaeological Services of Western Wyoming College, Rock Springs), 4. The *Code of Standards* also states, "This company wants the friends and relatives of employees in the service, but the greatest kindness an official can do those who are related to him is to give them a chance to develop their worth under some other official of the company. Many poor men are kept in position throughout the industrial world by favoritism, and an equally large number of good men are handicapped, their independence and initiative destroyed by working for their relatives. As the sons of employees and officials grow up, opportunity for service should be given them under men who will be free to judge them on merit alone."

[8] *The Rock Springs Daily Rocket*, February 11, 1953.

[9] *The Rock Springs Miner*, March 1, 1953.

[10] Ibid., February 2, 1954.

[11] *The Rock Springs Daily Rocket*, January 16, 1954.

[12] Ibid., February 27, 1954.

[13] Ibid., January 23, 1954.

[14] Frank Dernovich, Mike Duzik, Eugene Paoli, Norma Paoli, Antone Pivik, and Amy Pivik. Interview with author, Rock Springs, Wyoming, 1984 (Ms. on file, Archaeological Services of Western Wyoming College, Rock Springs), 35.

[15] *Wyoming Coal Mining and Wage Employment Survey 1982* (Cheyenne: Wyoming Department of Labor Statistics), 6.

[16] Ibid., *State Coal Mine Inspector's Report 1954*, 7; Robert H. Brown, *Wyoming, A Geography* (Boulder, Colorado: Westview Press, 1980), 259-254.

[17] *The Rock Springs Miner*, February 22, 1957. Information on number of mines operating available in *State Coal Mine Inspector's Report* 1945-1958.

[18] The February 22, 1957, *Rock Springs Miner* states that 190 men were laid off at Stansbury. Some of these were apparently transferred to Superior. The October 10 issue of the *Miner* states "150 men are being laid off as of October 13, 1957." The difficulty arises in determining how many Stansbury miners went to Superior and were subsequently laid off. The October 9 issue states, "all the men transferred to Superior when Stansbury closed . . . as well as 67 regular Superior miners" will be laid off. However, the October 9 issue only lists 100 layoffs. The figure given by the coal company in the October 10 issue of the *Miner* was 150 men; adding 150 to 190 gives the 340 figure. Some of the men lost their jobs at two different mines.

[19] *State Coal Mine Inspector's Report* 1889-1957.

[20] *The Rock Springs Daily Rocket*, April 1, 1962.

[21] *The Rock Springs Daily Rocket*, August 28, 1962.

[22] R. A. LeMassena, *Articulated Steam Locomotives of North America*, vol. 1 (Silverton, Colorado: Sundance Books, 1979), 114. The last steam engine in regular service on the Union Pacific mainline was a 4-8-8-4 Big Boy. It made its final run in the spring of 1959.

[23] Sol Williams, interview with Margie Krza, Superior, Wyoming, April 1982 (Ms. on file, Archaeological Services of Western Wyoming College, Rock Springs), 13.

[24] Joseph Stipanovich, *The South Slavs in Utah: A Social History* (Saratoga, California: R. and E. Research Associates, 1975), 25-27. "In Slovenia the Zadruga,

or extended family commune, had once been common to all the South Slavs. Males were not allowed to leave permanently. Women could leave only to marry. A rise in population and a lack of opportunities led to the break-up of the Zadruga as migration to urban centers and later to the United States began to grow in the nineteenth century. The traditional pattern was to live in one place amongst your family for your entire life."

[25] Larson, *Wyoming A History*, (New York: W. W. Norton, Inc.: 1984), 143.

[26] Paul Krza, *Casper Star Tribune*, September 10, 1984.

[27] Robert A. Divine, T. H. Breen, George M. Fredrickson, and R. Hal Williams, *America Past and Present*, vol. 2 (Glenview, Illinois: Scott Foresman and Company, 1987), 840.

[28] *State Coal Mine Inspector's Report 1965*, 4.

[29] *State Coal Mine Inspector's Report 1959*, 16.

[30] Duane Smith, *Mining America, The Industry and the Environment 1800-1980*, (Lawrence: University of Kansas, 1987), 137.

[31] Harry M. Caudill, *My Land is Dying*, (New York: E. P. Dutton and Company, 1971), 18.

[32] Ibid.

[33] Smith, *Mining America*, 136.

[34] Ibid.

[35] Robert W. Righter, *The Making of a Town, Wright, Wyoming* (Boulder, Colorado: Roberts Rinehart, 1985), 17-18.

[36] Ibid., 17.

[37] Ibid., 14.

[38] Caudill, *My Land is Dying*, 129-130.

[39] *State Coal Mine Inspector's Report 1945-1970*.

[40] Smith, *Mining America*, 140. Originally written by Arnold Miller, "The Energy Crisis as a Coal Miner Sees It," *Center Magazine* (Nov.-Dec. 1973): 33-45.

[41] Righter, *The Making of a Town*, 13.

[42] Ibid.

[43] Larson, *Wyoming, A History*, 162.

[44] *Wyoming Coal Mining and Wage Employment Survey 1984* (Cheyenne: Wyoming Department of Labor Statistics), 6.

[45] Righter, *The Making of a Town*, 35.

[46] Ibid.

[47] Ibid., 35-36.

[48] Brown, *Wyoming, A Geography*, 6. Brown gives federal ownership at 48.1 percent, state 5.9, and private 46 percent. Union Pacific still owns a large segment of the land granted under the original land grant.

[49] Righter, *The Making of a Town*, 36.

[50] Robert Rhode, *Booms and Busts on Bitter Creek*, (Boulder, Colorado: Pruett Press, 1987), 177-178.

[51] Larson, *Wyoming, A History*, 172.

[52] Ibid., 145.

[53] *The Rock Springs Miner*, January 27, 1957.

54 Dennis C. Stickley, "Mineral Wealth and Severance Taxes—A Public Policy Perspective," *Wyoming Issues* 1 (Fall 1978): 7.

55 Gregg Cowley, Janet Clark, Michael Horn, Maggi Murdock, Alan Schenker, and Oliver Walter Head, *The Equality State, Government and Politics in Wyoming* (Dubuque, Iowa: Eddie Bowers Publishing Company, 1988), 31.

56 Larson, *Wyoming, A History*, 563.

57 Larson, *Wyoming, A History*, 168; *Wyoming State Constitution* November 4, 1986. Article is Section 19, 45. The amendment reads, "Mineral excise tax: distribution.—The Legislature shall provide by law for an excise tax on the privilege of severing or extracting minerals of one and one-half percent on the value of the gross product extracted. The minerals subject to such excise tax shall be coal, petroleum, natural gas, oil shale, and such other minerals as may be designated by the Legislature. Such tax shall be in addition to any other excise, severance or ad valorem tax. The proceeds from such tax shall be deposited in the Permanent Wyoming Mineral Trust Fund, which fund shall remain inviolate. The monies in the fund shall be invested as prescribed by the Legislature and all income from fund investments shall be deposited by the State Treasurer in the general fund on an annual basis. The Legislature may also specify by law conditions and terms under which monies in the fund may be loaned to political subdivisions of the state."

58 Wyoming Ad Valorem and Severance Taxation: A History and Analysis of Trends. Prepared for Wyoming Coal Information Committee by Wyoming Taxpayers' Association, November 1985, 40-42, Tables 8.14 and 8.18.

59 *Mineral Severance Taxes, Friend or Foe*, League of Women Voters of Wyoming Publication No. 50 (Cheyenne, 1980), 1.

60 *Session Laws of the State of Wyoming Passed by the Forty-fifth State Legislature* (Cheyenne: Legislative Service Office, 1979), 184.

61 Larson, *Wyoming, A History*, 565.

62 Kenyon N. Griffin, Pledging Future Revenue: Financing Energy-Related Impact in Wyoming. Paper presented at the First National Energy Policy Conference, West Virginia University, Morgantown, May 1-3, 1980.

63 Wyoming Ad Valorem and Severence Taxation, 51.

64 Ibid., 40-42, Table 8.1; Cowley et al., *The Equality State*, 130.

65 Smith, *Mining America*, 150.

66 John D. Collins, "The Abandoned Mine Reclamation Fund: A View from the West," *Land and Water Review* 20 (1985): 1.

67 Smith, *Mining America*, 150.

68 *Wyoming Coal Mining and Wage Employment Survey 1984*, 6.

69 Keith Miller, "The Wyoming Human Services Project: an Experiment in Community Problem Solving," *Wyoming Issues* 2 (Spring 1979): 36.

70 Ibid.

71 Cynthia L. Guillume and Sylvia Ridlen Wenston, "Child Abuse in Impact Communities," In *The Boom Town Problems and Promises in the Energy Vortex*, edited by Joseph Davenport and Judith A. Davenport (Laramie: University of Wyoming Department of Social Work, 1980), 86.

72 James P. Streba, *The New York Times*, April 11, 1974. In "Problems and Policies of Energy Impacted Communities in Wyoming," (Ms. on file, Western Wyoming College History Department, Rock Springs, n.d.), 225.

73 Ibid., 226-227.

74 Ibid., 227.

75 Joseph Davenport and Judith A. Davenport, *The Boom Town Problems*, 43.

76 *New York Times*, April 11, 1974; "Energy Impacted Communities in Wyoming," 227.

77 Barbara Smith, "Sisters," *Writers Forum, New America Literature from the West*, 9 (Spring 1983): 205. Reprinted by permission of the author.

78 *Wyoming Coal Mining and Wage Employment Survey 1984*, 6.

79 *The Rock Springs Rocket Miner*, January 15, 1975.

80 Ibid.

81 *The Rock Springs Rocket Miner*, January 18, 1975.

82 Ibid.

83 *The Rock Springs Rocket Miner*, January 22, 1975.

84 *The Rock Springs Rocket Miner*, February 14, 1975.

85 Homer Alley interview, 29-30.

86 Linda Linn, interview with author, Rock Springs, Wyoming, October 27, 1988.

87 *The Rock Springs Rocket Miner*, July 1, 1975.

88 Ibid.

89 Ibid.

90 Paul Averitt, "Coal Resources of the United States," U.S. Geological Survey Bulletin 1412, January 1, 1974. Information reported in *Rock Springs Rocket Miner*, September 30, 1975. Also in Brown, *Wyoming, A Geography*, 201. Brown states Wyoming has 45 different coal fields with reserves of 935.9 billion tons.

91 *Wyoming Coal Mining and Wage Employment Survey 1984*, 6.

92 *Wyoming Data Handbook 1987*, (Cheyenne: Department of Administration and Fiscal Control, 1987), 22.

93 *Wyoming Coal Mining and Wage Employment Survey 1984*, 6. The drop in production for 1986 is shown in the *Wyoming Data Handbook 1987*, 51.

94 Wyoming Ad Valorem and Severance Taxation, 8.15.

95 Ibid.

96 Cowley et al., *The Equality State*, 131.

97 Larson, *Wyoming, A History*, 160.

98 *Wyoming Data Handbook 1987*, 22.

99 Homer Alley interview, 29-30.

100 Mary Wolney interview, 30.

Select Bibliography

Books

Allen, James B. *The Company Town in the American West.* Norman: University of Oklahoma Press, 1966.

American Institute of Mining and Metallurgical Engineers. *Mining Geology 1941.* York, Pennsylvania: The Maple Press, 1941.

_____. *Coal Division 1942.* York, Pennsylvania: The Maple Press, 1942.

Athearn, Robert G. *Union Pacific Country.* Lincoln: University of Nebraska Press, 1971.

Baldwin, W. W., ed. *Chicago, Burlington, and Quincy Railroad Company.* Vol. 3, *Documentary History: Lines West of the Missouri River.* Chicago: Chicago, Burlington, and Quincy Railroad Company, 1929.

Barrett, Glen. *Kemmerer, Wyoming: The Founding of an Independent Coal Town 1897-1902.* Kemmerer: Quealy Services, 1975.

Beard, Frances Birkhead. *Wyoming: From Territorial Days to the Present.* New York: The American Historical Society, 1933.

Bolognani, Bonifacio. *A Courageous People from the Dolomites.* Trento, Italy: Typolithography TEMI, 1981.

Bromely, Isaac Hill. *The Chinese Massacre at Rock Springs, Wyoming Territory.* Boston: Franklin Press, 1886.

Brown, Robert H. *Wyoming, A Geography.* Boulder, Colorado: Westview Press, 1980.

Bruff, Joseph Goldsborough. *Gold Rush: The Journals, Drawings, and other Papers of Joseph Goldsborough Bruff.* Edited by Georgia Willis Read and Ruth Gaines. New York: Columbia University Press, 1944.

Burroughs, John Rolfe. *Where the Old West Stayed Young.* New York: Bonanza Books, 1962.

Calvert, Jerry W. *The Gibraltar: Socialism and Labor in Butte, Montana, 1895-1920.* Helena: Montana Historical Society Press, 1988.

Caudill, Harry M. *My Land is Dying.* New York: E. P. Dutton and Company, 1971.

Clayton, William. *The Latter Day Saints Emigrant Guide.* St. Louis: Chambers and Knapp, 1848.

Coal Mining Notebook. New York: Coal Age, n.d.

Coleman, McAlister. *Men and Coal.* New York: Farrar and Rinehart, 1943.

Crawley, Greg, Janet Clark, Michael Horan, Maggi Murdock, Alan Schenker, Oliver Walter. *The Equality State: Government and Politics in Wyoming.* Dubuque: Eddie Bowers Publishing Company, 1988.

Dick, Everett. *The Sod-House Frontier 1854-1890.* Lincoln: University of Nebraska Press, 1979.

223

Divine, Robert A., T. H. Breen, George M. Fredrickson, and R. Hal Williams. *America, Past and Present*, vol. 2. Glenview, Illinois: Scott Foresman and Company, 1987.

Dix, Keith. *What's a Coal Miner to Do?: The Mechanization of Coal Mining*. Pittsburgh: University of Pittsburgh Press, 1988.

Eavenson, Howard N. *Coal Through the Ages*. New York: American Institute of Mining and Metallurgical Engineers, 1939.

Garreau, Joel. *The Nine Nations of North America*. Boston: Houghton Mifflin, 1981.

Gilmore, John S. and Mary K. Duff. *A Growth Management Case Study: Sweetwater County, Wyoming*. Denver: Rocky Mountain Energy Company, 1974.

Gitelman, Howard M. *Legacy of the Ludlow Massacre: A Chapter in American Industrial Relations*. Philadelphia: University of Pennsylvania Press, 1988.

Gradwohl, David M. and Nancy M. Osborn. *Exploring Buried Bruxton: Archaeology of an Abandoned Iowa Coal Mining Town with a Large Black Population*. Ames: The Iowa State University Press, 1984.

Groutage, Lorenzo. *Wyoming Mine Run*. Kemmerer, Wyoming: 1981.

Guillume, Cynthia L. and Sylvia Ridlen Wenston. "Child Abuse in Impact Communities." In *The Boom Town Problems and Promises in the Energy Vortex*, edited by Joseph Davenport and Judith A. Davenport. Laramie: University of Wyoming Department of Social Work, 1980.

Hall, R. Dawson and J. H. Edwards. *Coal Age Mining Manual*. New York: Coal Age, 1934.

Hendrickson, Gordon Olaf, ed. *Peopling the High Plains, Wyoming's European Heritage*. Cheyenne: Wyoming State Archives, 1977.

History of the Union Pacific Coal Mines 1868 to 1940. Omaha: The Colonial Press, 1940.

Holbrook, Stewart H. *The Story of American Railroads*. New York: Crown Publishers, 1947.

Irving, Washington. *Adventures of Captain Bonneville*. Reprint. Portland, Oregon: Binfords and Mort, 1950.

Isham, Dell. *Rock Springs Massacre 1885*. Lincoln City, Oregon: Quality Printing Service, 1985.

Jackson, Donald and Mary L. Spence. *Travels from 1838 to 1844, The Expeditions of John Charles Fremont*, vol. 1. Urbana, Illinois: University Press, 1970.

Jackson, W. Turrentine. *Wells Fargo in Colorado Territory*. Denver: Colorado Historical Society Monograph Series, 1982.

Justi, Herman. *Organization and Public Opinion*. Chicago: Coal Operators Association, 1903.

Kathka, David. "The Italian Experience in Wyoming." In *Peopling the High Plains, Wyoming's European Heritage*, edited by Gordon Olaf Hendrickson. Cheyenne: Wyoming State Archives and Historical Department, 1977.

Klein, Maury. *The Life and Legend of Jay Gould*. Baltimore: The John Hopkins University Press, 1986.

_____. *Union Pacific, Birth of a Railroad 1862-1893*. Garden City: Doubleday and Company, 1987.

Kuzara, Stanley A. *Black Diamonds of Sheridan, A Facet of Wyoming History.* Cheyenne: Pioneer Printing and Stationary Co., 1977.

Larson, Taft A. *History of Wyoming.* Lincoln: University of Nebraska Press, 1978.

_____. *Wyoming: A History.* New York: W. W. Norton and Company, 1984.

LeMassena, R. A. *Articulated Steam Locomotives of North America,* vol. 1, Silverton, Colorado: Sundance Books, 1979.

Malone, Michael P. *The Battle for Butte: Mining and Politics on the Northern Frontier, 1864-1906.* Seattle: University of Washington Press, 1981.

Margolis, Eric. *Coal Mining as a Way of Life: An Oral History of the Western Coal Miners.* Boulder, Colorado: University of Colorado Institute of Behavioral Science, 1984.

Miller, Tim R. *State Government: Politics in Wyoming.* Dubuque: Kendall/Hunt Publishing, 1981.

Nielson, Waldo. *Right of Way: A Guide to Abandoned Railroads in the United States.* Bend, Oregon: Old Bottle Magazine, 1974.

Palmer, Joel. *Journals of Travels over the Rocky Mountains.* Cincinnati: J. A. and U. P. James, 1847.

Puotinen, Arthur Edward. *Finnish Radicals and Religion in Midwestern Mining Towns, 1867-1914.* New York: Arno Press, 1973.

Rhode, Robert. *Booms and Busts on Bitter Creek.* Boulder, Colorado: Pruett Press, 1987.

Righter, Robert W. *The Making of a Town, Wright, Wyoming.* Boulder, Colorado: Roberts Rinehart, 1985.

Russell, Osborne. *Journal of a Trapper,* edited by Aubrey L. Haines. Lincoln: University of Nebraska Press, 1965.

Schwieder, Dorothy. *Black Diamonds: Life and Work in Iowa's Coal Mining Communities, 1895-1920.* Ames: Iowa State University Press, 1983.

Selekman, Ben M. and Mary Van Kleeck. *Employees Representation in Coal Mines, A Study of the Industrial Representation Plan of the Colorado Fuel and Iron Company.* New York: Russel Sage Foundation, 1924.

Smith, Duane. *Colorado Mining, A Photographic History.* Albuquerque: University of New Mexico Press, 1977.

_____. *Mining America, The Industry and the Environment 1800-1980.* Lawrence: University of Kansas, 1987.

_____. *When Coal was King, A History of Crested Butte, Colorado, 1880-1952.* Golden: Colorado School of Mines, 1984.

Stansbury, Howard. *Exploration and Survey of the Valley of the Great Salt Lake of Utah Including a Reconnaissance of a New Route Through the Rocky Mountains.* Washington, D.C.: Robert Armstrong Public, 1853.

Stennett, William H. *Yesterday and Today: A History of the Chicago and Northwestern Railway System.* Chicago: Chicago and Northwestern Railway Company, 1910.

Stipanovich, Joseph. *The South Slavs in Utah: A Social History.* Saratoga, California: R. and E. Research Associates, 1975.

Stone, E. A. *Uinta County: Its Place in History.* Laramie: The Laramie Printing Company, 1924.

Trenholm, Virginia Cole. *Wyoming Blue Book*, vol. 2. Cheyenne: Pioneer Printing, 1974.
Ubbelohde, Carl A., Maxine Benson, and Duane A. Smith. *A Colorado History.* Boulder, Colorado: Pruett Publishing Company, 1976.
Wallace, Anthony F. C. *St. Clair, A Nineteenth Century Coal Town's Experience with a Disaster-Prone Industry.* New York: Alfred A. Knopf, 1987.
Wheeler, Denise. *The Feminine Frontier: Wyoming Women 1850-1900.* Evanston, Wyoming: Denise Wheeler, 1987.
Wheeler, Keith. *The Railroaders.* New York: Time-Life Books, 1973.
Young, Otis E. Jr. *Black Powder and Hand Steel: Miners and Machines of the Old West Frontier.* Norman: University of Oklahoma Press, 1976.

Journals and Periodicals

"Americans Won't Work in Mines." *Coal Age* 8 (September 4, 1915): 393.
Beach, C. S. "The Susie, Wyoming Explosion." *Coal Age* 1 (April 20, 1912): 908.
Bishop, M. Guy. "More Than One Coal Road to Zion. The Utah Territory's Efforts to Ease Dependency on Wyoming Coal." *Annals of Wyoming* 60 (Spring 1988): 8-16.
"The Cambria Coal Field in Wyoming." *Coal Age* 1 (March 23, 1912): 766-768.
Cardoso, L. A. "Nativism in Wyoming, 1868 to 1930," *Annals of Wyoming* 58 (Spring 1986).
Collins, John D. "The Abandoned Mine Reclamation Fund: A View from the West." *Land and Water Review* (1985): 67-92.
Crawford, P. V. "Journal of a Trip Across the Plains in 1851." *Quarterly of the Oregon Historical Society* 25 (1924): 136-169.
Gardner, A. Dudley, Markia A. Matthews, and David E. Johnson. "Historic Japanese Sites of Southwestern Wyoming." *Wyoming Archaeologist* 31 (1988): 67-82.
Gilmore, John S. "Boom Towns May Hinder Energy Resource Development." *Science* 191 (February 13, 1976): 535-540.
"Housing Coal Miners." *Coal Age* 8 (July 24, 1915): 137-138.
Ichioka, Yuji. "Asian Immigrant Coal Miners and the United Mine Workers of America: Race and Class at Rock Springs, Wyoming, 1907." *Amerasia Journal* 6 (1979): 1-23.
Jones, Walter R. "Coal Mine Explosions at Almy, Their Influence on Wyoming's First Coal Mining Safety Laws." *Annals of Wyoming* 56, (Spring 1984): 54-65.
Kalish, P. A. "The Woebegone Miners of Wyoming: A History of Coal Mine Disasters in the Equality State," *Annals of Wyoming* 42 (October 1970): 237-242.
Lampi, Leona, "Red Lodge from a Frantic Past of Crows, Coal, and Boom and Bust Emerges a Unique Festival of Diverse National Groups," *Montana, the Magazine of Western History*, 11 (April 1961): 20-31.
Letter to the Editor. *Union Pacific Employees Magazine* (February 1886): 318.
Letter to the Editor. *Union Pacific Employees Magazine* (January 1887): 60, 272.

Letter to the Editor. *Union Pacific Employees Magazine* 3 (February 1888): 190, 328, 350.

Letter to the Editor. *Union Pacific Employees Magazine* 4 (February 1889): 30, 250.

Letter to the Editor. *Union Pacific Employees Magazine* 5 (February 1890): 59, 61, 381.

Letter to the Editor. *Union Pacific Employees Magazine* 6 (February 1891): 29, 125, 157, 254, 318, 351, 359, 379.

Letter to the Editor. *Union Pacific Employees Magazine* 8 (February 1893): 26, 59.

Letter to the Editor. *Union Pacific Employees Magazine* 9 (February 1894): 2-31.

Margolis, Eric. "Western Coal Mining as a Way of Life: An Oral History of the Colorado Coal Miners to 1914." *Journal of the West* 24 (July 1985): 1-129.

McAuliffe, Eugene. "Rock Springs: The Center of Wyomings Great Coal Industry." *Wyoming Labor Journal* (1929): 1-15.

McFarland, Mel. "Wyoming's First Coal Railroad." *Annals of Wyoming* 53 (Spring 1981): 34-37.

Miller, Arnold. "The Energy Crisis as a Coal Miner Sees It," *Center Magazine* (November-December 1973): 33-45.

Miller, Keith. "The Wyoming Human Services Project: An Experiment in Community Problem Solving," *Wyoming Issues* 2 (1979): 36.

Morgan, Dale L. "The Mormon Ferry on the North Platte, The Journal of William A. Emprey," *Annals of Wyoming* 21 (July-October 1949): 111-167.

Myler, Glade A. "Mitigating Boom Town Effects of Energy Development: A Survey." *Journal of Energy Law and Policy.* 2 (1982): 211-235.

Peltier, M. F. "Coal Mining in Northern Wyoming." *Coal Age* 10 (November 18, 1916): 832-833.

"A Plea for a Better House." *Coal Age* 8 (August 28, 1915): 328-329.

Plested, Delores. "Where Coal Was Once King." *Colorado Heritage* 2 (1987): 30-43.

"Questions Asked at Five Boss Examinations Held at Cumberland, Wyoming, January 29-31, 1912." *Coal Age* 1 (March 16, 1912): 720, 756, 788.

Simmons, Jesse. "The Sheridan Wyoming Coal Field." *Coal Age* 1 (April 13, 1912): 866-868.

_____. "The Sheridan Wyoming Coal Field." *Coal Age* 1 (April 27, 1912): 932-934.

_____. "The Acme Co.'s Plant in Wyoming." *Coal Age* 1 (May 11, 1912): 998-1001.

Smith, Barbara. "Sisters," *Writers Forum, New America Literature from the West* 9 (Spring 1983): 205.

Steeper, Steven. "Sales Tax and an Indicator of State Economic Progress." *Wyoming Issues* 1 (Fall 1978): 2-5.

Stickley, Dennis C. "Mineral Wealth and Severance Taxes—a Public Policy Perspective," *Wyoming Issues* 1 (Fall 1978): 6-10.

"Susie Mine Explosion." *Coal Age* 1 (February 24, 1912): 650-651.

Thompson, James G. "The Gillette Syndrome: A Myth Revisited?" *Wyoming Issues* 2 (Spring 1979): 30-36.

Veda, Giezentanner. "In Dugouts and Sod Houses," *The Chronicles of Oklahoma*, 39 (1961): 140-149.

Whiteside, James. "Protecting Life and Limb of Our Workingmen: Coal Mining Regulations in Colorado 1883-1920." *Essays and Monographs in Colorado History* 4 (1986): 1-24.

Newspapers

Alexander Gazette (Virginia), 1923.
Carbon County (Wyoming) Journal, 1886, 1899.
Casper (Wyoming) Star Tribune, 1984.
Cheyenne (Wyoming) Daily Leader, 1869-1881.
Cheyenne (Wyoming) Weekly Leader, 1881.
Deseret Evening News (Salt Lake City, Utah), 1886.
Fremont Clipper (Lander, Wyoming), 1890.
Frontier Index (Green River, Wyoming), 1868.
Kemmerer (Wyoming) Camera, 1907.
Laramie (Wyoming) Boomerang, 1891.
Newcastle (Wyoming) Newsletter Journal, 1984.
The New York Times, 1974.
The Omaha (Nebraska) Daily Bee, 1899.
The Rock Springs (Wyoming) Exposer, 1876.
The Rock Springs (Wyoming) Daily Rocket Miner, 1947-1957.
The Rock Springs (Wyoming) Daily Rocket, 1943-1946.
Rock Springs (Wyoming) Independent, 1885.
The Rock Springs (Wyoming) Miner, 1892-1952.
The Rock Springs (Wyoming) Rocket (weekly), 1907-1935.
The Rock Springs (Wyoming) Rocket (daily), 1936-1943.
The Salt Lake (Utah) Herald, 1881.
The Sheridan (Wyoming) Post, 1903-1910.
Wyoming Tribune, 1870.

Manuscripts and Letters

Nebraska State Museums and Archives, Lincoln

Biggs, Alexander. Letter to George L. Black, 1899.
Black, George L. Letter to D. O. Clark, 1899, 1900.
Burt, H. G. Letter to D. O. Clark, 1900.
Callaway, S. R. Letter to Charles F. Adams, 1885.
The Citizens' Alliance of Cheyenne, Wyoming, Constitution.
Clark, D. O. Letters to Horace G. Burt and other Union Pacific employees, various
    dates 1899 to 1903.
George, H. Letter to H. G. Burt, 1903.
Kangley, John. Report of an Experienced Coal Miner, on the U.P. Coal Department
    Mines in Wyoming and Colorado 1887.
Potter, T. J. Letter to Union Pacific President Charles F. Adams, 1887.
Stanton, Fred J. Letter to the Honorable Charles F. Adams, 1884.
Union Pacific Railway Company Coal Department Report for 1887.

University of Wyoming Archives, American Heritage Center, Laramie

Finfrock, J. W. Dairy of Ft. Halleck, Wyoming.
Hodgson, Mary E. History of Carbon, Wyoming.

Western Wyoming College, Rock Spring

Gardner, Jodie Voiles. A Childhood in Cambria, 1918-1928. Archaeological Services of Western Wyoming College, 1988.
Kathka, David. Problems and Policies of Energy Impacted Communities in Wyoming. Western Wyoming College History Department, n.d.
Union Pacific Coal Company Code of Standards, To Govern Safety Work, Including Construction and Operation, 1954. Archaeological Services of Western Wyoming College.
Union Pacific Coal Company various records, 1920-1963. Archaeological Services of Western Wyoming College.

Wyoming State Archives, Cheyenne

All territorial and state coal mine inspector reports.
Shaw, F. Memories of a Miner, 1936.

Various

Chadey, Henry F. The Chinese Story and Rock Springs, Wyoming. Green River: Sweetwater County Historical Museum, n.d.
Cutting, A. Howard. A Journal of an Overland Trip, 1863, Henry H. Huntington Library and Art Gallery, San Marino, California. June 2, 1863, entry.
Evans, James A. Report of Jas. A. Evans of Exploration from Camp Walbach to Green River, 1865. Union Pacific Historical Museum, Omaha, Nebraska.
Lawson, John R. Special Collections, Scrap Book. Denver Public Library, 1912.
Miners Monument Pamphlet, Union Pacific Railroad Company, Hanna Library, Hanna, Wyoming.
Nicholas, Thomas A. L. The Gebo Mine and Miners, Thermopolis, Wyoming, 1969.
United States National Archives. Special Orders No. 103, Headquarter Department of the Platte, Omaha, Nebraska, 1881-1889.
Warren, Francis E. Letter to S. R. Callaway. Microfilm National Archives, Denver, Territorial Communications, 1885.
Wells, N. E. A Brief Biographical Sketch of Some of My Experiences as a Country Doctor. Privately published, 1953.

Interviews

All interviews listed are on file at Archaeological Services of Western Wyoming College, Rock Springs.

Alley, Homer. Interview with author. Dayton, Wyoming, July 1987.

Antilla, Alice. Interview with author. Kemmerer, Wyoming, Fall 1983.

Bozovich, Joe. Interview with author. Rock Springs, Wyoming, December 1987.

Carter, Hack and Lola Carter. Interview with author. Rock Springs, Wyoming, Fall 1984.

Crouch, Elizabeth and Hugh Crouch. Interview with David Kathka. Rock Springs, Wyoming, 1975.

Dernovich, Frank, Mike Duzik, Eugene Paoli, Norma Paoli, Antone (Tony) Pivik, and Amy Pivik. Interview with author. Rock Springs, Wyoming, 1984.

Ellis, Cora. Interview with author. Medicine Bow, Wyoming, 1984.

Flaim, Caroline. Interview with Jodie Gardner. Rock Springs, Wyoming, May 1988.

Giorgis, Ernest. Interview with Linda Newman. Fort Bridger, Wyoming, November 1985.

Harris, William. Interview with author. Frontier, Wyoming, Fall 1983.

Kaczmarek, Marie Havens. Interview with author, Vernal, Utah, December 1983. In *Oral Historical Accounts of Northwestern Colorado*, edited by A. Dudley Gardner and Verla R. Flores. Rock Springs: Western Wyoming College Contributions to History No. 2, 1986.

Ketchum, Bernice. Interview with author. Sheridan, Wyoming, July 1987.

Korogi, Jack. Personal communication with author. Rock Springs, Wyoming, December 1987.

Kovach, Henry. Interview with Todd Horn. Rock Springs, Wyoming, March 1987.

Linn, Linda. Interview with author. Rock Springs, Wyoming, October 27, 1988.

Miller, Catherine and Joseph Miller. Interview with Shirley Black. Rock Springs, Wyoming, February 1987.

Okano, George. Interview with author. Rock Springs, Wyoming, 1984.

Silla, Guido and John Wolney. Interview with author. Sheridan, Wyoming, July 1987.

Sunada, Edith. Interview with author. Green River, Wyoming, 1986.

Tabuchi, Yoshio and Agnes Tabuchi. Interview with author. Reliance, Wyoming, Spring 1986.

Williams, Sol. Interview with Margie Krza. Superior, Wyoming, April 1982.

Wolney, Mary. Interview with author. Dayton, Wyoming, July 1987.

Zampedri, Henry. Interview with author. Rock Springs, Wyoming, 1984.

Dissertations and Theses

Bryans, William S. A History of Transcontinental Railroads and Coal Mining on the Northern Plains to 1920. Ph.D. dissertation, University of Wyoming, 1987.

Dickinson, S. C. The Geology and Coal Mines of Hanna, Carbon County, Wyoming. B.S. thesis, Mine Engineering, University of Wyoming, 1913.

Fletcher, Erma A. The History of the Labor Movement in Wyoming, 1870-1940. Master's thesis, Department of Economics and Sociology, University of Wyoming, 1945.

Frazer, Marie Milligan. Some Phases in the History of the Union Pacific Railroad in Wyoming. Master's thesis, University of Wyoming, 1927.

Headlee, Richard. An Architectural History of Southern Wyoming, 1867-1887. Master's thesis, University of Wyoming, 1977.

Krueger, Thomas Arthur. Populism in Wyoming. Master's thesis, Department of History, University of Wyoming, 1960.

Smith, David. An Economic History of the Coal Industry of Southwestern Wyoming, 1868-1965. Master's thesis, Department of Economics, University of Wyoming, 1966.

Sharzehi, Gholamali. Optimal Public Investment for Boomtowns: A Welfare-Economic Analysis. Ph.D. dissertation, University of Illinois.

Trevor, Marjorie C. History of Carter: Sweetwater County, Wyoming to 1875. Master's thesis, University of Wyoming, 1954.

Wilson, Arlen Ray. The Rock Springs, Wyoming, Chinese Massacre, 1885. Master's thesis, University of Wyoming, 1967.

Technical Reports

Bryans, William S. (Bill). *Deer Creek: Frontier Crossroad in Pre-Territorial Wyoming.* Glencock, The Glenrock Historical Commission, n.d.

Gardner, A. Dudley and David E. Johnson. Mining and Homesteading in the Intermountain West. Paper presented at the 42nd Annual Plains Conference, Lincoln, Nebraska.

_____. Results of *Test Excavations at 48AB349, 48CR4105, and 48CR4116 (DEQ Project 7).* Rock Springs: Archaeological Services of Western Wyoming College, 1985.

_____. *Cultural Resource Inventory of the Department of Environmental Quality AML Project 6C.* Cultural Resource Management Report No. 17. Rock Springs: Archaeological Services of Western Wyoming College, 1985.

_____. *Archaeological Investigations at South Cumberland.* Rock Springs: Archaeological Services of Western Wyoming College, 1986.

_____. *Cultural Resource Inventory and Mitigation of Thirty-Seven Mine Reclamation Sites in Sweetwater County, Wyoming.* Cultural Resource Management Report No. 29. Rock Springs: Archaeological Services of Western Wyoming College, 1986.

_____. Ore Carts, Coffee Cups, and Wagon Mines. A Discussion of 19th-century and Early 20th-century Coal Mines in Southern Wyoming. Paper presented at the 1986 Conference of the Society for Historic Archaeology/Conference of Underwater Archaeology. Sacramento, California, January 1986.

_____. *Historic Overview of the Bitter Creek Valley from Rock Springs to Green River.* Cultural Resource Management Report No. 47. Rock Springs: Archaeological Services of Western Wyoming College, 1988.

_____. *The Restoration of the Reliance Tipple.* Proceedings: Symposium on Evaluation of Abandoned Mine Land Technologies, Wyoming DEQ, Riverton, Wyoming, June 1989.

Gardner, A. Dudley, David E. Johnson, and Marilyn Christiansen. *Archaeological and Historical Survey of 31 Mine Reclamation Sites in Carbon and Albany Counties, Wyoming.* Cultural Resource Management Report No. 14. Rock Springs: Archaeological Services of Western Wyoming College, 1985.

Gardner, A. Dudley and Robert Rosenberg. *Archaeological and Historical Survey of 26 Mine Reclamation Sites in Uinta and Lincoln Counties, Wyoming.* Cultural Resource Management Report No. 13. Rock Springs: Archaeological Services of Western Wyoming College, 1984.

Griffin, Kenyon N. Pledging Future Revenue: Financing Energy-related Impact in Wyoming. Paper presented at the First National Energy Policy Conference, West Virginia University, Morgantown, May 1-3, 1980.

Hauff, Jeffrey L., and Skylar S. Scott. *Cultural Resource Investigations and Historic Evaluation of 15 Abandoned Mine Sites, Hot Springs County, Wyoming.* Laramie: Office of the Wyoming State Archaeologist, 1984.

Markoft, Dena. *Site Documentation of the Hamilton Homestead Site in Southern Campbell County, Wyoming.* Manuscript on file, State Historic Preservation Office, Fort Mead, South Dakota, 1982.

Mineral Severance Taxes, Friend or Foe. Cheyenne: League of Women Voters, 1980.

Rosenberg, Robert G. *Class I Historical Cultural Resource Overview of the Rock Springs Known Recoverable Coal Resource Area (KRCRA), Sweetwater County, Wyoming.* Bismark: Cultural Research and Management, Inc., 1984.

_____. *Historic Overview for DEQ Abandoned Mine Lands Project No. 8, Sheridan, Johnson, Campbell, Natrona, and Converse Counties, Wyoming.* Bismark: Cultural Research and Management, Inc., 1984.

_____. *Archaeological and Historical Survey of Mine Reclamation Sites in Fremont County, Wyoming: Historic Overview,* vol. 2, Department of Environmental Quality, Abandoned Mine Lands Project No. 9. Bismark: Cultural Research and Management, Inc., 1984.

Sanders, Paul H. *An Archaeological Inventory in the Hodges Pass Area of the Overthrust Belt in Western Wyoming.* Laramie: Larson Tibesar Associates, 1985.

Schweigert, Kurt. *Historic Site Feasibility Study, Superior Mining District and the Town of Superior, Sweetwater County, Wyoming.* Cheyenne: Department of Environmental Quality, 1987.

Simon, Arleyn and Kelly Keim. *The Marsh Hawk Site, 32BI317, Billings County, North Dakota,* vol. 1. Department of Anthropology and Archaeology, Grand Forks, North Dakota, 1983.

An Update of the Comprehensive Plan for Rock Springs, Wyoming, August 1975. Englewood: John Dempsey and Associates, 1975.

Whissen, Steven R. *Report of Class III Cultural Resource Investigations of Abandoned Mines (Goshen, Platte, Converse, Albany, Sweetwater, Carbon, Lincoln, and Uinta Counties).* Cheyenne: Department of Environmental Quality, 1989.

_____. *Historic Overview for DEQ Abandoned Mine Lands, Project No. 16 (Fremont and Natrona Counties, Wyoming).* Cheyenne: Department of Environmental Quality, 1987.

Whissen, Steven R. and David Y. Boon. *Report of Class III Cultural Resource Investigations of Abandoned Mines (Albany, Laramie, Goshen, Platte, and Niobrara Counties).* Department of Environmental Quality Abandoned Mine Lands Project No. 10. Cheyenne: Wyoming Department of Environmental Quality, 1985.

Whissen, Steven R., and Gregory P. Smith. *Report of Class III Cultural Resource Investigations of Abandoned Mines (Fremont and Hot Springs Counties, Wyoming).* Department of Environmental Quality Abandoned Mine Lands Project No. 9B. Cheyenne: Wyoming Department of Environmental Quality, 1986.

Wyoming Ad Valorem and Severance Taxation: A History and Analysis of Trends, Wyoming Assessed Valuation. Prepared for Wyoming Coal Information Committee by Wyoming Taxpayers Association, November 1985.

Federal Documents

Ashley, George H. *The Valuation of Public Coal Lands.* United States Geological Survey Bulletin 424. Washington, D.C.: U.S. Government Printing Office, 1910.

Averitt, Paul. "Coal Resources of the United States." U.S. Geological Survey Bulletin 1412, January 1, 1974.

Berryhill, Henry L. Jr., Donald M. Brown, Andrew Brown, and Dorothy A. Taylor. *Coal Resources of Wyoming.* Washington, D.C.: United States Department of the Interior, Geological Survey.

Davis, J.A. *The Little Powder River Coal Field.* Contributions to Economic Geology, 1910. Washington, D.C.: U.S. Government Printing Office, 1912.

Day, David T. *Mineral Resources of the United States, Calendar Year 1889.* Washington, D.C.: U.S. Government Printing Office, 1891.

_____. *Mineral Resources of the United States, Calendar Year 1890.* Washington, D.C.: U.S. Government Printing Office, 1892.

_____. *Mineral Resources of the United States, Calendar Year 1900.* Washington, D.C.: U.S. Government Printing Office, 1892.

_____. *Mineral Resources of the United States, Calendar Year 1905.* Washington, D.C.: U.S. Government Printing Office, 1906.

Dobbin, C. E. and V. H. Barnett. *The Gillette Coal Field, Northeastern Wyoming.* U.S.G.S. Bulletin 796-A. Washington, D.C.: U.S. Government Printing Office, 1927.

Emmons, S. F. and E. C. Eckel. *Contributions to Economic Geology 1905.* Washington, D.C.: U.S. Government Printing Office, 1906.

Hague, J. D. and C. King. *Mining Industry: United States Geological Exploration of the Fortieth Parallel.* Washington, D.C.: U.S. Government Printing Office, 1870.

Hayden, Ferdinand V. *Fifth Annual Report of the U.S. Geological Survey of Montana and Portions of Adjacent Territories.* Washington, D.C.: U.S. Government Printing Office, 1872.

Humphrey, H. B. *Historical Summary of Coal Mine Explosions in the United States, 1810-1958.* Washington, D.C.: U.S. Government Printing Office, 1960.

Hunt, Edward Eyre, F. G. Tryon, and Joseph H. Willits, eds., *What the Coal Commission Found.* Baltimore: The Williams and Wilkins Co., 1925.

Knight, W. C. *Geology of the Wyoming Experimental Farms and Notes on the Resources of the State.* University of Wyoming Agricultural Department Bulletin No. 14, Laramie, 1893.

Reed, Silas. *Report of the Surveyor General of Wyoming Territory for the Year 1871.* Washington, D.C.: U.S. Government Printing Office, 1871.

Shaw, E. Wesley. *The Glenrock Coal Field, Wyoming.* Contributions to Economic Geology, 1907. Washington, D.C.: U.S. Government Printing Office, 1909.

Stansbury, Howard. *Exploration and Survey of the Valley of the Great Salt Lake of Utah Including a Reconnaissance of a New Route Through the Rocky Mountains.* Washington, D.C.: Robert Armstrong Public Printer, 1853.

Stone, R. W. and C. T. Lupton. *The Powder River Coal Field, Wyoming, Adjacent to the Burlington Railroad.* Contributions to Economic Geology 1908. Washington, D.C.: U.S. Government Printing Office, 1910.

Stone, R. W., C. T. Lupton, H. S. Gale, C. H. Wegemann, E. G. Woodruff, M. W. Ball, Eugene Stebinger, and A. R. Schultz. *Investigations of the Coal Fields in Wyoming by the United States Geological Survey in 1908.* Washington, D.C.: U.S. Government Printing Office, 1910.

Taft, J. A., E. W. Shaw, C. W. Washburne, E. G. Woodruff, E. E. Smith, M. W. Ball, and A. R. Schultz. *Investigations of the Coal Fields of Wyoming by the United States Geological Survey in 1907.* Washington, D.C.: U.S. Government Printing Office, 1909.

U.S. Department of the Census. *Eighth Census of the United States, 1860.* Washington, D.C.: U.S. Government Printing Office, 1864.

_____. *Ninth Census of the United States, 1870.* Washington, D.C.: U.S. Government Printing Office, 1872.

_____. *Tenth Census of the United States, 1880.* Washington, D.C.: U.S. Government Printing Office, 1883.

_____. *Eleventh Census of the United States, 1890.* Washington, D.C.: U.S. Government Printing Office, 1892.

_____. *Twelfth Census of the United States, 1900.* Washington, D.C.: U.S. Government Printing Office, 1901.

_____. *Thirteenth Census of the United States, 1910.* Washington, D.C.: U.S. Government Printing Office, 1913.

_____. *Fourteenth Census of the United States, 1920.* Washington, D.C.: U.S. Government Printing Office, 1922.

_____. *Fifteenth Census of the United States, 1930.* Washington, D.C.: U.S. Government Printing Office, 1931.

_____. *Sixteenth Census of the United States, 1940.* Washington, D.C.: U.S. Government Printing Office, 1942.

_____. *Seventeenth Census of the United States, 1950.* Washington, D.C.: U.S. Government Printing Office, 1952.

_____. *Eighteenth Census of the United States, 1960.* Washington, D.C.: U.S. Government Printing Office, 1952.

U.S. Congress. House of Representatives Committee on Foreign Affairs. "Providing Indemnity to Certain Chinese Subjects: Report to Accompany H.R. 147." 49th Congress 1st session, 1886.

U.S. Department of the Interior. *America 200, The Legacy of our Lands.* Washington, D.C., 1976.

_____. *Draft Green River-Hams Fork Regional Coal Environmental Impact Statement.* Denver, 1978.

U.S. Government Printing Office. *Mineral Resources of the United   States, Calendar Year 1912.* Washington, D.C., 1913.

_____. *Historical Statistics of the United States, Colonial Times to 1957.* Washington, D.C., 1961.

_____. *Report of Surveyor General of Wyoming Territory for the Year 1871.* Washington, D.C., 1871.

_____. *Mineral Resources of the United States, Calendar Year 1909.* Washington, D.C., 1911.

_____. *Mineral Resources of the United States, Calendar Year 1912.* Washington, D.C., 1913.

_____. *Report of the Mining Industries of the United States.* Washington, D.C., 1886.

_____. *Special Reports: Mines and Quarries, 1902.* Washington, D.C., 1905.

_____. *Special Reports: Mines and Quarries, 1919.* Washington, D.C., 1922.

_____. *Special Reports: Mines and Quarries, 1929.* Washington, D.C., 1933.

_____. *Special Reports: Mines and Quarries, 1939.* Washington, D.C., 1944.

Veatch, A. R. "Geography and Geology of a Portion of Southwestern Wyoming." U.S. Geological Survey Professional Paper No. 56. Washington, D.C.: U.S. Government Printing Office, 1907.

Walsh, Frank P. "Final Report of the Commission on Industrial Relations." Washington, D.C.: Barnard and Miller Print, 1915.

Wegemann, C. H. *The Sussex Coal Field, Johnson, Natrona, and Converse Counties, Wyoming.* Contributions to Economic Geology, 1910. Washington, D.C.: U.S. Government Printing Office, 1912.

Winchester, D. E. *The Lost Spring Coal Field, Converse County, Wyoming.* Contributions to Economic Geology, 1910. Washington, D.C.: U.S. Government Printing Office, 1912.

Woodruff, E. G. and D. E. Winchester. *Coal Fields of the Wind River Region, Fremont and Natrona Counties, Wyoming.* Contributions to Economic Geology, 1910. Washington, D.C.: U.S. Government Printing Office, 1912.

State Documents

House Journal of the Fourth Legislative Assembly of the Territory of Wyoming. Cheyenne: Leader Steam Book and Job Printing House, 1875.

Ricketts, L. D. *Annual Report of the Territorial Geologist to the Governor of Wyoming.* Cheyenne: Cheyenne Daily Leader Steam Book Print, 1890.

Session Laws of the State of Wyoming, First State Legislature, Cheyenne: The Daily Sun Publishing House, 1891.

Session Laws of the State of Wyoming, Tenth State Legislature, Sheridan, Wyoming: Post Printing Co., 1909.

Session Laws of the State of Wyoming Passed by the Eighteenth State Legislature, 1924, Sheridan, Wyoming: The Mills Company, 1925.

Session Laws of the State of Wyoming Passed by the Forty-fifth State Legislature, Cheyenne: Legislative Service Office, 1979.

Session Laws of Wyoming Territory, passed by the Ninth Legislative Assembly. Cheyenne: Vaughn Montomery Printers and Binders, Democratic Leader Office, 1886.

Wyoming Department of Administration and Fiscal Control, *Wyoming Data Handbook 1987,* Cheyenne.

Wyoming Board of Immigration. *The Territory of Wyoming, Its History, Soil, Climate, Resources, etc.* Laramie: Daily Sentinel Print, Laramie, 1874.

Wyoming Department of Labor Statistics. *Wyoming Coal Mine Wage and Employment Survey,* Cheyenne, 1982.

_____. *Wyoming Coal Mine Wage and Employment Survey,* Cheyenne, 1984.

Wyoming Geological Survey. *Wyoming Coal Directory,* Public Information Circular No. 3. By G. B. Glass, Laramie, n.d.

_____. *State-owned Coal Lands in Wyoming,* Public Information Series No. 2. By G. B. Glass, Laramie, n.d.

_____. *Analyses and Measured Sections of 54 Wyoming Coal Samples (Collected in 1974),* Report of Investigations No. 11. By G. B. Glass, Laramie, 1975.

_____. *Wyoming Coal Fields,* Circular No. 9. By G. B. Glass, Laramie, 1978.

_____. *Coal Analyses and Lithologies Descriptions of Five Core Holes Drilled in the Carbon Basin of Southcentral Wyoming,* Report of Investigations No. 16. By G. B. Glass, Laramie, 1978.

_____. *Wyoming Coal Production and Summary of Coal Contracts.* Public Information Circular No. 12. By G. B. Glass, Laramie, 1980.

_____. *Guidebook to the Coal Geology of the Powder River Coal Basin, Wyoming,* Public Information Circular No. 14. Ed. G. B. Glass, Laramie, 1980.

_____. *Description of Wyoming Coal Fields and Seam Analyses,* Reprint No. 43. By G. B. Glass, Laramie, 1982.

_____. *Coal Deposits of Wyoming,* Reprint No. 39. By G. B. Glass, Laramie, 1981.

_____. *Remaining Strippable Coal Resources and Strippable Reserve Base of the Hanna Coal Field in Southcentral Wyoming,* Report of Investigations No. 17. By G. B. Glass and J. T. Roberts, Laramie, 1979.

_____. *Coal and Coal-Bearing Rocks of the Hanna Coal Field, Wyoming.* Report of Investigations No. 22. By G. B. Glass and J. T. Roberts, Laramie, 1980.

_____. *Analyses and Measured Sections of 25 Coal Samples from the Hanna Coal Field of Southcentral Wyoming (collected between 1975 and 1979)*, Report of Investigations No. 27. By G. B. Glass and J. T. Roberts, Laramie, 1984.

_____. *The Jackson Hole Coal Field*, Reprint No. 42. By R. W. Jones, Laramie, 1982.

Wyoming Secretary of State, *Wyoming State Constitution*. Cheyenne, 1986.

Wyoming Secretary of the Territory. *Reserves of Wyoming: The Vacant Public Lands and How to Obtain Them*. By S. D. Shannon, Cheyenne, 1889.

Wyoming State Coal Mine Inspector. *Annual Report of the State Coal Mine Inspector*, 1891-1970. Cheyenne, Wyoming.

Wyoming Territorial Inspector of Mines. *Annual Report of the Territorial Coal Mine Inspector*, 1886-1890. Cheyenne, Wyoming.

Index

New Mexico, 192
Newcastle, 67
New York, 123
Nixon, Richard M., President of U.S., 193
North Dakota, 194-195

Oakley (mine and town), 188
Ohio, 192
Ohio Oil, 199
Oil, 196-197; severance tax, 200-203, 214
Oklahoma, 170
"Okies," 170-171
Oregon, 4, 10, 66
Oregon-California Trail, 4-6, 8
Oregon Short Line, 66
Organization of Petroleum Exporting Coun-
    tries (OPEC), 194-195
Overland Trail and Stage Line, 6-8, 11
Owl Creek Coal Company, 120, 123-124

Pacific Power and Light, 191
Pacific Railroad Act of 1862 and 1864, 12-13
Panic of 1893, 71-76
Paoli, Eugene, 137, 172
Peerless mine, 159
Pennsylvania, 20, 77, 113, 115
Peter Kiewit and Sons, 179, 209-212
Pinedale, Wyoming, 189
Pinkerton agents, 112
Pivik, Amy, vii, 171
Pivik, Antone, 134, 137
Point of Rocks, 6, 7, 15
Polish miners and families, 82, 86, 113, 136-
    137, 180-181
Powder River, 4, 8-9
Powder River Basin, 8, 62, 66-67, 69, 159, 194,
    205-207, 209
Progressive Mine Workers Union (PMW),
    210-213
Prohibition, 137-139
Prop pulling, 42, 180-181

Quarry mine, 34, 159
Quealy, Michael, 15
Quealy mines and town, 125, 134, 189
Quealy, P. J., 70, 77, 89-90, 121, 158

Rawlins, Wyoming, 209
Raynolds, William, 8
Red Lodge, Montana, 88
Reliance mines and town, 127, 135, 141, 147,
    165, 170-171, 184, 187
Respirators, 181-182

Righter, Robert, 194, 196
Riverside mine, 167, 179
Rock Springs, 6, 18-21, 40, 46-52, 79, 83, 86-87,
    100, 109, 112, 115-119, 125-126, 137-138,
    140, 151, 162, 165-166, 170-171, 184, 188,
    195, 197, 205, 217
Rocky Mountain Coal and Iron Co., 24, 42
Room and pillar, 34, 152
Rooms in coal mines, 35, 37, 46-47
Roosevelt, Theodore, President of U.S., 119
Rope rider, 37
Rosebud Coal Company, 209-210
Russel, Osborne, 4

Safety teams, 154
Sage, Wyoming, 64
Sawyers, James, A., 8-9
Schwieder, Dorothy, 37, 87
Scrip used for wages, 72-73
Scrubbers (in power plants), 193
Severance taxes, 199-203
Shaft mine, 34-35
Shakers and panlines, 148
Sheridan, 66, 69, 71, 79-80, 82, 100, 105, 109,
    113, 125, 134, 151, 162, 167, 181-182, 188,
    195, 210-212, 217-218
Sheridan County, 69, 89, 120, 167, 179-180, 182
Sheridan-Wyoming Coal, 182
Shot firer, 36
Shot inspectors, 156
"Sisters" (poem), 208
Slope mine, 34, 35
Slovenian miners and families, 82, 85-86, 110,
    135-136, 140, 142-143, 154-155, 188
Slovinski Doms, 143
Slowdowns in mining, 144-145, 164-165
Smith, Barbara, 207
Smith, Duane, vii, 40, 167, 191, 193
Snell, William, vii
Socialists and labor, 107, 124-126
Soldiers scrip, 121
South Cumberland, 136
South Dakota, 67
Spring Valley, Wyoming, 88, 103-104, 121
Squib, 36
Stansbury, Howard, 4-6, 217
Stansbury mine, 185, 188
State Coal Mine Inspectors, 98-100
State Constitutional Convention, 199
State Legislature and Coal Issues, 72, 100, 118-
    119, 124-125, 156, 199-203
State Penitentiary, 209
Stone, Elizabeth, 23